GREAT
IRISH
HEROES

Stuart Pearson, after many varied careers over decades in law enforcement, education, government and business, has finally found his calling in writing. His first book *Bittersweet: The Memoir of a Chinese Indonesian Family in the Twentieth Century* (released globally in 2009) was published by Singapore University Press to much critical acclaim, and was nominated for the New South Wales Premier's Prize for Literature in 2010. *Great Irish Heroes*, a companion volume to his *Great Scottish Heroes* (John Blake, 2015) is his fourth book; his second (with Bob Mitchell), *Blood on the Thistle: The tragic story of the Cranston family and their remarkable sacrifice in the Great War*, was published (also by John Blake) in the summer of 2014, to universal approval and strong sales. He is married, and lives in Sydney, Australia.

STUART PEARSON

GREAT IRISH HEROES

FIFTY IRISHMEN AND WOMEN WHO SHAPED THE WORLD

JOHN BLAKE

Published by John Blake Publishing Ltd,
3 Bramber Court, 2 Bramber Road,
London W14 9PB, England

www.johnblakebooks.com

www.facebook.com/johnblakebooks ⬛
twitter.com/jblakebooks ⬛

First published in paperback in 2016.

ISBN: 978-1-78418-997-6

British Library Cataloguing-in-Publication Data:

A catalogue record for this book is available from the British Library.

Design by www.envydesign.co.uk

Printed in Great Britain by CPI Group (UK) Ltd

1 3 5 7 9 10 8 6 4 2

© Text copyright Stuart Pearson 2016

The right of Stuart Pearson to be identified as the author of this work has been asserted
by him in accordance with the Copyright, Designs and Patents Act 1988.

Papers used by John Blake Publishing are natural, recyclable products made from
wood grown in sustainable forests. The manufacturing processes conform to the
environmental regulations of the country of origin.

Every attempt has been made to contact the relevant copyright-holders, but some were
unobtainable. We would be grateful if the appropriate people could contact us.

This book is dedicated to Glenice Aiken, a close friend, staunch trade unionist and long-term partner to my wife's adopted brother. Glenice reminded me that women make up half the world's population and that I should really try to increase the number of women represented in this book. Thanks to Glenice, I am pleased to say that my masculine bias in the selection process has been somewhat corrected, although my overall transformation to a sensitive New-Age guy is still a work in progress!

CONTENTS

INTRODUCTION   XI

SAINT COLUMBA (COLUMCILLE) (c.521–97): Irish saint and   1
    missionary to Scotland

BRIAN BORU (c.941–1014): Last High King of Ireland   9

GRACE O'MALLEY (c.1530–1603): Sea trader and pirate queen   15

ROBERT BOYLE (1627–91): Natural philosopher and chemist   22

PATRICK SARSFIELD, 1ST EARL OF LUCAN (c.1655–93):   28
    Jacobite commander

KIT CAVANAGH (1667–1739): Soldier   34

TURLOUGH O'CAROLAN (1670–1738): Harpist and composer   39
    of Irish folk music

AMBROSIO O'HIGGINS (c.1720–1801): Viceroy of Chile   44
    and Marqués de Osorno

WOLFE TONE (1763–98): Irish patriot   49

MARY ANN MCCRACKEN (1770–1866): Radical and philanthropist 56

SIR FRANCIS BEAUFORT (1774–1857): Admiral and hydrographer 62

DANIEL O'CONNELL (1775–1847): 'The Liberator' 67

CHARLES (CARLO) BIANCONI (1786–1875): Pioneer of public 75
transport in Ireland

MARY AIKENHEAD (1787–1858): Founder of the Sisters 81
of Charity

JAMES GAMBLE (1803–91): Industrialist, co-founder of 88
Procter & Gamble

GEORGE BOOLE (1815–64): Mathematician 92

CATHERINE HAYES (1818–61): First Irish diva 98

WILLIAM THOMSON, 1ST BARON KELVIN (1824–1907): 104
Mathematical physicist and engineer

THOMAS D'ARCY MCGEE (1825–68): One of the 'Fathers' of 109
Canadian Confederation

ELIZA LYNCH (1835–86): 'Queen' of Paraguay 115

JOHN PHILIP HOLLAND (1841–1914): Inventor of the 122
modern submarine

THOMAS JOHN BARNARDO (1845–1905): Philanthropist 128

MICHAEL DAVITT (1846–1906): Founder of the Irish 134
Land League

CHARLES STEWART PARNELL (1846–91): Politician and nationalist 142

MICHAEL CUSACK (1847–1906): Founder of the Gaelic 149
Athletic Association

OSCAR WILDE (1854–1900): Man of letters 155

GEORGE BERNARD SHAW (1856–1950): Playwright and 161
Nobel laureate

WILLIAM BUTLER YEATS (1865–1939): Poet, playwright and 168
Ireland's first Nobel laureate

CONSTANCE, COUNTESS MARKIEVICZ (1868–1927): 174
Revolutionary and politician

EVA GORE-BOOTH (1870–1926): Labour reformer, poet and suffragist   183

KATHLEEN LYNN (1874–1955): Medical doctor and political activist   189

SIR ERNEST SHACKLETON (1874–1922): Antarctic explorer   195

HANNA SHEEHY-SKEFFINGTON (1877–1946): Feminist and nationalist   202

MARGARET COUSINS (1878–1954): Suffragist, educator and theosophist   210

PATRICK PEARSE (PÁDRAIG MACPIARAIS) (1879–1916): Writer, educator and revolutionary   216

ÉAMON DE VALERA (1882–1975): Dominant Irish politician of the twentieth century   224

HARRY FERGUSON (1884–1960): Engineer and developer of the modern agricultural tractor   232

MICHAEL COLLINS (1890–1922): Revolutionary leader and military commander   238

MONSIGNOR HUGH O'FLAHERTY (1898–1963): Roman Catholic priest and Vatican official   246

DAME NINETTE DE VALOIS (1898–2001): Ballet dancer and founder of the Royal Ballet   253

ERNEST WALTON (1903–95): Physicist and Nobel laureate   259

SEÁN MACBRIDE (1904–88): Lawyer, statesman and Nobel Peace laureate   265

CHAIM HERZOG (1918–97): Soldier, lawyer and President of Israel   271

JOHN HUME (1937–): Politician and Nobel Peace laureate   277

MARY ROBINSON (1944–): Human rights lawyer and first female President of Ireland   283

GEORGE BEST (1946–2005): Football legend   290

PIERCE BROSNAN (1953–): Actor and social activist   295

VERONICA GUERIN (1958–96): Investigative journalist 301

BONO (PAUL HEWSON) (1960–): Musician and social activist 308

BRIAN O'DRISCOLL (1979–): International rugby star 313

BIBLIOGRAPHY AND SOURCES 318

INTRODUCTION

When I was commissioned to write *Great Irish Heroes*, the first two questions that sprang to mind were definitional. What defines being Irish, and then, what does the word 'hero' mean?

The first question can be answered fairly quickly and easily. In this book, an Irishman or Irishwoman is defined by a person's birth or adoption. In other words, if a person was born in Ireland – either Northern Ireland or the Republic of Ireland – then they are automatically Irish. If they were born elsewhere but have chosen to live in Ireland and adopt its culture, heritage, laws and customs, then they are Irish by adoption.

This last point is relevant for four people I've included in the list of fifty *Great Irish Heroes*. The first is Charles Bianconi, who was born in northern Italy in the late eighteenth century, but adopted Ireland in 1802 at the age of eighteen and went on to become a pioneer of road transport. The second is Éamon de Valera, who was born in New York, but lived most of his life in Ireland, becoming one of the most dominant figures in Irish history in the last century. The third person is Seán McBride who was born in Paris, but who rose to become one of the most influential and controversial figures of the twentieth century.

The fourth person (and arguably the most contentious choice) is George Boole, who was born and lived most of his life in England, but relocated to Ireland when he was appointed a Professor of Mathematics at Cork University. He produced his finest work in Ireland, married and raised an Irish family and would have happily lived a long and fruitful life in Ireland if it was not for the fact that he died prematurely of pneumonia, caused by circumstances that were entirely avoidable.

The second definitional issue that needs to be addressed is the meaning of the word 'hero'. The word has become much overused in modern society. When a sport star scores the match-winning goal or runs a personal best, that person is called a hero by the press and media. In artistic terms the hero is the central character in a story, play or film. When emergency workers in uniform save lives, the public often declare them to be heroes. In some countries it can also be the name of a sandwich!

But can an inanimate object, a character in a book and people merely doing the job they were trained and paid for, really be heroes?

According to the *Collins English Dictionary* a hero is a person who is, 'idealised for possessing superior qualities in any field'. The *Oxford English Dictionary* says, 'a person, typically a man, who is admired for their courage, outstanding achievements, or noble qualities'. Finally the *Macquarie Dictionary* defines a hero as, 'a person of distinguished courage or performance'.

From these three sources the common features are:

Courage + noble qualities = role model for others.

I have tried to select men and women from Ireland's past and present who exemplify the characteristics of being courageous and having noble qualities. Synonyms that could be used interchangeably with courage and nobility would be: influential, noteworthy, remarkable, outstanding, important, significant, memorable, striking, impressive, uncommon or exceptional. A hero is a larger-than-life character who can achieve great things, sometimes even alter the course of history of nations, if not the world. I hope that the fifty Irish people I have chosen, not only provide interesting reading, but also can act as role models for people everywhere.

One more issue that must be addressed is the actual selection of the people who appear in the following pages. If people had to select their own list of fifty Great Irish Heroes, I dare say there would be little unanimity. I suspect everyone would have different names and no two lists would match exactly.

So it is for me. The fifty names I have chosen represent my choice and my choice alone. It was not forced on me, nor was it the work of a committee. If you do not like my selection, you are perfectly welcome to publish a list of your own!

In truth I could have picked one hundred Great Irish Heroes, possibly even two hundred or more. There are so many Irish men and woman who have made significant contributions to the world that it is unfortunate such a large number must be omitted.

But there is a final comment that needs to be made before we commence to read the following individual biographies and that is about the perception of Ireland as a land of 'Saints and Scholars'. So much time, energy and money has been devoted on these themes that people often forget that Ireland is much more than just a place for 'Religion, Writers and Revolutionaries'.

It is the contention of this book that Ireland has been a vibrant,

ST COLUMBA (COLUMCILLE)
(c.521–97)

IRISH SAINT AND MISSIONARY
TO SCOTLAND

Christianity was declared the official state religion of the Roman Empire in AD 380. However, Christianity had been growing in popularity throughout the empire for at least two centuries prior to that. Tertullian (c.155 to c.240), the Bishop of Carthage, believed Christian communities were present in Romano-Britain from at least AD 200 (Tertullian, *Adversus Judaeos*, Chapter VII).

In 431, Pope Celestine I sent Bishop Palladius to Ireland to preach to the increasing number of Christians there. His mission, interpreted from the writings of Prosper of Aquitaine, a fourth-century chronicler, seemed to concentrate on Leinster and the western midlands of Ireland with apparent success. Saint Patrick who came after Palladius, worked as an evangelist mainly in the north of Ireland. Even though there is disagreement about which Christian missionary came first and indeed who actually converted the people of Ireland, all the records agree on one point, that by the late 400s most of Ireland had been converted to Christianity.

Fifty or so years later, in about AD 521, a young nobleman was born in Gartan, Co. Donegal into one of Ireland's many ruling houses. It is not known what Celtic name he was given at birth, but some historians speculate it was Crimthann ('Fox'). From an early age, he was placed under the tutelage of a priest and became thoroughly imbued with Catholic doctrine. When he was at the age to claim his hereditary title, he renounced his noble status and became ordained as a priest instead.

Following his ordination, he was given another Celtic name, Columcille (Dove of the Church). Finally, when he dedicated his life to mission work, his name was Latinised to Columba.

Columcille spent the next fifteen years or so, preaching and teaching in Ireland. As was the custom in those days he combined study and prayer with manual labour and good Christian deeds. He was a gifted orator, perhaps even charismatic, because people seemed drawn to him and to what he preached.

These personal traits when coupled with an unbreakable faith in God, set him apart as a force of nature and as a priest of extra-ordinary distinction. By the time he was twenty-five, Columcille had founded no less than twenty-seven Irish monasteries, including those at Derry, Durrow and Kells, the latter both in the County of Meath. The monasteries at Durrow and Kells will feature again later in this book.

Even though Columcille took on the new religion of Christianity without reservation and devoted his life to being a personal manifestation of its beliefs, he did not abandon his Celtic roots and heritage. In fact, he learnt as much about Irish history as he could, studied poetry and became something of an accomplished poet himself. He wrote in Latin and yet could easily speak in ancient Gaelic to his fellow countrymen.

Columcille was slowly fusing love for his Christian religion with the heritage and culture of Ireland's pagan and Celtic past. He could have adopted a more Roman way of life, like others before him, but for Columcille, there was something rich and powerful about Celtic symbols, art and culture that only added to being a Christian, and did not detract from it.

At around this time, Columcille found himself in conflict with one of Ireland's most powerful chiefs, a disagreement which very quickly descended into an armed struggle between tribes, who either supported or opposed Chief Diarmaid. Matters came to a head at the Battle of Cul Drebne (modern Cooldrevny, Co. of Sligo), in which it was said that the Chief and some 3,000 of his followers were slaughtered.

Columcille was appalled at the losses caused by his opposition to the slain chief and vowed that he would bring as many souls to Christ as had been killed at Cul Drebne. But where was he to find such a large number of potential converts? Ireland's population was relatively small at the time and a sizeable percentage had already become Christian. However, it was common knowledge that across the Irish Sea there were more people, of whom few were Christians. Some tribes beyond Hadrian's Wall in Scotland and in the wild hills of Wales had never even seen a priest.

As he contemplated his future, historic documents say he underwent a profound and irresistible call to preach to the heathen. He accepted without question that God was calling him to become a missionary and spread the word of God to new people in foreign lands. In 563, Columba crossed over the Irish Sea with a dozen companions to the western coast of northern Britain, driven to convert as many pagans to Christ as he could, or die in the process.

Landing in what is now Scotland, Columba established a pattern of overseas missionary behaviour for fellow Irishmen that would continue to today. For the last millennia and a half, tens of thousands of Catholic priests have taken an Irish brand of Christianity beyond their own shores to the four corners of the world.

Columba had landed on the tiny island now known as Iona in the Inner Hebrides of Scotland. Then, it was called 'The Island of the Druids' and belonged to the King of Dál Riata, which luckily for Columba he was distantly related to. The king granted him a parcel of land on Iona to build a monastery and a school. From this location, Columba made it his mission to convert the heathens of western Scotland, then known as Picts, to Christianity.

In 565, shortly after the settlement at Iona was established, Columba went to see the Pictish King Brude at his hill fort in Inverness to try and convert him. As was the custom then, if the ruler of a tribe changed his faith so would all his clansmen, as their oaths of allegiance made them duty-bound to follow his lead. The king refused to see Columba and locked the heavy wooden gates to prevent his entry.

But as a legendary story states, when Columba stood in front of the gates and made the sign of the cross, the gates miraculously opened. This version of events went on to say that the king was so impressed, that he converted to Christianity, as did all the people of his Caledonian tribe, giving up Druidism for Christ. It was more likely that Columba's connection by birth to the Kingdom of Dál Riata would have been enough to at least gain him an audience with King Brude.

The interconnection between the Irish and Scottish Kingdoms

continued to work in Columba's favour, for he was allowed to establish many more monasteries throughout the Hebrides and Scottish mainland. All the time his reputation for doing good deeds and even miracles was growing, as was the number of converts to Christ.

According to chroniclers, Columba at one time turned water into wine, and on another occasion he revived the dead. He was said to be prescient – what the Scots still call 'fey' today – and could foresee events before they happened. It was reported that he successfully battled demons, evil spirits and on one climactic occasion, even the devil himself. A famous legend has it that Columba was the first Christian to see a 'monster' in Loch Ness, which threatened him until it was banished when Columba gave the sign of the cross.

Columba was as fiercely committed to learning as he was to winning souls, which is why most of his monasteries had school buildings built beside them. Literacy was not common outside the borders of the Roman Empire. Traditionally, Ireland, Scotland and Wales were part of a wider Celtic civilisation that honoured the oral, not written language. Columba was determined to change this situation and through his intense efforts, Columba and a growing band of disciples turned Iona into a thriving centre of Christian worship and learning with one unique difference – it was promoting a distinctly Celtic form of Christianity.

The earliest Celtic crosses existing today can be dated to the late 500s and early 600s in both Scotland and Ireland. These dates coincide with the time of Columba's mission work. There have been a number of accounts put forward over the years for the design of the Celtic cross, including one claiming that St Patrick carved the sign onto a pagan altar stone, but there is an alternative explanation that possibly points to Columba.

Some scholars believe that the unique, attractive design of the Celtic cross is a deliberate merger of two powerful symbols – the Christian cross of the new religion with the pagan 'circle of the sun' from the ancient religion. If that is so, then it tends to support the contention that it might have been the work of Columba, or one of his disciples influenced by his master's ideas.

One day in 597, Columba was at his writing desk copying yet another exquisitely illustrated religious book, when he suddenly felt sharp stabbing pains in his chest. He stopped work and went to his bed. A few hours later he managed to rise and go to the nearby church, where he collapsed. By the time help arrived he was already dead, at the age of seventy-six.

The spirit of Columba's teaching and beliefs seemed to enthuse his followers to even greater achievements and Iona went on to become a dominant religious and educational institution in the region for centuries.

Two magnificent publications created over the course of the next several generations have survived to today. The first is the *Book of Durrow*, an illuminated manuscript said to be initially started at either Iona or Lindisfarne in England's north-east coast and brought to the monastery of Durrow in Ireland for completion sometime between AD 650–700. The second is the *Book of Kells*, again started elsewhere in Scotland or perhaps England but removed for safekeeping to the monastery at Kells in Ireland when the Vikings started raiding and pillaging the coast of Britain. *The Book of Kells* is thought to have been completed at about AD 800.

What makes these two publications remarkable is that they surpass the quality of any other illustrated manuscripts at the time for their complexity and their sheer extravagance of presentation.

There are illustrations of animals, mythical beasts and fantastic drawings of people, spirits and Christ. The most outstanding feature of these manuscripts is that they clearly demonstrate the combination of traditional Christian iconography with the ornate swirling motifs of Celtic art. This is something which would have been dear to Columba's heart and shows how his legacy of blending the old symbols with the new religion continued for centuries after his death. The manuscripts are classified as irreplaceable national treasures and are securely displayed permanently at the Trinity College Library, Dublin.

Columba was admired, even revered, for his heroic and energetic missionary work, his founding of many Hebridean churches and his authorship of several hymns. It is said that he personally copied over 300 books in his lifetime on beautiful parchment, using a new and distinctive style of writing in which the religious texts were interspersed with glorious, wonderful images from a Celtic heritage.

Over time, Iona became a place of pilgrimage where royalty and commoners alike would come to pay their respects at the grave of Columba. An inventory in the 1500s recorded the graves of sixty early Scottish kings, as well as kings from Ireland, Norway, and even France who were buried at Iona.

Columba was canonised as a saint shortly after his death. He is also the Patron Saint of Derry, converter of the Picts and one of the Twelve Apostles of Ireland.

St Columba may have been the founder of several major themes in Irish history. His desire to preach and educate with equal determination has led to Ireland being long-regarded as a nation of 'Saints and Scholars'. Finally, a willingness to conserve Celtic customs, culture and symbols rather than destroy them, meant

BRIAN BORU (c.941–1014)

LAST HIGH KING
OF IRELAND

Brian mac Cennétig, was born in Munster, Ireland, the youngest of twelve sons to Cennétig mac Lorcáin, who was the dynastic head of the Dál Cais tribe, which had become a powerful influence in Munster by the tenth century.

Even though the population of Ireland was relatively small at the time – some say as few as 500,000 – there were over 150 kings claiming control over a patchwork of small-to-medium sized territories. In essence these self-proclaimed kings were in fact chiefs of tribes, but they wielded so much power over their people and territory that they were like absolute monarchs. The power of life and death was in their hands and the rule of law was as capricious as the king's regard for you.

Needless to say with so many kingdoms squeezed up against each other, there were many serious disputes between rulers. The actions of neighbouring kings were often perceived as insults that required an immediate armed response, which simply fed a cycle of revenge and more violence that existed in Ireland at the time. It would be fair to say that Ireland was not a safe place to live in during this period, the average life expectancy from famine, disease or war being as low as thirty-five years.

To maintain some order, Ireland was further divided into a hierarchy of territories in which several smaller kingdoms were grouped together under the control of an 'overking' that roughly corresponded to the modern provinces of Ireland. The overkings of the regions in turn all supposedly gave their allegiance to the largely ceremonial positon of 'High King' of Ireland. But not all the overkings gave their oaths of fealty to the same High King, and there were lengthy periods of time when the position was never filled because of a dispute. Despite this, the northern dynasty of the Uí Néill tribe had come to dominate the occasional position by the tenth century.

Into this situation came a new and powerful influence from overseas – the Vikings. During the ninth and tenth centuries, Vikings arrived in their longboats from Scandinavia in increasing numbers. First they raided, but over time they stayed and established settlements at Dublin, Wexford, Waterford, Cork and Limerick, and these grew to become the first large towns of Ireland.

In 965, Brian's older brother seized the throne of Munster from a weak king and over the next fifteen years launched a campaign to rid the land of the Viking settlement at Limerick, but he was captured in 976 and killed. Brian then assumed leadership of the province, and, fuelled by revenge, launched an immediate attack against the town. Brian managed to breach the walls and when the Viking leader and his sons sought sanctuary in the town's monastery, Brian broke in and slaughtered them all.

For the next several years he consolidated his reign over Munster, but when he started expanding his influence into the rival provinces of Leinster and Connacht he came up against Máel Sechnaill II, then the High King of Ireland of the Uí Néill dynasty.

Both launched raids into each other's territory over the next fifteen years, but neither side gained the upper hand. Meanwhile the Viking occupiers in their towns were consolidating their control over their territory, growing stronger and watching the only people who potentially threatened them, fight each other to a standstill.

Eventually, a compromise was reached between Brian mac Cennétig and Máel Sechnaill II when they agreed to a fragile peace treaty in 996 in which the Uí Néills maintained their control over the north and west, and Brian was declared ruler of newly-conquered Leinster, as well as confirming his authority over Munster in the south. But the treaty did not last, and within a year the rival Irish forces were fighting again. This time, the troops loyal to the Uí Néills had joined forces with the Hiberno-Norse leader of Dublin, Sigtrygg Silkbeard, to defeat Brian once and for all.

Brian's response was decisive and rapid. He collected a large force of battle-hardened warriors and made off to attack Dublin. The defenders marched out to meet him and in the ensuing fierce and bloody battle outside the city walls it was Brian who proved the better tactician. The soldiers of Dublin and Uí Néill retreated in disarray, chased mercilessly by Brian's forces as they raced back to Dublin. Brian gave the routed troops no respite by attacking the city before they could man the walls in defence. It was a one-sided conflict and Dublin was plundered and then sacked, with both leaders of the defeated armies captured.

Cleverly, Brian made an ally of Sigtrygg Silkbeard by saving his life, and reinstating him as ruler of Dublin for as long as he swore allegiance to Brian. Finally, to confirm his status as new-found ally, Brian gave Silkbeard the hand of one of his daughters in marriage. As for the leader of the Uí Néill forces, he was held hostage until a handsome ransom had been paid for his eventual release.

Buoyed up with success and with his coffers replenished, Brian now added the title of Bóruma (Boru for short) to his name, meaning 'Lord of cattle tributes'. Cattle were then the most expensive commodity in Ireland and this was a direct reference to Brian possessing more cattle from tribute than anyone else in Ireland.

In the year 1000, with the southern half of Ireland now firmly under his control and pacified, Brian Boru led a combined force from Munster, Leinster and Dublin in a campaign to overthrow the Uí Néills in the north. In 1002, Boru had conquered the county of Meath in the centre of Ireland, which caused his old enemy, Máel Sechnaill II, to surrender the title High King of Ireland to Boru. Only the heartland of the Uí Néill dynasty in Ulster still stubbornly refused to accept Boru's overlordship, and it would take almost another decade before cunning, diplomacy and the combined strength of three-quarters of Ireland finally subdued the powerful province in 1011.

Brian Boru intended the title of High King of Ireland to become more than just a name. He wanted a united Ireland under one ruler and, like the Romans before him in antiquity, wanted to use the title Emperor. But the unification of Ireland that had taken him several decades to achieve did not last. Ongoing bitterness and resentment festered into open rebellion just one year later in 1012, when Leinster and Dublin rose up against him in open revolt.

It took Brian Boru another two years before he had subdued Leinster, during which the Vikings in Dublin had enough time to call for reinforcements from their kinfolk overseas. In the spring of

1014 Brian's army assembled outside the walls of Dublin for a long siege, when a large fleet of longships came in view carrying many hundreds of Viking warriors from the Orkneys and the Isle of Man in support of the blockaded city.

Battle was joined at a place called Clontarf (now a prosperous suburb) on Good Friday 1014. The two sides were evenly matched numerically and the ferocious battle swung back and forth all day. However, in the late afternoon Brian Boru's forces gained the upper hand and the rebel ranks broke, fleeing back to the boats and the city walls.

Legend has it that the victorious forces pursued them and cut them down as they fled. So many died that it was said that the waters around Dublin Bay were red with blood and choked with rotting corpses for weeks. But among the dead was also Brian Boru, hacked to death at the age of seventy, by the strokes of an axe to the head. His body is reported to have been ceremonially marched north to a burial fit for a king at the cathedral in Armagh, which had been the ecclesial centre of Christianity in Ireland for centuries.

The true legacy that Brian Boru left behind is that through effective military skills and astute political know-how he had demonstrated that kingship of all of Ireland was no mere symbolic office. It wielded much power, and if the throne was joined with the Church, as Brian had shrewdly done, it could also be a source of great wealth. Many kings now fought each other to follow in Brian's footsteps and become the next ruler of the whole island. But none were successful before the Normans invaded nearly two centuries later. Brian Boru was therefore the last High King of Ireland.

Yet what Boru's actions led to was a gradual centralisation of power within the upper echelons of Ireland's ruling classes. The number of kingdoms decreased, especially petty kingdoms that were no larger than districts, and a new caste of administrators grew up, people who could serve these more complex and powerful administrative areas. Provinces were now at the apex of authority and two families in particular would wield significant power over them, and these were descendants of the Uí Néill tribe and of Brian Boru. They would be known as the O'Neills and O'Briens and go on to be two of Ireland's most popular surnames.

For a brief moment in Ireland's history Brian Boru showed that Ireland could be a unified and independent nation under one administration. Not a country consisting of petty and fractious rulers fighting each other. Brian Boru's unified Ireland lasted for just a few short years and is yet to be repeated a thousand years later.

GRACE O'MALLEY
(c.1530–1603)

SEA TRADER AND
PIRATE QUEEN

This person had many names in her lifetime, including Gráinne Ui Mháille (Grace of the O'Malley clan), Gráinne Mhaol (Grace the bald), and Gráinne O'Mailey. But the name that is chosen for this biography is her English name of Grace O'Malley.

Grace O'Malley was born around 1530, one of only two daughters to the hereditary Chief of the O'Malley clan whose territory surrounded Clew Bay in Co. Mayo. The O'Malleys derived their income mainly from maritime pursuits, such as fishing, trading and 'taxing' passing ships. The O'Malley roots went back to ancient times and the family considered themselves to be of genuine Gaelic Irish nobility. While the O'Malleys controlled the seas, another powerful family, the Bourkes, controlled the hinterland of Co. Mayo. The Bourke clan (alternate spelling Burke) were descended from an Anglo-Norman family who had resided in the area since the thirteenth century. They also regarded themselves as a noble family, but of superior standing to the native Irish around them.

During her childhood, Grace received a formal education at the family's castle stronghold on Clare Island at the entrance of Clew Bay. It is believed she was taught Latin and possibly French, though her native tongue would have been Gaelic. Apparently Grace showed an independent and impetuous spirit from a young age, which is born out in the following, possibly apocryphal story. One day when Grace was still a young girl, she wanted to accompany her father on a trading mission to Spain, but he refused, citing the dangers of her long red hair easily catching in the ship's ropes and rigging. Overnight, Grace cut off all her hair and defiantly insisted on going. This earned her one of the many nicknames she would have during her life. Until her hair grew back, she was called, Gráinne Mhaol (Grace the bald).

Importantly, Grace also learnt her family's trade of stopping and 'taxing' sea traffic that ranged within control of the clan's fast boats. O'Malley's ships would stop and board vessels, demanding either cash or a portion of the cargo as payment for safe passage. Any resistance was met with violence or even death. Today, this behaviour would be classified as 'protection money' or extortion, but in the sixteenth century extracting money from people passing through your territory was considered a semi-legitimate source of income.

In 1546, when Grace was about sixteen, she was married off to the heir of the O'Flaherty clan, whose territory was further south along the west coast of Ireland. It was a political union designed to bolster the power of both clans and provide a counter to the growing influence of the Bourke nobility. Over the next twenty years, Grace gave birth to two sons and a daughter and watched over them as they grew up. However she was not an idle mother.

The traditional seat of the O'Flaherty clan was Bunowen Castle on the far western coast of Connacht, which had access to a vast sway of the Atlantic Ocean and coastline. It is from here that Grace began to run her own maritime operations far enough away from her family's sphere of influence to be completely independent. She was in her thirties and was building up a solid, lucrative business when disaster struck.

In one of the many internecine power struggles between rival clans in western Ireland, Grace's husband was murdered while out hunting. The assailants then marched on to the O'Flaherty castle thinking that Grace would surrender without a fight, but she defended it so vigorously that it was the attackers in the end who had to surrender.

Nevertheless, without a husband, Grace's social and legal position was weak. She returned to the O'Malley castle on Clare Island and there arranged another political wedding. Her second marriage was to Richard Bourke in 1566, the senior heir to the Bourke family lands and recipient of considerable income. She gave birth to a son in about 1567, but the union was not strong and it was said both parents would go on to have relationships with other partners.

Her activities on the seas continued transporting freight around the coast of Ireland and preying on shipping caught off the coast of Mayo. At the height of her activities in the 1560s–80s it is believed that Grace O'Malley employed over two hundred men and more than twenty ships that conducted both lawful and unlawful activity on the seas. Her ocean-going boats were mainly carracks, capable of sailing as far away as Spain and Portugal, exporting products from the Irish Sea and land, and then returning fully laden with copper, wine and spices. Her in-shore boats were fast and nimble galleys, rowed by up to twenty men, which could rapidly chase down and board any lumbering trading vessel that passed by. O'Malley became the most dominant sea trader and pirate along the entire western seaboard of Ireland.

At this point of time, English control over Ireland was light and in many areas non-existent. In the west and north of Ireland for example, the English authorities had been content to let the various local clan chiefs manage the countryside with little interference from Dublin, the seat of English power in Ireland. However, the English increasingly came to view these autonomous regions with suspicion, especially when many of the activities led by the Irish chiefs bordered on lawless banditry and piracy. When it came to piracy, the O'Malley name was mentioned loudly and frequently.

Once, in 1574, the English tried to suppress her activities by launching an amphibious assault on her stronghold of Clare Island, but, if the stories are to be believed, Grace called for the lead on the castle's roof to be removed, heated to a molten liquid and then poured onto the heads of her besiegers. The English left in disarray, not to return for decades.

From the mid-to-late 1500s, English power steadily increased over Ireland and along with this expansion of power came the spread of Protestantism, which further alarmed the devoutly Catholic Irish. In 1584, Sir Richard Bingham, a career soldier and mariner, was appointed Lord Lieutenant (Governor) of Connaught by Queen Elizabeth I, with specific instructions to rid the seas of the scourge of piracy and impose English rule in this region. This meant that that the focus of his campaign would be against the O'Malley and O'Flaherty clans, with Grace as the lynchpin between these two families.

That same year, Richard Bourke died and Grace was left to face Bingham's campaign alone, though at this stage, Bingham did not have a large contingent of soldiers at his disposal. In 1586, she was arrested briefly by Bingham's brother and released only after another family member was offered as a substitute, together with surrendering much of her cattle and livestock. Later that year, her son was murdered by Bingham's men. Tensions exploded into open revolt and O'Malley went on a splurge of raiding every English ship she could find. A temporary truce was arranged only after O'Malley gave her other son, Theobald Bourke, as a hostage to Sir Richard Bingham.

The peace was short-lived. In 1589, Theobald killed the Sherriff of Mayo and rebellion broke out again. Grace O'Malley supported the rebellion by supplying Catholic fighters she transported from Scotland as reinforcements. To crush the rebellion, the English now sent large numbers of troops into the countryside beyond Dublin ('beyond the Pale' or marker fence, an expression still used today). In the end, armed resistance was crushed.

However, for Grace O'Malley the conflict was not over. In 1593, Sir Richard Bingham arrested Grace's son, Theobald, for the second time. On this occasion it was on the most serious charge of treason. For good measure, Grace O'Malley's half-brother was arrested too. Quite clearly Bingham thought the threat of executing the last members of Grace's immediate family would force her to stop her piracy once and for all.

Instead, Grace wrote a letter of complaint to Queen Elizabeth I, seeking to have Bingham removed from office and the O'Malley relatives freed. The Queen was intrigued enough to summon O'Malley to an audience in London in 1593. Grace wore a fine gown that almost outshone the Queen's dress and she argued her case forcefully, clearly and in the end, successfully. Queen Elizabeth must have been impressed with Grace O'Malley because Bingham was withdrawn from Connaught within weeks and her son and brother were freed without charge.

Grace O'Malley must have been impressed by Queen Elizabeth too. The following year another open rebellion broke out that became war between the Irish nobles and the ever-expanding rule of the English. During the Nine Years' War (1594–1603), Grace O'Malley sided with the English, much to the surprise of everyone. While the war was still being fought, Queen Elizabeth authorised a pension of £200 to be paid to Grace and her family for services to the Crown.

Grace O'Malley was now in her seventies and tired of all the fighting, raiding and piracy. She withdrew from the world and saw out her last days in one of her castles. It is believed Grace died in 1603 and was buried on her home island of Clare off the Mayo coast.

O'Malley's life has since inspired musicians, novelists and play-wrights to create works based on her adventures. She lived at a time when it was simply unheard of for women to engage in commerce, let alone piracy and armed rebellion. Grace O'Malley was a woman of singular strength and character, determined not to let something as trivial as her gender stand in the way of accomplishing great achievements.

Centuries later she would become a female role model for Irish nationalism. A good example of which is the following stanzas of a poem written during the Great Rebellion of 1798:

'Twas a proud and stately castle
In the years of long ago
When the dauntless Grace O'Malley
Ruled a queen in fair Mayo.
And from Bernham's lofty summit

GRACE O'MALLEY (c.1530–1603)

To the waves a Galway bay
And from Castlebar to Ballintra
Her unconquered flag held sway.

She had strongholds on her headlands
And brave galleys on the seas
And no warlike chief or Viking
E'er had bolder heart than she.
She unfurled her country's banner
High o'er battlements and mast
And 'gainst all the might of England
Kept it flying 'til the last.

(James Hardiman, *Irish Minstrelsy,* Vol. II, p. 65.)

ROBERT BOYLE (1627–91)

NATURAL PHILOSOPHER AND CHEMIST

Robert was born in Lismore Castle, Co. of Waterford, to the extremely wealthy 1st Earl of Cork (Richard Boyle) and his second wife, Catherine (née Fenton). Richard Boyle had arrived in Ireland from England in 1588 as a twenty-two-year-old adventurer and through a series of judicious appointments, purchases and two marriages amassed enormous landholdings in the south of Ireland that exceeded 20,000 hectares and included thirteen castles, much productive farmland and many settlements. Richard Boyle was ennobled by Queen Elizabeth I in 1620 as the 1st as Earl of Cork.

Robert, his son, began his education by receiving private tutoring in the classics at Lismore Castle, and when he was eight years old, was sent off to Eton College to continue his schooling. It seemed formal education did not suit Robert Boyle because his grades were mediocre and after three years at Eton, his parents decided it was time for a change. He was sent away on a 'grand tour' of Italy in 1638 at the age of eleven, accompanied by his brother Francis, and both boys were escorted by a tutor.

While away, Boyle underwent a profound life-changing experience. One night, he was woken by a violent lightning storm of such intensity, he imagined that this would be how the world would end on the Day of Judgement. He vowed that from this moment in his life, he would lead the life of a committed Christian and perform works that brought him and others closer to God. Only he did not know how he should express this new-found religious commitment. Shortly after in Florence, Robert met a person who would provide him with the direction he would take to serve God for the rest of his life.

Robert Boyle visited the famed astronomer Galileo Galilei, who was seventy-four, going blind and in ill health. Galileo had just published one of his most important works, *Discourses and Mathematical Demonstrations Relating to Two New Sciences*, which was a testament to much of Galileo's scientific observations over his previous forty years. Before then, in 1632, the Italian Inquisition had found Galileo guilty of heresy and had restricted his movements. The Inquisition had even tried to ban all Galileo's writing, but *Discourses* was published in the Netherlands, whose national religion was Protestantism, therefore outside the control of the Roman Catholic Church. Even though Galileo was effectively under house arrest, the authorities allowed visitors such as young Robert, and it would appear that he was greatly impressed and influenced by the man.

By the time Boyle returned to England in 1644 he was fired with an all-consuming interest in scientific research. Something had unlocked a dormant genius in the man, and he was now determined to pursue and build upon the scientific work of others, such as Pascal, Copernicus, Descartes, Bacon, and of course, Galileo.

The profound experience he underwent on tour also shaped his view of religion. He dismissed the extremes of puritanical Calvinism on one hand, and also the dogmatic, anti-intellectual aspects of extreme Catholicism on the other. He became a moderate, tolerant and inclusive person who would rather pursue a higher purpose in life instead of wasting time on dwelling on the petty differences between individuals. Philosophically, Boyle believed that ultimately a greater understanding of the world would lead to a greater understanding of God, for he sincerely believed that a divine hand had created the universe and everything in it. His personal search for Divinity included morning devotional Bible readings as part of his daily schedule for the rest of his life.

Robert's father died in 1643 and left the younger Boyle substantial property in both England and Ireland, from which he drew a considerable income, allowing him the freedom to spend his time discussing his ideas and making observations with a group of like-minded intellectuals in London. It was at about this time that his scientific direction started to coalesce around a relatively new science called chemistry. Before this time, chemistry had been the domain of alchemists who mixed potions, elixirs and balms for both medical and spiritual purposes.

Boyle pioneered the use of a scientific methodology in chemical investigations. He would measure ingredients, record the temperature, describe his methods and anything else he thought might prove relevant. Then he would record the chemical reaction between these, if any. This approach became the foundation of the modern science of chemistry, and would lead to Boyle being dubbed its 'Father' in the future.

Robert moved back to Ireland in 1652, where he thought he could continue his research into chemistry, but he was disappointed at the poor state of scientific advancement in the country. He described Ireland to a friend as, 'a barbarous country where chemical spirits were so misunderstood and chemical instruments so unprocurable, that it was hard to have any Hermetic [scientific and verifiable] thoughts in it.' He returned to England and took part in the intellectually charged atmosphere of Oxford in 1654, where he continued his work.

In Oxford, Boyle set up a laboratory over an apothecary's shop, chosen for the convenience of obtaining high quality samples of chemicals, and there he began the most productive and important phase of his life. He read about a primitive air pump and immediately set about devising improvements to its construction and performance, with the result that Boyle's 'pneumatic engine' was presented to the eager public in 1660.

Boyle continued extensive research and experimentation into the properties of gases and in 1662 published his findings in which he stated that the volume of gas varies inversely to its pressure, known today universally as Boyle's Law. The following year, the young scientist became a founding member of the Royal Society, commissioned in a Royal Charter from Charles II, and he sat on its inaugural Council.

Robert was appointed a Director of the East India Company and used his position to spread Christianity in the East. He contributed liberally to the sending of missionaries to Britain's new colonies and also to the translation of the Bible into local languages. Boyle thought that the introduction of one of the first English-speaking versions of the Holy Bible in 1611 by King James II was such a good idea, that he authorised and paid for a Gaelic version to be distributed throughout his native Ireland. At the time, the Roman Catholic Church resolutely spoke Latin at Mass, and Boyle hoped that by presenting the Bible to the general population in a language that they could readily understand, might serve to 'de-mystify' religion and allow the individuals to get closer to God.

For the last twenty years of his life, Robert lived in London at the house of his elder sister Katherine Jones, Lady Ranelagh, in Pall Mall. The relationship between Katherine and Robert appears to be one of equals, in which they shared medical remedies, promoted each other's scientific ideas, and edited each other's manuscripts. He coined the word 'analysis' and introduced the use of litmus paper to indicate acids and alkalis, thereby inadvertently lending the phrase, 'the litmus test' to the English language – this term meaning 'to scientifically prove a concept'.

Because of his considerable wealth, Boyle became somewhat of a patron himself. He financially sponsored up to a half a dozen young, aspiring inventors and scientists during the latter period of his life. He was graciously acknowledged in a number of publications as the financial contributor to their work.

He never married, preferring to lead a life devoted to science in pursuit of a greater appreciation of God.

Boyle was a prolific writer of books, treaties, monograms and even a set of poems, but his seminal work is said to be *The Sceptical Chymist* in 1661. Boyle proposed that the basic building blocks of chemistry were elements, that he called 'corpuscles', which arranged themselves into groups. This theory is close to our modern understanding of the atomic structure of elements, but was totally foreign to the scientific community of his day.

The pioneering scientist suffered a severe stroke in 1670, but continued to work in a diminished capacity until 1691, when his health deteriorated rapidly. He died of paralysis on the last day of that year. His burial was a memorable affair, for Boyle had already been elevated to the pantheon of all-time greats in science. He had become the leading exponent of the 'experimental method' as a way of conducting scientific research and as such laid the platform for all major scientific discoveries in the future.

In his will, Boyle left money for a series of lectures to be given on the relationship between Christianity and the new natural philosophy (what we today term 'science'). Over three centuries later, the Boyle Lectures still take place annually at the beautiful St Mary-le-Bow Church in the heart of London.

Of all Irish-born scientists, Boyle was, and still is, the most distinguished and prodigious. Even though Ireland in the mid-to-late 1600s was not a conducive location for advanced scientific research, he still loved the country and took a great deal of interest in its affairs and his Irish estates until his death. Robert Boyle and Sir Isaac Newton are considered by many to be the two greatest scientific minds of the seventeenth century.

PATRICK SARSFIELD, IST EARL OF LUCAN (c.1655–93)

JACOBITE COMMANDER

Sarsfield was born in Lucan, Co. Dublin in about 1655, a second son to a landed family of status and wealth who had estates in both counties of Dublin and Kildare. The family had been present in Ireland from the twelfth century, when an ancestor arrived along with other knights during the Anglo-Norman invasion of Ireland. In the centuries that followed, the family intermarried with other noble local families, so that by the seventeenth century it had become thoroughly Irish, and resolutely Catholic.

The Sarsfield family had been occasional supporters and sympathisers in a long-running campaign against English rule for at least a century, but matters took a dramatic turn for the worse when Patrick Sarsfield's father actively led an armed rebellion in 1641. This uprising was ruthlessly crushed by Oliver Cromwell, who authorised the killing of many thousands of rebels, as well as the forceful deportation of thousands more as indentured servants.

All the Sarsfield estates in Ireland were confiscated and the family was forced to live in humble circumstances for a number of years.

In 1661, the Sarsfield lands were thankfully restored to the family by King Charles II after he came to the British throne as a result of the restoration of the Royal House of Stewart (spelt 'Stuart' in French) in 1660. But the political situation was still volatile and the family felt it was safer if Patrick went overseas. He went to France and spent his youth studying in a French military academy. In the 1670s, when he was still a teenager, Patrick received his first commission as an ensign (junior officer) with the 'Irish Brigade' (a mercenary unit of Irish exiles) fighting for France. At the end of the Franco-Dutch War in 1678, Sarsfield and many other exiled Irish heeded the English King's offer of amnesty and returned home, where he was immediately commissioned as a lieutenant in an English infantry regiment.

During the last years of the reign of King Charles II (1684–85), Sarsfield fought for English regiments alongside the French, who were then allies in a war against the Dutch. He was promoted to the rank of captain.

As an experienced officer under King James II, Sarsfield was ordered to suppress a rebellion by the Duke of Monmouth in the south of England. He acquitted himself with distinction during the early stages of the Battle of Sedgemoor (1685), which saw the forces of Monmouth routed. Towards the end of the conflict, Sarsfield was clubbed from his horse and left for dead, only recovering after the victory had been won. Because of his bravery he was promoted to the rank of colonel and given his own cavalry regiment to command. In 1687, he was sent to Ireland to help re-model the Irish forces into a Catholic-led army. Previous Protestant monarchs had purged the Irish troops of Catholic officers in case they became a threat against their sovereign. Now, King James II, a Catholic, was reversing that process and cleansing the ranks of Protestant officers.

In Ireland, King James II enjoyed growing popularity, especially among the mainly Catholic population, but in England and Scotland, it was a very different story. These two overwhelmingly Protestant countries viewed the monarch's moves to re-assert Catholicism with at first alarm, and then with panic, which led to Parliament conspiring to have him removed.

In 1688, in what was called 'The Glorious Revolution', the Dutch Protestant William of Orange invaded England at the invitation of influential English politicians and clerics. He was met with rousing enthusiasm by the population and many units of the English army defected to his side. Patrick Sarsfield assembled his troops and returned to England in haste to fight for King James, but by the time he arrived, the cause was lost and he was only involved in minor skirmishes before he was able to escort his troops and King James II from England.

He accompanied King James II to France and the following year came back to Ireland with the monarch, where the majority of the population still supported James. In the Latin language, James translates to Jacobus, thus giving the name 'Jacobite' to the supporters of the exiled monarch. It was hoped that an army might be raised in Ireland to retake the English throne, and Sarsfield was one of several high-ranking officers tasked with the responsibility of whipping this army into shape.

Sarsfield was promoted to brigadier and then major-general by King James II, but even though the King relied heavily on Sarsfield's experience and successes, he regarded him as somewhat lacking in intelligence, saying, 'he is brave, but no head'. The French, however, had a very different opinion. The French Ambassador wrote in his diary that Sarsfield, 'is greater than that of any man I know. He is brave, but above all he has a sense of honour and integrity in all that he does.'

The Jacobite monarch's personal assessment of Sarsfield would cost the King dearly, for the following year in 1690, William (of Orange) attacked James in Ireland at the Battle of the Boyne, where he decisively defeated the combined Jacobite and French forces. During the battle, Sarsfield was relegated to a minor role in reserve, despite the fact that he commanded a 'crack' cavalry regiment and was obviously one of the most competent and experienced men fighting on the Jacobite side.

After the battle, the Jacobite King fled to France, urging his senior officers to fight on while he obtained further French reinforcements from King Louis XIV. The remnants of the Jacobite-French army rallied around Sarsfield, who retreated to Limerick where he intended to make a last stand. William's forces arrived some weeks later and laid siege to the city. As regards numbers it was not an even fight. Inside Limerick were about 15,000 French and Irish infantry, of which the Irish were poorly equipped and trained. Outside the city and camped a little distance away was Sarsfield at the head of 2,500 hardened cavalry troops, ready to annoy and harry the besieging army of William, which was comprised of 25,000 well-trained and well-equipped soldiers.

However, a siege requires artillery and accordingly, the heavy artillery needed to breach the solid walls of Limerick was transported under light escort, as it slowly made its way from Dublin. Sarsfield was aware of this arriving convoy, and he seized the moment by launching a brilliantly executed lightning raid on the siege train, which caught the escort completely by surprise. The guns were destroyed, many of William's troops were killed and a large quantity of vital ammunition and military stores was captured, much to the delight of those besieged in Limerick when the material was distributed to the Catholic troops.

Days later there was an all-out attack on the walls without the use of heavy artillery, but Sarsfield saw the impending danger and attacked the offenders with his dragoons as they were about to breach the walls. The attack failed with much loss of life on the attackers' side and William refused to order any further assaults until a second battery of heavy artillery was delivered.

However, before the new artillery arrived the winter rains set in and the English were forced to retire, having been unable to dislodge the Jacobite forces from Limerick. Sarsfield was now a popular hero throughout Ireland and regarded as a genius for his personal daring and shrewdness in leadership.

William's army had suffered about 3,000 casualties so far in the Limerick siege, including many of its best English, Dutch, Danish, and German troops. The defenders inside the walls of Limerick, together with Sarsfield's marauding dragoons outside, had lost only 400. Even William's General was impressed by the way Sarsfield had conducted himself, describing him as, 'a gallant champion for his cause'. In October 1691, when Sarsfield realised that further actions in Ireland in support of King James II were hopeless, he negotiated a very favourable surrender, whereby French troops would be returned to their homeland unharmed and the Irish defenders would disband without recriminations.

However, Patrick Sarsfield was ordered into exile. He returned to France, having succeeded in bringing more than 12,000 Irish soldiers to that country to join King James. And all of these potential enemies transported at English expense! He joined the army of Louis XIV, where he was awarded the rank of lieutenant-general

(*Maréchal-de-camp*) and placed at the head of the Irish troops. He was also given the title of Earl of Lucan by the exiled King James, perhaps in belated recognition that Sarsfield had indeed been one of the King's most effective generals. He fought with distinction in Flanders until mortally wounded at the Battle of Landen in 1693, where he was fighting the English, Scots and Dutch on behalf of the French (*see* Kit Cavanagh, p. 34).

He was struck by a musket-ball to the chest and died three days later. As he breathed his last, he purportedly cried out, 'Oh, that this were for Ireland!'

Sarsfield had married Lady Honora Burke, the daughter of the Earl of Clanricarde, another Irish noble family, at the end of 1689 and they had one son who died childless in 1718.

A biography of Patrick Sarsfield was published in 1992, by Piers Wauchope, who said, 'By the time of his death, Patrick Sarsfield was by far the best known and most loved of all the Irishmen … none … have been written about as much as he has been and no Irish leader [will be] until the times of Wolfe Tone a century later.' (Wauchope, *Patrick Sarsfield and the Williamite War*, p. 1.)

He is still remembered fondly in Ireland, especially in Limerick where he is regarded as a romantic hero in his fight against the English. He has streets, bridges and the army barracks in Limerick named after him. But Patrick Sarsfield's true legacy is that he was a Catholic and came from a long line of Irish Catholic nobility. Everything he did in his brief life of thirty-eight years was to further the cause of Catholicism. Whether it was fighting against Protestantism in Europe, England or Ireland, Patrick had an abiding love for his faith and was prepared to die for it. In the end, he did.

KIT CAVANAGH
(1667–1739)

SOLDIER

This woman used several names throughout her life, some through marriage but others as aliases. She was variously known by the surname Welch, Ross, Jones and finally Davies. This biography will use the name of Kit (as she preferred) Cavanagh – Catherine was her official name.

Kit was born to a family of maltsters and brewers in Dublin in 1667. Her father was a Protestant, but died from wounds inflicted while fighting for the Catholic King James II in the Jacobite wars of 1689. The public house which her father owned passed into the hands of his wife, who together with young Kit served the rough and tough element of Dublin's poor. When she was a teenager she was sexually assaulted by a relative and by the time she was twenty, she was married to one of the hotel's servants and had a child.

The young woman inherited the hotel when she was twenty-one and despite her relative inexperience was apparently making a good living when in 1692, her husband Richard Welch (some say Walsh) suddenly disappeared one day, leaving Kit with two young children and pregnant with a third.

For a whole year she heard nothing about his whereabouts, but then she received a letter from the Netherlands. It was from her husband Richard, describing how he had been drunk and then 'press-ganged' (forcefully conscripted) into the army on the last day she had seen him. However, he did not identify which regiment he was fighting with, so Kit had no way of writing back to him. If she wanted to see him she had to go and search for him, but Britain was at war with the Netherlands and all civilian transport was embargoed. The only way a person could get transport there was to join the military as a soldier.

Kit left her children with her mother, cut her hair, dressed in one of Richard's suits and enlisted in the Duke of Marlborough's infantry under the name Christopher Welch. She was twenty-six years old.

For the next three years she fought as an infantryman while occasionally making enquiries regarding her husband's whereabouts. She was slightly wounded at the Battle of Landen (1693) in Belgium, where Patrick Sarsfield was killed (*see* p. 33), but only needed minimal medical attention. Days after the battle, she was captured by the French in another skirmish, though returned in a prisoner exchange a week later. At no stage did the British (nor the French for that matter) discover that she was a woman.

Once returned to her unit, she continued her life as a soldier, which included the customary drinking sessions, moments of sheer terror and the making of money out of plunder. She once wrote later, 'We spared nothing, killing, burning, and otherwise destroying whatever we could not carry off.'

Soldiers need to urinate, sometimes in public, while on active service. To maintain her subterfuge, Kit devised a silver tube that funnelled the flow of her urine, thereby allowing her to stand and urinate like a man.

In 1697 she became embroiled in a dispute with a sergeant in her regiment over, of all things, a woman. Cavanagh defended the woman against the unwanted advances of the sergeant and wounded him in a subsequent duel. She was forced to resign from the army, but immediately re-enlisted in the cavalry (the Scots Greys).

Later that same year, the Peace of Ryswick (1697) was declared and Cavanagh found herself back in Ireland, demobilised at the end of the war. By now it had been five years since her husband had gone missing and she became resigned to the prospect that she would probably never see him again.

The peace did not last and in 1701 hostilities broke out again between the major powers of Europe in the War of Spanish Succession. On the pretext of still trying to find her husband, Kit Cavanagh once again enlisted in the Dragoons of the Scots Greys, again as Christopher Welch. However, it would be more correct to say that a military life now excited her and filled her with a sense of adventure.

She was so successful at passing herself off as a male British soldier in war that on one occasion a prostitute claimed she was the 'father' of her child. Rather than give proof that this was impossible, Cavanagh paid child support to the woman. Riding with the Scots Greys she was slightly wounded in the thigh during the Battle of Schellenberg (1704), but she refused medical treatment, because such attention would have uncovered her secret.

After the Battle of Blenheim (1704), she was assigned to guard French prisoners when she happened to recognise her long-missing husband in the amorous embrace of a woman. Initially angry at finding Richard Welch cheating, Kit eventually calmed down and the two resolved to continue their lives separately. She asked Richard to keep her secret safe so that she could continue her charade, and he agreed.

In 1706 Kit was wounded again during the Battle of Ramillies in Belgium. This time the injury was serious: a fractured skull. During the subsequent operation it was discovered to everyone's astonishment that the apparently male trooper was, in fact, a woman.

Kit quickly became a celebrity throughout the British army and her husband was summoned from his regiment to remarry Kit in a rare battlefield wedding. Kit expected to be sent home to Britain, but to her surprise she was allowed to stay on and serve the cavalry unit as a 'sutleress' (civilian cook and provider of provisions). However, she had to now dress openly as a woman.

When her husband was killed in 1709 along with over 20,000 others at the Battle of Malplaquet in France, it was Cavanagh who found his body. Deeply distraught, she was consoled by a captain named Ross and quickly became his companion, and was referred to in the regiment as 'Mother Ross'. But the liaison did not last and within three months Kit married Hugh Jones, a grenadier with the Royal Scots Greys. However, this relationship did not last either, for Jones was killed in battle in 1710.

Two years later, with the war now over, Kit returned to London where she found that her fame had preceded her. She was presented at the court of Queen Anne, who granted her a bounty of £50, plus a shilling a day for the rest of her life, which allowed her to start another pub back in Dublin. She had been away for ten years and sadly during that time, two of her three children had died and the third was in the workhouse as a pauper. She promptly retrieved her surviving child and commenced to start life afresh in her new hotel.

Unfortunately, she continued her poor choice of partners when she embarked on her third marriage, to an ex-soldier named Davies. Her new husband was dissolute and spent most of her profits of her business on drink. She remained unsettled, and for the next twenty-seven years she moved constantly between Ireland and England, starting and losing several hotel businesses. Eventually, she managed to get her husband a job in the Chelsea Hospital (a retirement home for ex-soldiers who were broken by age or war), where she herself became a pensioner. She ended her days there and was buried with full military honours in Westminster.

In 1740, one year after her death, a biography appeared under the hand of British Army Surgeon John Wilson, who had served as a medic in the same campaigns as Cavanagh. It is entirely speculative, but it is possible that Wilson may have even assisted in the operation that uncovered her true identity in 1706. Wilson said of Cavanagh that she was, 'the most remarkable person this or any other nation ever produced.' (J. Wilson, *The British Heroine*, p. ii. – *see* references at the end)

Perhaps these sentiments border on the side of hyperbole, but today young female recruits into the army are reminded that 300 years ago a young, feisty, female joined the military, fought alongside men and distinguished herself on the battlefield, being wounded several times.

These recruits are reminded that if Kit Cavanagh could achieve success in what was exclusively a man's profession 300 years ago, imagine what a young woman could do today in a world of equal opportunity.

TURLOUGH O'CAROLAN
(1670–1738)

HARPIST AND COMPOSER
OF IRISH FOLK MUSIC

Turlough was born near Nobber, Co. Meath where his father was the town's blacksmith, or according to one source, ran an iron foundry. When Turlough (Terry in English) was a teenager, the family moved to Ballyfarnon in Co. Roscommon where his father took up employment with the MacDermott-Roe family of Alderford House in 1684.

The MacDermott-Roes were an ancient Irish family who had prospered in medieval times, but as English control strengthened throughout Ireland in the sixteenth and seventeenth centuries the family's influence had declined. Nevertheless, when the O'Carolan family arrived at Alderford House in 1684 the MacDermott-Roes were still wealthy farmers, who held substantial land holdings throughout the north-west of Ireland.

The MacDermott-Roe family was staunchly Catholic and backed James II during the Jacobite War against William of

Orange (1689–1691). This resulted in the family being stripped of its official titles by the English and Mr MacDermott-Roe senior fleeing to France in exile. Several tracts of land were confiscated by the Crown, but the family was allowed to keep its substantial estate of 1,250 hectares at Ballyfarnon, which was now run by Mrs MacDermott-Roe.

She befriended the teenager Turlough and gave him a basic education. To everyone's delight it was found that Turlough had a natural gift for poetry and music. Unfortunately, when he was eighteen he contracted smallpox and was left permanently blind in both eyes. Mrs MacDermott-Roe arranged for Turlough to have harp lessons and paid for his tuition from a local harpist over the next three years. At the age of twenty-one, with his musical apprenticeship completed, Mrs MacDermott-Roe gave him an Irish harp, a horse, some money and a guide, and sent him out to travel the roads of Ireland.

For a millennium the harp had been held in the highest regard in Ireland and competent players were honoured. A tradition had developed over centuries whereby Irish nobility patronised harpists, who were often paid to compose sentimental ballads about Irish nationhood, freedom and praise of their Gaelic lifestyle. But with the expansion of English control over much of the countryside, the English authorities considered harpists, poets and story-tellers to be dangerous. By the close of the seventeenth century, when O'Carolan was setting forth on his travels, laws had been enacted forbidding the support of harpists and their like.

The suppression of Irish traditional culture was deliberately designed to obliterate any sense of Irish pride and independence that the people might have, and to replace it with a dependence on English culture. This was why O'Carolan was sent out into the world by Mrs MacDermott-Roe, for this was an attempt to capture, maintain and compose as much Irish traditional music as possible. Turlough became one of the last Irish harpists to do so.

Turlough travelled widely throughout Ireland, composing and singing songs in return for a night of food and shelter. Being blind meant that he was unable to write down his music, but thankfully he not only possessed a great musical ability, but he also had a phenomenal memory. When he composed or heard a tune he could play it again perfectly, even decades later. Once he was challenged by another player to replay a tune O'Carolan had heard only once many years earlier. Not only did he replay it note for note, but then he played it again, adding his own enhancements that made it a far superior composition.

O'Carolan's genius was that he was able to successfully merge traditional Irish folk music with more modern elements, such as the 'Italian baroque' style of musical presentation. The underlying melody was still instantly recognisable as an old Irish tune, but the presentation had a modern, timeless feel about it. His tunes were written down by others, including his son, and many still survive today.

O'Carolan married Maggie Maguire in 1720 and they had several children, though it was well known that he 'knew' many other women. The family settled down on land near the town of Mohill, in Co. Leitrim. But when his wife died in 1733, he took to the road again at the age of sixty-three, being warmly greeted by the Irish population wherever he went. He had by now become the pre-eminent harp player in Ireland and even the English dared not interfere with his popularity or performances.

But age and the hardships of years of travelling finally caught up with the man and in 1738 the ailing sixty-eight-year old Turlough returned to the home of his first benefactor, Mr MacDermott-Roe in Co. Roscommon. He was led to an upstairs bed and cared for. A few days later, he called for his harp, and lifting his beloved instrument, composed one last beautiful melody – 'O'Carolan's Farewell to Music'. Then he died.

Gráinne Yeats, musician, historian and daughter-in-law of the poet William B. Yeats (*see* p. 168) wrote extensively about O'Carolan in *The Complete Collection of Carolan's Irish Tunes* in which she said, 'At his best he wrote music that is distinctively Irish, yet has an international flavour as well. It is this achievement that suggests Turlough O'Carolan does indeed deserve the title of Ireland's National Composer.' (p. 6)

Turlough O'Carolan left a legacy of over 220 tunes, the first of which were published in Dublin in 1762 after the English had lifted their restrictions on promoting Irish culture. From this point there was a resurgence of interest in Irish traditional music, culminating in harp festivals being held in Ireland during the last decades of the eighteenth century. The first was held in Granard, in Co. Longford (1781–1785) and then Belfast in 1792.

Since then, the revitalisation of all things Irish has gathered pace and is part of a broader movement now called the 'Celtic Revival', though it would be true to say that Irish harp music has not enjoyed the same popular success as other forms of music. In fact in some parts of Ireland harp playing has all by died out over the last century. Yet the mystical allure of the harp, especially the Irish harp played by Turlough O'Carolan, continues to attract attention. O'Carolan is regarded as one of the last of the great Irish harpists and the harp itself takes pride of place on not only the Royal coat of arms of the United Kingdom, but as the only symbol on the Republic of Ireland's coat of arms.

AMBROSIO O'HIGGINS
(c.1720–1801)

VICEROY OF CHILE AND MARQUÉS DE OSORNO

When this man was born at around 1720 in Ballinary, Co. Sligo, he was called Ambrose. The O'Higgins family were minor Irish nobility with ancient roots going back to a time before the Vikings. Although the family had little money, he received a good education through an uncle who was a Jesuit priest.

When Ambrose was still young, he was sent to Spain to continue his education with a view to perhaps becoming a priest himself. At the time Irish Catholic seminaries had been closed by the English and Spain was one of the few countries that welcomed young Irishmen into its religious institutions. Spain and Ireland not only shared a common religion, but much of Ireland's native population and that of Spain also shared a common animosity against the English.

Ambrosio (the Spanish form of Ambrose) showed little academic aptitude however, and for the next few years drifted in and out of a number of unsuccessful commercial ventures in the Spanish port city of Cadiz. In 1756, frustrated at his lack of success, Ambrosio took a galleon across the Atlantic Ocean to try his luck in the Spanish New World. He started a small business in Lima, Peru, which had become the most important city in the New World for Spain. But his business failed, like all his previous business ventures had, and after four fruitless years he returned to Spain again.

In 1760, the year Ambrosio returned to Spain, an important event occurred that would alter his circumstances. The Order of Jesuits were expelled from South America and their lands confiscated by the Portuguese. To counter growing territorial expansion by the Portuguese, the newly crowned Spanish Emperor, Charles III, decided to consolidate Spain's dominion over the New World by encouraging Spanish citizens to take up government positons in the colonies. Ambrosio set off once again to South America, this time resolutely determined to make his fame and fortune by working for the Spanish government.

His first break came in 1766 when he successfully established a year-round, all-weather, overland postal route between Spain's possessions in modern-day Chile and Argentina. O'Higgins achieved this by following and improving upon ancient Inca paths that crossed the snow-covered Andes. This new track cut communication time between the major cities of Lima and Buenos Aires from being months by sea, to weeks via the overland route. Such competence brought O'Higgins the reward of being commissioned into the Spanish colonial cavalry as a captain and in 1770 he was dispatched to subdue the native Indian tribes along Chile's southern frontier.

Later that same year he won a key victory against the Araucanian Indians and established a fort at San Carlos in southern Chile.

Unlike many other officers, O'Higgins showed respect and fairness towards the native populations he subdued. The Spanish authorities had comparatively few military leaders in their officer-class to control its huge South American empire. So men who could expand Spain's dominion and then maintain a lasting peace, received steady promotions. Over the next fifteen years Ambrosio O'Higgins rose rapidly through the ranks of the military.

O'Higgins was promoted first to Lieutenant-Colonel and then Brigadier in charge of Chile's southern frontier region. By 1786 he had become *Intendente* (Government Administrator) of Concepción, Spain's most important city in southern Chile. After showing that he was very capable in the role, he was appointed to the high post of Captain-General (Governor) of Chile, which reported directly to the Viceroy of Peru.

As Captain-General of Chile, O'Higgins made changes that were to have an important long-term impact on the country. He abolished the system of *encomienda*, which had virtually reduced the legal status of native workers to that of slaves. He grew Chile's economy by developing old and new industries, such as the production of rice and tobacco, mining, and fishing. He erected permanent dykes and levee banks along the Mapocho River to prevent the capital city, Santiago, from being frequently flooded. After rebuilding the far-southern city of Osorno in 1788, which had been left abandoned for almost 200 years, the King of Spain awarded him the title of Marqués de Osorno.

In 1793, O'Higgins sponsored a famous council on the plains of Negrete in southern Chile, at which 161 native chiefs swore their allegiance to the King of Spain in return for an upgrading in their legal status, allowing them to share in the growing prosperity of the colony.

Again promoted to Lieutenant-General in 1794, 'Don Ambrosio' as he was now popularly and affectionately called, became the Viceroy of Peru in 1795. The territory controlled by him took in great swathes of land covering all or parts of what is now Ecuador, Peru, Chile, Columbia, Bolivia, north-west Argentina and some of western Brazil. For the Spanish, it was the most important possession outside Spain itself and was built on the proceeds of centuries of massive exports of silver and gold. The capital of Lima was a distinguished and aristocratic settlement, with the largest population of any city in South America.

It was the most important strategic location of the Spanish Empire and Don Ambrosio de O'Higgins, Marqués de Osorno, was in sole charge. He was seventy-five when he was appointed Viceroy, but was still energetic and organised.

He needed to be, for when war broke out between Britain and Spain in 1797, as a result of Spain allying itself with Napoleonic France, O'Higgins devoted himself tirelessly to the area's defence, building up fortifications along the coast to prevent a naval attack, which O'Higgins rightly believed was inevitable. Britain had been seeking to expand its influence in South America since the loss of its North American colonies in the War of Independence (1775–1783), but as enticing as the west coast of South America was, Ambrosio's efforts at shoring up defences caused the British to rethink their plans. Instead of invading from the sea, the British authorities devised an audacious strategy to attack overland from Argentina ('The Maitland Plan'), something which was never implemented because of their forces twice failing to capture Buenos Aires. However, twenty years later Ambrosio's son, Bernardo, together with General San Martin, would use the Maitland Plan in their successful struggle for Chilean independence from the Spanish Empire.

Ambrosio O'Higgins died suddenly after a short illness in 1801.

He had never married, but had enjoyed a brief relationship with Isabel Riquelme, the attractive daughter of close family friends. She was only eighteen at the time, while Ambrosio was fifty-seven years old. In 1778, Isabel gave birth to a boy, Bernardo, who was never officially recognised as a son and heir until Ambrosio was on his deathbed. Ambrosio did send Bernardo to Spain and then to England for a decent education and made provisions for him in his will, but there was no relationship between father and son.

Bernardo would go on to liberate Chile from Spanish rule in 1817 and to appoint himself Supreme Dictator of Chile from 1817–1823, after which opponents of his autocratic style forced him from office. He lived in exile in neighbouring Peru until his death in 1842. Bernardo O'Higgins is still regarded in Chile as 'The Great Liberator'.

Today, there are roads, bridges, parks and buildings named after either Ambrosio O'Higgins or his son Bernardo in South America. Administrative areas of government in Argentina and Chile are called O'Higgins. Geographical features including navigable bays along the coast, a lake, a glacier and a base for research in Antarctica bear the O'Higgins name. Finally, a football club in the Chilean Premier Division is called the O'Higgins Fútbol Club.

WOLFE TONE
(1763–98)

IRISH PATRIOT

Tone was born in Dublin, the eldest of sixteen children to Peter Tone, a successful coach-builder and his wife Margaret (née Lamport). The family was middle-class and Protestant. Baptised Theobald Wolfe Tone, he preferred to use his middle name. From his youth, Wolfe demonstrated a powerful and inquiring mind, which he used to start examining the world around him. His father made many financial sacrifices to enable Wolfe to become a lawyer, including finding tuition at expensive schools after his business interests failed. In 1780, he was accepted into the Law faculty of Trinity College, Dublin, but Tone was restless and thought that a career in the military was more to his liking.

His passage though university was punctuated with a suspension for a year for duelling; he had a whirlwind elopement and marriage to Martha Witherington, the daughter of a local draper, and discovered that he possessed remarkable debating and oratory skills, for which he won several medals. When he graduated from Trinity College in 1786, Tone had developed a keen desire to know more about the political world he was about to enter.

Leaving his wife in the care of his own family, Tone journeyed to London to further his law career as a barrister, but he was bored and allowed himself to be distracted by gossip, novel writing and an adventurous scheme to found a colony in Hawaii. The tea houses, pubs and gentlemen's clubs he attended started to fuel his yearning for political knowledge.

Despite a lack of application, Tone managed to qualify as a barrister in 1788 but his heart was no longer in law, it was in politics. When he returned to Dublin in 1789 he became a pamphleteer (writer of opinion pieces), and his pamphlets were crudely printed on cheap paper and widely distributed to the masses. These documents were poorly composed when he began producing them, but Tone slowly began honing his skills, arguing and stating his thoughts, thereby making steady improvements. At the same time he also developed his ideas on the political situation in Ireland and concluded that the Irish were being unjustly repressed by the English. He considered that something needed to be done about it.

Wolfe Tone was not alone in this opinion. In fact by the second half of the eighteenth century many Irish people – both Catholic and Protestant – had become militant in opposition to English rule. What was particularly galling for many was that the discrimination was based on religious grounds and nothing more.

While some easing of restrictions occurred in the 1780s and 1790s, Irish Catholics were still prevented from holding senior government posts, owning horses and buying Protestant land. They continued to face restrictions on trade and voting, including exclusion from political participation at a meaningful level.

Finally, resentment reached a critical point after the American War of Independence (1765–1783) followed by the start of the French Revolution in 1789, which wrought powerful changes in those two countries. Wolfe Tone was greatly influenced by the writings of Thomas Paine, an English-American Philosopher who wrote the *Rights of Man* in 1791. The publication was eagerly read by many Irish people, who devoured its central message promoting representative democracy and republicanism.

Tone came to the radical conclusion that Ireland should totally separate from Britain to achieve true democracy through independence. He penned off another pamphlet, titled *'An argument on behalf of Catholics in Ireland'*, stating his views that Ireland must, 'break the connection with England, the never failing source of all our political evils'. He reassured the Irish Protestants that they had as much to gain from an independent Ireland as the Catholics and in any event he wanted people to think of themselves as 'Irishmen' rather than 'Catholics or Protestants'.

This pamphlet caused a sensation throughout Ireland and within months 16,000 copies had been sold. With one stroke of his pen, Wolfe Tone had become the spokesperson for the people wanting radical change. He was invited to Belfast to attend the inauguration of a new society designed to give effect to Tone's dream of an independent Irish republic. It was called the Society of United Irishmen, and Tone became one of its founding members in 1791.

The Society of United Irishmen had struck a nerve with the Irish people and membership grew exponentially to approximately 200,000 within a few years, with branches across Ireland. Tone felt so assured that he led a delegation to London in 1792, where he handed a petition of grievances directly to King George III.

Everything seemed to be going Tone's way. Even the English

Parliament was moved to enact legislation offering voting rights to Irish Catholics on the same basis as Irish Protestants, but then France declared War on Britain in 1793. Overnight, Tone found that sympathy for his campaign among the English authorities had been replaced by cries of sedition.

The government instituted a crackdown on dissent in Ireland and rounded up leaders it thought would undermine its war effort against France. As well as leaders of several other militant organisations, arrests also included those of one or two office bearers of the Society of United Irishmen. Tone was somehow overlooked during the first lot of arrests, but understood quite clearly that his time at large was in jeopardy. He was thinking of fleeing to America in 1794, when he was approached in secret by a French spy who was authorised in writing to offer significant military assistance if Tone could assure him the people of Ireland would also rise up in rebellion. Tone jumped at the chance and satisfied the secret agent that all the Irish, Protestant and Catholic alike, were ready to fight and die for their freedom.

The government uncovered evidence of this clandestine meeting, outlawed the Society of United Irishmen as a revolutionary organisation and made several arrests. To head off an arrest, Wolfe Tone went directly to the authorities and made a deal. He would confirm what the government already knew in return for not being transported to the penal colony of Botany Bay and would agree to leave Ireland voluntarily. Within the year he had settled his affairs as promised and went into self-exile in America.

However, the French had not lost interest in Tone and a representative caught up with Wolfe in Philadelphia in 1795. There were two meetings spread out over several months while the French representative sought further instructions from Paris, but at the second meeting Tone was warmly invited to the French capital to formalise plans for a French invasion of Ireland.

From the moment he arrived in France in 1796, he fell in love with the country and immediately made arrangements for his wife and family to join him. During meetings with the military and civil authorities in Paris, Tone authoritatively laid out his plans for a joint French invasion and simultaneous Irish insurrection of Ireland. For some time the French had believed an invasion of Ireland was a brilliant strategy to attack England, through the weakly defended 'back door', but now Tone's skilful advocacy turned them into wildly enthusiastic supporters of such a policy.

The French rapidly assembled a fleet of forty-three ships and crammed them with almost 15,000 soldiers. Then it set sail for Bantry Bay in Cork, Ireland, with Wolfe Tone, now appointed *Chef de Brigade* (Brigadier-General), at its helm. This fulfilled his younger romantic notions of being in the military. But the invasion was a disaster. Severe winds and rough seas prevented the army from landing. The ships sailed back and forth for several days frustratingly in sight of the coast, until food and water ran out and they had to return to France.

The French agreed to launch a second invasion attempt the following year in 1797, but this time unfavourable weather prevented the fleet from even leaving the French harbour. Later that year Napoleon Bonaparte seized power in France and, even though he met Wolfe Tone over several meetings to discuss yet another Irish invasion, it was clear that Napoleon had no interest in the project. Instead, his eyes were firmly set in the direction of the Mediterranean Sea, and Ireland in the Atlantic Ocean was an unnecessary distraction.

Meanwhile, patriots in Ireland had grown frustrated at the

two failed attempts to land French troops and in a risky gesture decided to launch a rebellion without French military support. It was doomed to fail. Over the previous years, much of the leadership of the United Irishmen had been rounded up, gaoled or executed. There was no effective control of the rebels.

Further, the mood of some of the Irish people had altered. After years of armed struggle against France, in which many Irish men fought for the British, it seemed grossly disloyal, even traitorous, to welcome enemy troops onto Irish streets. Nevertheless, the pathetic rump of United Irishman's governance decided they could wait no longer and launched a general uprising to commence in mid-June 1798.

In Paris, Tone and the French were caught completely off-guard. No one knew about the rebellion until three-weeks after it had started. A small fleet was hastily assembled, manned with an expeditionary force of about 4,000 troops and instructed to lend any assistance they could when they landed in Ireland. Tone went with them, but it was too late. The rebellion had been crushed at a cost of over 30,000 lives even before the French landed. As poorly organised as it was, it still ranks as one of the bloodiest uprisings in Ireland's history, which clearly demonstrated that parts of the country still harboured deep anti-English feelings. There was some sporadic fighting, but it was in short order, the French soldiers surrendered and among those captured was Wolfe Tone.

He was conveyed to Dublin in chains and under armed escort where he was swiftly tried under Martial Law, something that had been declared since the uprising. There was never any doubt that the court would find Wolfe Tone guilty of treason. His last request was to be executed by firing squad as a uniformed officer in the French army. This was denied; instead it was ordered that he was going to be hanged like a common civilian criminal. The next morning he was found in his cell, fatally wounded from a self-inflicted knife cut to the throat.

He left behind a wife he had married thirteen years previously, and four young children. He was buried in Bodenstown, Co. Kildare, where his grave has become a site of annual commemorations. His autobiography and many journals were published posthumously by his widow and they helped to establish his reputation as the 'father' of Irish republicanism.

In his short thirty-five years, Wolfe Tone did not achieve what he intended and dearly yearned for: an independent united Irish republic. What he did achieve was to start the dream of one. His dream became Ireland's dream and over the next century this idea would grow in fits and starts, sometimes coming tantalisingly within reach and at other times seemingly completely unattainable. But during this period, Wolfe Tone's dream for Ireland remained alive in the hearts of a growing number of like-minded Irish men and women. The idea planted by Wolfe Tone, a Protestant, for an independent Irish republic would finally became a reality 120 years later.

Some historians have speculated what might have occurred if Tone had successfully landed at the head of 15,000 seasoned French troops at the first planned invasion two years earlier in 1796. The leadership of the Society of United Irishmen would have been more intact, the planned uprising would have been better co-ordinated and, most importantly, a greater proportion of the Irish people would have been willing to rise up against the English.

MARY ANN MCCRACKEN
(1770–1866)

RADICAL AND PHILANTHROPIST

Mary was born into a prominent Belfast Presbyterian family, the fifth of six children to sea Captain John McCracken and his wife Ann (née Joy). The family were prosperous merchants and known for their liberal, Protestant ideals. Capt. McCracken enjoyed a profitable trade sailing his merchant vessel between Belfast and the Americas.

The McCracken and Joy families had had roots in Belfast for a number of generations before the marriage of Capt. John and Anne Joy. Anne's father, Francis Joy, started Belfast's first newspaper, *The Belfast Newsletter*, in 1737 and both families had been involved in the then thriving linen and cotton industry for decades.

Being outward-looking and progressive, Capt. John McCracken and his wife made sure that all their children were educated at the very best schools available, where female pupils received exactly the same education as their male counterparts. This was most unusual for its time, but was typical of the McCrackens, who believed that everyone – men and women, Catholics and Protestants – should have an equal opportunity to succeed in life.

When Mary was in her late teens, she and her older brother Henry started Belfast's first Sunday school. It was open to boys and girls as well as men and women, and taught students how to read and write as well as conducting Bible studies. The local authority – controlled by an Anglican vicar who was also the long-serving Mayor of Belfast – shut the school down because in his opinion it was 'too subversive'. This caused some resentment within the two siblings and started a chain of events in their championing of causes for the poor and underprivileged that would ultimately lead to the execution of one and a lifelong commitment to social causes for the other.

In Ireland, during the 1790s, there was growing unrest among many citizens who were influenced by the revolutionary spirit and ideals of both the American Revolutionary War (1775–1783) and the French Revolution (1788–1789). Most of the McCracken family agreed with the progressive ideals of liberty and freedom that underpinned these movements. The three eldest McCracken sons were founding members of the Belfast branch of the Society of United Irishmen in 1795. The society was started as a liberal political organisation that initially sought parliamentary reform, such as the ideas of extending the voting franchise to Catholics and having limited self-government for the Irish Parliament.

However, this organisation quickly evolved into a more radical movement for Irish independence. It appears that at least two of Mary's older brothers became caught up in the more drastic aspects of the United Irishmen, for Henry and William found themselves arrested and gaoled for being part of an outlawed organisation in 1797.

Mary wrote a series of letters to her brothers that have remarkably survived to this day, in which she supported the cause of a United Ireland, but insisted on the following condition: that the desire for liberty and equality for men of Ireland had to be extended to the women of Ireland as well! She wrote:

'Is it not time for the clouds of error and prejudice to disperse … and that the female part as well as the male … rise to the situation for which they were designed' (Madden papers, p. 151).

The concept of women's equality, including allowing women the right to vote, may not appear controversial today, but in Mary McCracken's day these notions were considered extremely radical, even dangerous to society. At the time, few countries granted voting rights to men, and none to women. Even in the United States of America and France, the very models used by the United Irishmen to promote independence for Ireland, suffrage would not be granted to women until 1920 (USA) and 1944 (France).

The McCracken brothers were released on bail at the end of 1797 because of ill-health and the efforts of family lawyers, but they continued to work, secretly formulating plans for the soon-to-be-announced rebellion against British rule. In February 1798 Henry McCracken and another were appointed as the Ulster delegates to the national executive of the United Irishmen, where Henry plotted strategy with other leaders of the organisation, including Wolfe Tone (see p.49). Everyone present agreed that the organisation would lead Ireland in an open rebellion at a date yet to be fixed.

The rebellion, when it came some months later in June 1798, was an abject failure. Informers had passed on details of the plans to the British authorities and many leaders had been arrested. The French, who had been at war with Britain since 1793, promised to lend their considerable weight behind the rebellion, but arrived too late and with too small a force to influence the outcome. Earlier, the Catholic Church had been cynically 'bought off' by the British authorities with promises of a new university seminary for Roman Catholic priests, which would be known as the Royal College of St Patrick.

The seminary was built near Dublin at great expense by the British Government and opened in 1795. This commitment was enough to make the Catholic Church hierarchy openly condemn the 1798 rebellion.

With the rebellion falling apart around him, Henry McCracken decided that one dramatic gesture might yet turn the hopeless cause around. He decided to lead an attack on the British garrison in Antrim. Armed with only pitchforks and pikes the insurgents were no match for the rifles and artillery of the well-defended garrison and the attack failed within minutes.

Henry McCracken fled and hid in the hills of south Antrim, where Mary visited him and brought him much-needed clothes and money. Mary then arranged for a ship to take her brother to America, but he was arrested on his way to the port. Mary visited Henry in prison and attended his court martial, as Ireland was temporarily under martial law. Having refused an offer of clemency in return for informing on his comrades, Henry was hanged immediately after his trial, but Mary was not ready to say farewell to her beloved brother at that point in time.

Mary was given permission for a medical doctor to be present at the execution and as soon as Henry was dropped through the hangman's door of the gallows, she arranged for the body to be hastily removed. Away from the prying eyes of the British soldiers, the doctor attempted to resuscitate Henry, but despite his best efforts and Mary's desperate urgings, the body of Henry stubbornly refused to come to life.

Following the death of her brother, Mary channelled her considerable energies into charitable and educational work with the poor of the rapidly industrialising town of Belfast. Even so, she was never far from controversy with her continued support for an independent Republic of Ireland. She was close friends (some say lovers) with Thomas Russell, another revolutionary, whom she supported. Russell was executed in 1803 for trying to organise another rebellion. Mary paid for the defence at his trial and, after he was executed, paid for the headstone that was placed on his grave.

During the 1790s, Mary and her sister Margaret started a small business manufacturing and selling muslins. For a while it was successful and employed a growing number of local women from socio-economically disadvantaged areas of Belfast. This allowed Mary to campaign for industrial reform and she occasionally wrote to the *Belfast Newsletter* (the paper was still in the hands of relatives) pointing out ways to improve the health and hygiene of employees.

Mary also took an active interest in the cultural life of Belfast. In particular, she was a founding member and financial benefactor of the Belfast Harp Society, which contributed to the revival of interest in the Irish language, music, poetry and literature.

Ireland suffered a recession after the Napoleonic Wars and the two sisters Mary and Margaret McCracken found it impossible to keep the muslin business afloat. But Mary was more concerned about the fate of her workers than that of herself or her sister. She knew that she and Margaret would survive, but the women factory workers would find it impossible to get other jobs. When the debts were finally cleared in 1815, there was very little money left.

In response to the catastrophic Irish Potato Famine of 1845–1847, in which up to a million people died, Mary, now in her seventies, established the Belfast Ladies Association for the Relief of Irish Destitution. She became its first president and toiled ceaselessly, raising money for this and other organisations she was involved in, such as the Belfast Ladies Clothing Society and the Society for the Relief of the Destitute Sick.

Her commitment to political causes never wavered throughout her life. Although her public support for an independent Irish Republic became less strident as she grew older, Mary found her energies directed into another cause – slavery. Mary had been a supporter of the anti-slavery movement from its early days, when the United Irishmen called for a boycott of sugar products from the slave plantations of the West Indies. In 1859, at eighty-nine years of age, she was still handing out leaflets to emigrants about what she called, 'the diabolical system of slavery', at the docks in Belfast as they were departing for the Americas. It was not until 1865 that slavery was abolished in the United States.

She wrote to a friend near the end of her life saying, 'I have allowed my out-of-door avocations to increase so much, that I have less command of my time now than when I was occupied with [the muslin] business.' In 1866, just a few weeks after her ninety-sixth birthday, Mary Ann McCracken died peacefully in her sleep. A radical, who campaigned tirelessly for social and political causes all her life, she was now finally at rest.

SIR FRANCIS BEAUFORT
(1774–1857)

ADMIRAL AND HYDROGRAPHER

Francis was born in Navan, Co. Meath to Reverend Daniel Beaufort and his wife Mary (née Waller). He had an older brother, William, and three sisters: Frances, Harriet and Louisa. Francis's grandfather was a French Huguenot (Protestant) who fled France with his family during the religious wars of persecution in the 1600s. The Beaufort family originally settled in London, but the grandfather moved his family to Ireland in 1747 to accompany Lord Harrington, upon the latter's appointment as Lord Lieutenant of Ireland.

The Beaufort family was deeply involved in the Protestant church, with the grandfather, father and the brother of Francis all becoming Rectors (Ministers) in the Church of England and then the Church of Ireland (which has similar Anglican beliefs), after the family's relocation to Ireland.

Francis was educated at the David Bates' Military and Naval

Academy in Dublin and spent several months studying astronomy at Dunsink Observatory, part of Trinity College, Dublin. But at the age of fourteen his formal education ended when Francis was sent to sea on a Dutch East-Indies vessel for a trading and surveying voyage to the then Dutch East Indies (Indonesia). Because of poor navigation charts Francis almost lost his life when the Dutch vessel ran aground on an uncharted reef off the coast of Sumatra and he was shipwrecked.

Daniel Beaufort had an abiding interest in cartography, which was shared by his son. For most of the 1780s, Reverend Beaufort had been preparing a new and detailed map of Ireland from his own personal observations and surveys, which was published in 1792. It is believed that his young son Francis accompanied him on many of his surveys. It was from these beginnings that Francis developed a deep and abiding love of cartography.

When Francis returned to Britain from his trip to the East Indies, he had already formulated the idea that the world needed accurate sea charts for safe navigation. At the time, the British Royal Navy was producing some of the most precise sea charts in the world, known as Admiralty charts. Francis wanted to be part of this development. In 1790, Francis joined the Royal Navy as a midshipman. Over the next ten years he saw much action, including a major battle during the French Revolutionary War, in which a British fleet of seven ships was attacked by twenty-two French vessels (Admiral Cornwallis's Retreat, 1795).

In 1800, when Francis was twenty-six and now a Lieutenant on HMS *Phaeton*, he used daring and guile to capture a valuable prize ship from under the heavy guns of a Spanish fort along the Mediterranean coast. He received a total number of nineteen wounds from grapeshot in the successful attack and spent months recuperating in the family home in Ireland.

To assist in his recovery, he helped his brother-in-law Richard Edgeworth (who had married his sister Frances in 1798) establish a line of semaphore signal stations from Dublin to Galway. The route Edgeworth took in constructing his semaphore stations needed to be surveyed accurately, and Francis Beaufort took great delight in assisting in this task, which furthered his passion for mapping, cartography and charts.

In 1807, while in charge of HMS *Woolwich* and now promoted to commander, Beaufort was ordered to conduct a hydrographic survey of the coast of Rio de la Plata in South America and the charts he produced impressed many in the Admiralty, including Alexander Dalrymple (the first hydrographer of the British Admiralty) who wrote: 'we have few officers (indeed I do not know one) in our Service who have half his professional knowledge and ability, and in zeal and perseverance he cannot be excelled.' (John de Courcy Ireland, 'Francis Beaufort (Wind Scale)', found online at *National Maritime Museum of Ireland*.)

He was promoted again to Post-Captain and from 1810–12 he completed a major survey of the entire coastline of Turkey, then the homeland of the Ottoman Empire and often at war with other European powers. His charts were so accurate that they were not surpassed for 150 years. While fighting pirates, he was shot and seriously wounded in the hip. During his convalescence back in Ireland, he wrote about his experiences in what would become one of the first travel books about Turkey, which became mildly popular.

It was during this period of enforced homestay, that Beaufort began revising and refining a Wind scale that he had first developed back in 1805. He was interested in scientifically determining the most appropriate amount of sail that could be safely unfurled on a full-rigged sailing ship during various strengths of wind. But first he needed an accurate scale of wind velocity and to this end he took many observations and samples, which were refined over the years.

By 1835, the recording of wind strength using the Beaufort scale had become mandatory on all Royal Navy ships, and in 1874 the practice was adopted by the International Meteorological Committee for international use on all shipping worldwide.

Meanwhile, the repeated injuries he had sustained over his years on active service prevented Beaufort from progressing further as the captain of an operational naval vessel. His body was no longer up to the rigours of life on the open sea, but other opportunities opened themselves up to Beaufort by way of important positions onshore.

He became the Admiralty's main liaison between that organisation and a growing number of scientists who were producing an increasing amount of scientific data for the navy's benefit. In 1829, at the age of fifty-five, Beaufort reached the pinnacle of his profession when he was appointed as the 'Hydrographer of the Royal Navy' by the British Admiralty.

Beaufort served in that post for twenty-six years, converting a minor repository for naval charts into the finest surveying and charting institution in the world. He was responsible for producing over 1,000 navigational maps of the highest precision, covering all the world's oceans. British Admiralty charts still remain the most trusted navigational documents available in the world today.

Francis was also given the task of managing the Greenwich and Capetown Observatories, both of which were vitally important for maintaining Britain's position as the pre-eminent global naval power. He was elected Fellow of the Royal Astronomical Society,

Member of the Royal Society and finally Member of the Royal Geographical Society. It was Beaufort who secured government funds for the second voyage of HMS *Beagle* and invited Charles Darwin to accompany the ship. This action would lead directly to one of the seminal scientific breakthroughs for man: Darwin's Theory of Evolution.

Beaufort retired from the Royal Navy with the rank of Rear Admiral in 1846 and was knighted by Queen Victoria two years later. He died at the age of eighty-three in England, having had the 'Beaufort Sea' in the Arctic and 'Beaufort Island' in the Antarctic named after him.

This talented cartographer and innovator married Alicia Wilson, the daughter of his first captain, in 1812 and they had seven children. After her death from breast cancer in 1834, he invited his two unmarried sisters, Harriet and Louisa, to reside with him and look after the household. This arrangement lasted until 1838, when Beaufort married Honora Edgeworth, the stepdaughter of Richard Edgeworth. There was no issue from the second marriage.

It would be fair to say that the Beaufort wind scale (referred to officially today as the 'Beaufort wind force scale' or abbreviated to the 'Beaufort scale'), together with his production of the world's most accurate sea charts, has meant that Sir Francis Beaufort has saved the lives of a countless number of sailors and passengers on the oceans.

DANIEL O'CONNELL
(1775–1847)

'THE LIBERATOR'

Daniel was born on a small farm called 'Carhen', near the town of Cahersiveen in Co. Kerry. The O'Connells were once proud, Catholic gentry of old Gaelic stock, but had suffered significant decline over the previous century at the hands of discriminatory English laws. When Daniel was born, the family were lucky to still have a farm as the Penal Laws of the early 1700s should have worked against them maintaining their hold on the land, but their very remoteness on the western coast of Ireland probably acted in their favour.

The junior O'Connell's immediate family were not wealthy, but an uncle by the name of Maurice O'Connell lived about thirty kilometres away at Derrynane, and he had skilfully managed to prosper. Daniel was first sent to live with Maurice for a number of years and subsequently to France at the uncle's expense to continue his education when Daniel was about fifteen years old. The young man's intelligence and drive were noticed from the beginning by his tutors, who predicted he would achieve remarkable things in the future.

Daniel was in France for only three years, but during that time he witnessed first-hand the deteriorating political situation that would soon lead to the French revolution. He also absorbed the rhetoric and ideals of those advocating a new order and by the time he returned to the comparative safety of England in 1793, the year that France declared War on Britain, he had become somewhat of a revolutionary himself. Yet there was one important distinction between his views and that of other like-minded souls: O'Connell believed that ideals such as fairness, equality and liberty could be achieved through lawful means, not by bloodshed and outbursts of mindless violence.

By the mid-1790s, some discriminatory laws against Catholics had been repealed and O'Connell took advantage of them to go to London and become a lawyer. He was studious and eager to learn, so eager that he devoured the contents of books that were devoted to philosophy, economics and politics as well as those relating to Law. Writers such as Voltaire, Gibbon, Paine, and Adam Smith were shaping his thoughts and helping him move from ideas such as revolution to those of the evolution of humanity.

Appalled at the violence and futility of the 1798 Irish rebellion (see Wolfe Tone, p. 49) and the threatened French invasions at around this period, he joined a militia group to defend law and order. It was also at about this time that he was admitted to the Irish Bar and decided that a career in the Law would only be a stepping stone to an eventual poisition in politics. It was never going to be a case of either working as a lawyer or as a politician, as the ever-changing political atmosphere in Ireland offered Daniel plenty of scope to embrace both of these areas of interest.

He did not have to wait long to venture into the political landscape because in 1800, the Irish Parliament had voted itself out of existence by accepting an offer from London to become an integral part of the United Kingdom of England, Scotland, Wales and Ireland. O'Connell immediately launched criticism of both the dissolution of the Irish Parliament and of the enactment of the Act of Union.

The negotiated deal between London and Dublin was that if the Irish Parliament would give up any pretence of independence, the British Government would treat the Irish people as equals and return all the rights and privileges to them that had been removed over the previous century or so: meaning that Catholics would be treated the same as Protestants.

O'Connell rejected this proposal because it meant that Ireland would never be free and independent – a goal that he had come to embrace passionately. He voiced his opposition in the strongest terms possible, but it was not as a firebrand, headstrong patriot. It was the cold, clear, logic of an articulate, educated lawyer who was using reason, not emotion, to win his argument. And win it he did. People were impressed by his rhetoric and persuasive logic and at the age of twenty-five, O'Connell was making his mark in Ireland as a political reformer of the future.

During this time, his law practice was growing and his presence arguing cases before the courts was constantly in demand. In 1806, his professional income from Law was reputed to be £600, when the average wage was just £30 per year. By the mid-1820s, when O'Connell was at the height of his career as a lawyer, his annual income was said to be in excess of £6,000. But as his income grew so did his expenses.

In 1802, O'Connell married a third-cousin, Mary O'Donnell, and moved from one large and expensive home in Dublin to an even larger and more expensive home near the centre of the city. An ever-growing number of children (there would be eight in all), required more nannies and servants. Then there were friends, relatives and charity cases that Daniel generously supported. The O'Connell family should have been well-off, but throughout most of his adult life, Daniel had difficulty managing his finances.

From the second decade of the 1800s, O'Connell started campaigning for a change in the 'Oath of Allegiance', something which all new parliamentarians had to swear before they could take their seat in Westminster. The oath required the individual to acknowledge the paramountcy of the British monarch as head of the Church of England over any other religion. Catholics, Jews and some Protestants felt unable to take this oath and were therefore prevented from entering parliament. O'Connell did not want the oath discarded, he just wanted the religious connotations removed.

Catholic 'emancipation' is what O'Connell started calling the campaign against the oaths act, and from this point onwards he began adding other areas of discrimination where Catholics were also prevented or discouraged from taking an active part in society. In 1823, he formed the Catholic Association and organised for ordinary Irish Catholics to contribute a small levy of a penny per month into a fighting fund. By 1825, the Catholic Association had evolved into a vast and powerful organisation that had spread across Ireland.

Thanks to the fighting fund, the Association was able to stand candidates in a number of electorates in the 1826 elections. Against all odds four candidates were successful in Monaghan, Westmeath, Louth and the city of Waterford. Waterford was a particularly pleasing result, because it had been previously held by the wealthy and influential Beresford family, who had considered the seat to be theirs.

O'Connell was teaching the Irish that change could be achieved through peaceful means and in the process, he was giving the people a voice. He decided to test the resolve of the Westminster Parliament by running as a candidate at the 1828 election. If he won, and was turned away from parliament because he would not take the oath, he wondered what would the government in London do?

The campaigner lawyer was overwhelmingly elected to the seat of Clare by a two-to-one majority and, as planned, was debarred from taking his seat when he presented himself at Westminster and refused to take the oath. So adroit was his management of the issue and so agitated were the Irish that it seemed to the British Government that the majority of the estimated 6 million people of Ireland were about to rise up in rebellion. After the horrors of 1798, this was simply unthinkable. To avoid this potential calamity, Prime Minister Wellington backed down and in 1829 the Catholic Relief Act was passed. This was an Act which repealed virtually all previous discriminatory legislation that had been aimed against Catholics.

In Ireland, O'Connell was now regarded as the undisputed leader of Irish nationalism and to the amazement of many, had achieved significant advancements without resorting to bloodshed. Because he had emancipated the Catholics, he would be called by the sobriquet 'The Liberator' for the rest of his life. One other, very important lesson was learnt – the English could be beaten using parliamentary democracy and the British legal system.

In the 1830s, O'Connell was at the apex of his political career and his reform agenda seemed unstoppable. He had successfully reformed the poor laws, eliminated the ancient and repressive regime of tithes in Ireland, achieved changes to municipal elections and co-founded the National Bank of Ireland. Outside the United Kingdom, O'Connell campaigned for the abolition of slavery and the liberation movement in South America.

And in 1840, O'Connell turned his full attention back to the issue that had been dogging him for the past four decades – the Act of Union of 1800. He thought the Union was a disaster for Ireland, a means by which it threw away its sovereignty and any chance of independence in return for having England merely reverse some discriminatory policies that should not have been implemented in the first place.

He called for a repeal of the Act of Union and set out to use exactly the same tactics that had worked so successfully twenty years earlier. He founded the Repeal Association in 1840, and the powerful voice of 'The Liberator' began drawing the Catholic population to his cause. To bolster his campaign he ran for, and was elected, as Mayor of Dublin. O'Connell held 'Monster Meetings' across the country, which attracted enormous crowds that started to worry the government in London. One gigantic meeting was attended by 750,000 men and the one after that, O'Connell promised, would be even larger.

This next meeting was scheduled to be held outside Dublin at Clontarf in 1843 and many in authority believed that it would quickly get out of hand and possibly lead to rioting in Ireland's capital. There was also some evidence from informers that militant elements within the Repeal Association would actually use the expected crowd of up to one million people to unleash something far more sinister than rioting, perhaps even a rebellion. This last piece of information would be disputed later, but nevertheless the authorities were deeply worried about what such a huge number of people could be capable of, especially if O'Connell lost control over the crowd. The meeting was banned at the last moment.

O'Connell could have easily gone ahead with the meeting. After all, his tactics of brinkmanship had always worked in the past. But something about the number and mood of the people predicted to attend, caused him to pause. O'Connell backed down and cancelled the meeting, following which he was arrested, tried and convicted of sedition. The conviction was quashed on appeal by the House of Lords, but in the meantime he had spent seven months in gaol. When he was finally released the aura of invincibility that had followed him all his adult life had evaporated.

The Repeal movement now faltered as the potato harvest of 1845 was ruined by blight. The young hard-line radicals within the movement started to talk about using violence to achieve their goals if it became necessary and O'Connell, now in his seventies, no longer had the willpower and conviction to convince them otherwise. 'Obey my advice … no violence,' he demanded, but they were no longer listening.

As hunger began to spread across the land, the Repeal Association split and for once, O'Connell was not able to unite it again. In truth, the population and the young radicals they now turned to for leadership had lost interest in pursuing high, lofty ideals; they just wanted food instead. O'Connell was also concerned about the gathering calamity of famine. In his last speech to the House of Commons, his once powerful voice had been reduced to hardly a whisper, when he pleaded: 'Ireland is in your hands … she cannot save herself.'

Daniel O'Connell was devastated when his wife Mary died

in 1836, leaving him quite alone and companionless for the last eleven years of his life. By 1845 his health had deteriorated quite dramatically. Knowing that time was not on his side, he left Ireland for what would be his final trip – a pilgrimage to Rome. He died in Genoa, Italy, in 1847 at the age of seventy-two from meningitis. His body was brought back to Dublin for burial.

O'Connell was a champion of civil and religious liberty; of an Ireland in which all people could be equal. He was also an advocate of non-violent protest, but was prepared to use every political trick in parliament to achieve his objectives. Today, he would be called a pragmatic idealist. His non-violent approach to reform would become the model adopted by Mahatma Ghandi, Martin Luther King and Nelson Mandela in their struggles for freedom and social justice.

Writing in 1889, Prime Minister William Gladstone eulogised O'Connell as, 'the greatest popular leader of the present century and the greatest Irishman that ever lived ... who never for a moment changed his end [and] never hesitated to change his means.' (*Nineteenth Century*, Jan. 1889.)

CHARLES (CARLO) BIANCONI
(1786–1875)

PIONEER OF PUBLIC
TRANSPORT IN IRELAND

Charles (Carlo) was born in a nondescript village near Como in northern Italy. He was the second of five children to Pietro and Maria Bianconi, who ran a small silk farm. Carlo was destined to become a priest, but when he was a teenager Napoleon Bonaparte's armies attacked northern Italy in 1798, forcing the Austrian rulers of the region at the time to raise an army by conscription.

Many Italian families had long objected to Austrian rule, which had been imposed fifty years earlier. They were certainly not willing to send their sons to fight Bonaparte, whom a sizeable number of Italians secretly admired. Dozens and then hundreds of teenage males quietly left for overseas and Carlo Bianconi was one of them. To pay for the trip, Carlo was apprenticed to an engraver and printer for eighteen months and shipped off to London.

When Carlo arrived there he discovered that his sponsor,

Andrea Faroni, had coincidentally made a decision to relocate his business to Dublin and in short order, Carlo found himself living in crowded conditions in Temple Bar on the south bank of the River Liffey in central Dublin. It was 1802 and Carlo was only sixteen years old in a city that was completely foreign to him. He could not even speak the language.

The first thing that Carlo did was anglicise his name to Charles and then to earn his keep he started selling engravings and other art work on the streets of Dublin. A year later, and with his language skills improving all the time, he was selling art works throughout the countryside as well. On one trip overland to Waterford he was arrested for selling images of Napoleon, who was at the time Britain's main enemy. He managed to avoid punishment by speaking Italian only until the soldiers let him go.

When his eighteen-month apprenticeship (more an indenture really) had expired, Andrea Faroni agreed to help Charles establish his own business. He took to the road as a travelling salesman, selling pictures and frames on his own account, and carried everything he had in a large box strapped to his shoulders. It was back-breaking work, lugging twenty or thirty kilograms' worth of wares day-after-day along dirty, uneven country tracks and lanes for kilometres during the wet, the windy and the cold conditions. Yet Charles continued to trudge the highways and byways of Ireland on foot for the next thirteen years, coming to the growing realisation that he needed to buy a pony and cart to alleviate his hardship.

Bianconi had based his business in Clonmel, Co. Tipperary when in 1815 he had saved enough money to purchase a two-wheel horse-drawn cart. The small cart could take three or four passengers and every day there was no shortage of people willing to pay for the privilege of riding with him to the next town of Cahir, about eighteen kilometres away, thereby turning a three-hour journey on foot into a one-hour journey by horse and cart.

Bianconi quickly realised he could make more money out of transporting passengers than by selling pictures, and changed his business into the Bianconi Coach Service. Soon there was demand from passengers to be taken to different locations further afield, and Bianconi started purchasing more carts and hiring more drivers. In 1833 he introduced the 'long car' which he manufactured in his bustling workshop in Clonmel. It was pulled by up to four horses and could carry sixteen passengers comfortably, plus cargo and Royal Mail bags for Post Offices along the routes that criss-crossed Ireland.

The highway system throughout Ireland in the early-to-mid nineteenth century was appalling. The roads were either rutted in dry weather or became a quagmire after rain, but thanks to representations from a growing chorus of people, including Bianconi, the roads started to improve when a new system called 'Macadamisation' sealed the surfaces against the worst effects of weather and traffic.

Consequently, improvements to the roads helped Bianconi's business significantly. A more comfortable ride in better quality coaches made coach transport more attractive to the general population. And Bianconi's Coach Service continued to grow. Over the next thirty years, Charles would become the 'King of Irish transport' with over one hundred coaches and 1,300 horses taking passengers from Belfast to Cork, and Dublin to Galway. At its peak in the mid-1840s, Bianconi's coaches covered around 6,000 kilometres a day, connecting over one hundred-and-twenty towns and cities in Ireland to each other.

Bianconi introduced several classes of horse-drawn vehicles. The light, two-wheeled carts became known as *faugh-a-ballagh* meaning 'clear the way', named after the phrase shouted by the drivers as they raced through the narrow streets of towns. The next in size carried five-to-ten passengers and finally there was the 'long car' described above. Bianconi also introduced a heavy goods cart for the transportation of farm produce. Together, all his vehicles became affectionately known as 'Bians' (short for Bianconi).

To ensure that his passengers had a restful night's sleep on long journeys, he built a series of inns, called naturally enough 'Bianconi Inns', of which several still exist today including those in: Piltown, Co. Kilkenny (renamed Anthony's Inn), Durrow, Co. Laois (renamed The Ashbrooke Arms) and Killorglin, Co. Kerry (still named The Bianconi Inn).

Bianconi always maintained a watchful eye on his competition, which he never thought was limited to other coach firms. When he started his coach business in 1815, he realised then that his main competition came from Ireland's waterways, namely the rivers and more recently the canals, whose construction started in the 1770s. In the 1840s, Bianconi saw the first railway lines begin to snake their way across the country and understood that another competitor had just entered the market.

This practical businessman could have ignored the threat posed by railways, or even attempted to stop its progress. Instead he decided to invest in it, and began to buy shares in the different railway lines as they were being built. He was having an 'each way' bet on two forms of competing transport, which meant that even as coach transport declined in the mid-nineteenth century his wealth continued to increase from his investment in rail.

In the 1840s and 1850s, Charles became a director of the National

CHARLES (CARLO) BIANCONI (1786–1875)

Bank of Ireland and was elected twice Mayor of Clonmel. During the Great Irish Famine (1845–1852), he gave employment to all who wanted it and was liberal in his charitable donations to the hungry and the poor. This included distributing large quantities of food to the starving, items which he had imported at his own expense from overseas. In 1854, he was a significant financial benefactor to the founding of the Catholic University of Dublin, going on to become a long-term trustee of this educational institution.

In 1863, his services to Ireland were recognised when he was appointed Deputy Lieutenant of the Co. of Tipperary by the British authorities. After a serious accident that severely broke his thigh in 1865, Bianconi wound back his day-to-day involvement in the coach business, selling many of his coaches to his employees on very generous terms and retiring to what would grow into a 3,500 hectare estate outside Cashel, Co. Tipperary. He lived there for another twenty-nine years until he died in 1875 at the age of eighty-nine, a millionaire.

In 1832, Charles married Eliza Hayes, the daughter of a wealthy stockbroker. They had one son, Charles and two daughters: Kate and Mary. Kate died in 1854 and her brother Charles died ten years later. The only surviving daughter married Morgan O'Connell, nephew of Daniel O'Connell, 'The 'Liberator' (*see* p. 67).

Charles Bianconi, an immigrant to Ireland, became the founder of public transport on Irish roads before railways dominated the economy. His coaches opened up Ireland to trade, commerce, tourism and the exchange of ideas across the land. His agitation for better roads improved the quality and speed of transport links throughout Ireland and during the Great Famine may have actually helped many starving families, as thousands of men were employed on government relief schemes improving Ireland's roads

MARY AIKENHEAD (1787–1858)

FOUNDER OF THE SISTERS OF CHARITY

Mary was born in Cork city, the eldest of four children, to David Aikenhead – a physician and apothecary – and his wife Mary (née Stacpole). The marriage between David, a Protestant and Mary, a Catholic, was forbidden according to the repressive Penal Laws of 1695, though by the mid-to-late 1700s, these laws were gradually being relaxed. One way to convince authorities that a mixed marriage was not worth punishing was if the children of this union were baptised Protestants. So it was that young Mary was duly taken to the Anglican Church in Cork and baptised as a Protestant.

Soon after her birth, Mary was placed into the care of a local family who lived on the outskirts of Cork. There are a number of reasons why the Aikenhead parents might have chosen to take this course of action with the infant, yet it remains unclear what may have been the real motivating factor.

The city streets of Cork were unhealthy and the parents may have wanted their firstborn to be raised in a semi-rural environment on the outskirts of the city, which was comparatively healthier. Or perhaps Mary was handed over to a staunchly Irish Catholic family because it may well always have been the intention of her mother to raise Mary as a Catholic, notwithstanding her being baptised a Protestant. The final reason may have been because it had been the custom for centuries in Ireland for the elite to 'foster' their children to local families who were so grateful for the extra money they received to look after the child, that it often resulted in a superior level of care and protection being given, compared to what the infants may have normally received.

Mary's upbringing was idyllic and her 'foster' family treated her as if Mary was one of their own. Along the way, Mary went to Mass every Sunday and prayed the Rosary with the rest of her foster family every night. The parents came to see Mary every week and Dr Aikenhead, her father, often attended the poor and the sick while he was visiting.

In 1793, when Mary was six, she returned to live full-time with her parents, who had in the meantime produced two more daughters (and a brother would be born in 1796). Mary's foster parents came to work there as house servants. It was at around this time that Dr Aikenhead became a supporter of the Society of United Irishmen (*see* Wolfe Tone, p. 49) and on one occasion leading up to the rebellion of 1798, even harboured one of the ringleaders in the Aikenhead house so as to avoid arrest.

The actual rebellion was a complete disaster for the cause of a free and united Ireland. Political ramifications against sympathisers were severe. Dr Aikenhead's health deteriorated under the stress and he sold his practice at the age of fifty to retire. But his health continued to decline and in 1801 he became seriously ill. On his deathbed he converted to the Roman Catholic faith in the presence of his family and the Bishop of Cork. Within six months Mary had converted to Catholicism as well. At the time she was only fifteen and all her siblings became Catholics shortly afterwards.

With the death of her father and her mother's health failing, it fell to Mary to look after her younger siblings. She studied accountancy and bookkeeping and learned to run a household. She also found time to socialise and the young, attractive teenager became a well-known society girl in her home town.

In her late teens, Mary heard the parable of the Rich Man and Lazarus (Luke 16:19-31), in which the miserly rich man goes to Hell, while the poor, sick man goes to Heaven. Mary sensed parallels in the lives of people around her and felt a calling to serve the poor and sick of Cork, just as her father had done. At the time all the religious orders in Ireland for women were cloistered (enclosed behind walls), but she wanted to go out into the community and visit the people who most desperately needed help.

In 1807, Mary accepted an invitation to leave Cork and join Anna O'Brien, a close friend and the daughter of a prosperous silk merchant, who was already bringing food and comfort to Dublin's destitute underclass. Mary's mother died in 1809, which required her to return to Cork and tend to the family's affairs. Following the funeral and a period of mourning, she returned to Dublin to renew her efforts to tend to the poor.

The activities of Anna O'Brien and Mary Aikenhead had not gone unnoticed during these years and the assistant Bishop of Dublin, Dr Daniel Murray, concluded it was time to create the first non-cloistered (open) order of nuns in Ireland. He would call the new order the Sisters of Charity. In 1811, he invited Mary to head up the organisation, which Mary accepted after much thought and with the condition that she first became a nun.

After three years of religious training in York, England, Mary returned to Ireland and in 1815, as the head of the Religious Sisters of Charity, she opened the organisation's first convent in an orphanage in Dublin. Although Mary's full religious name was now Sister Mary Augustine, she would be better known as Mary Aikenhead for the rest of her life.

From the moment she was appointed head (Superior General) of the order, Mary threw herself into codifying the Order's rules and objectives, raising much needed funds from Dublin's Catholic wealthy, and spending the money on building new facilities. Mary first built a school for the poor children of Dublin, then a women's refuge, and all the while she was continuing to visit the needy.

In 1823, the Archbishop of Dublin asked Mary and her Sisters of Charity to take over a refuge for prostitutes that was being poorly run in Dublin. Originally designed as a shelter for 'fallen women' it was a way of fulfilling Mary Aikenhead's original dream to help women find a way out of poverty and prostitution through attaining alternative means of earning money. Over a hundred years later and long after her death, Aikenhead's honourable intentions had been perversely morphed into industrial-sized factories extracting profit mainly by the labour of children, who were often abused and ill-treated. This would turn out to be one of the darkest chapters in an otherwise outstanding and benevolent history of the Sisters of Charity.

The Sisters of Charity also received an invitation from the prison authorities at Kilmainham gaol, Dublin, to visit and give comfort to the women prisoners. Aikenhead personally attended to two young women convicted of murder until they were executed.

The physical exertion of such a life took its toll on Mary and she was confined to a wheelchair from the age of forty-four, with a chronic spinal disease. However, she continued to direct her growing Order during a cholera epidemic that struck the major cities of Ireland in 1832, killing an estimated 50,000 people across the country. At the height of the epidemic in Dublin, Mary Aikenhead threw open the doors to the convent and her Sisters nursed thousands of sick and dying people without giving a thought to their own well-being.

Mary had long held a dream to open a hospital for the poor and the cholera epidemic only strengthened her resolve. In 1834, she had somehow raised the significant sums needed to purchase and convert a property in St Stephens Green, Dublin, and later that year she opened St Vincent's hospital. It was named after St Vincent de Paul (1581–1660), who dedicated himself to serving the poor. St Vincent's in Dublin was the first hospital in the English-speaking world to be staffed by nuns. The first procedure done in the new hospital was performed on a small boy, called Danny, who needed an operation on a badly infected leg. There was no anaesthetic at the time (this was not invented until 1846), so Danny and all those who followed him for another ten years would have to be strapped down to the tables and held down prior to surgery. Mary Aikenhead heard of the boy's distress and held Danny's hand throughout the procedure. Ironically she was ill herself at the time, and had to be wheeled into the operating theatre in a wheelchair.

In 1835, Mary decided to expand the Order beyond the shores of Ireland. She dispatched five sisters to Australia to work among the women convicts and their children. They were the first women from any religious order to set foot on Australian soil.

During the dreadful Irish Potato Famine (1845–1852), also referred to as the Great Famine, when up to a half a million people died of either starvation or disease, the Sisters of Charity laboured against impossible odds to tend to the dying and the sick. The extent of the problem was enormous and even though the Sisters of Charity did what they could for the destitute from the countryside who flooded into the cities, even the government of the day was overwhelmed by the calamity. Nevertheless, Mary Aikenhead and her growing band of nuns did manage to relieve suffering in places where they had a presence.

Having spent the best part of three decades as an invalid, Mary Aikenhead passed away in 1858, aged seventy-one. Men from the slums of Dublin volunteered to carry her coffin past the thousands of mourners. One of them was Danny O'Connell, now a young man, who twelve years earlier had been comforted by Mary during the first ever operation at St Vincent's.

By the time of Mary's death, the Sisters of Charity had grown to thirteen institutions in Ireland, England and Australia, with over one hundred nuns working on numerous charitable missions. Today the Order has continued to grow and now has a presence in more than twenty countries on five continents: Africa, Europe, Australia, North and South America. The Sisters of Charity operate large schools, orphanages, hospitals and hospices for the dying. Although the number of nuns has diminished over the past several decades, the organisation itself, staffed by thousands of lay people, continues to grow and perform good deeds every day.

Recently, there has begun a renewed campaign to have the Vatican recognise Mary's extraordinary life of service and sacrifice by having her canonised. The process can be arduous and painstakingly slow. In this particular case the original application was lodged with the

Vatican in 1911, but it was not until 2015 that the Church in Rome announced Mary's elevation from 'Servant' to 'Venerable' in what is the second of four steps to sainthood.

JAMES GAMBLE (1803–91)

INDUSTRIALIST, CO-FOUNDER OF PROCTER & GAMBLE

James was born near Enniskillen, Co. Fermanagh in present-day Northern Ireland. He was the eldest of six children born to George Gamble and his wife Mary (née Norris). The family was related to prosperous farmers and merchants, but George Gamble had chosen the comparatively poorly paid profession of being a Methodist preacher.

While young James was educated at the Portora Royal School in Enniskillen, Britain suffered an economic downturn following the Napoleonic wars. The Gamble family decided to immigrate to the United States for a better life. In 1819 the family settled in Cincinnati, on the Ohio River, where George set up a horticultural nursery instead of continuing with his career as a Methodist preacher.

James attended the then newly-opened Kenyon College in Cincinnati in 1824 and was soon apprenticed to a soap-maker.

JAMES GAMBLE (1803–91)

In about 1826 he set himself up in business and was moderately successful from the start. After a few years he felt financially comfortable enough to start looking for a wife. James courted a local woman, Elizabeth Norris (no relation to James's mother) and discovered that her sister, Olivia, was engaged to an English-born candle maker, named William Procter. The two couples were married in 1835 and 1833 respectively, and it was James's father-in-law who in 1836 suggested that the two men should form a partnership and go into business together.

The suggestion made a great deal of sense since the main raw materials of both products – lye (sodium hydroxide) and animal oils – were in plentiful supply in Cincinnati, because the town had become a meat-packing centre. If the two manufacturers joined forces they could together negotiate a lower price for purchasing the ingredients in bulk than they could do separately.

The two men agreed on the partnership and Procter & Gamble first opened its doors for business in 1837. Gamble handled the manufacturing side of the enterprise and Procter looked after the money.

From the start, the company embarked on the highly successful strategy of using the advent of the railways to market its products widely across the United States. Just two decades later, in 1859, Procter & Gamble employed eighty members of staff and generated sales over US$1 million, the first time such a company had achieved such success, making it one of the largest soap and candle manufacturers in the USA. Which was just as well, for the following year, when Civil War broke out between the Unionist north and the Confederate south, Procter & Gamble was able to secure a contract from the union army to supply all the soap and candles it could manufacture.

The boost in sales caused by securing a government contract during the Civil War, brought Procter & Gamble to national prominence in the early 1870s. It was at about this time that the company slowly wound back its interests in candle making to concentrate on soap manufacture, which James Gamble believed would grow to become the mainstay of the company's future profitability. This was a very wise decision, for with the invention of the electric light in 1878, candles declined in popularity in an inverse ratio to the increased adoption of the electric 'incandescent light', until in 1920 Procter & Gamble discontinued candle manufacturing altogether.

Procter & Gamble was one of the first companies in the United States to invest in a research laboratory to produce purer, better soap products. It is thought, but not confirmed, that James Gamble was behind this development. What gives this assertion credence is that Gamble's eldest son, James Jr, was educated as a chemist and set to work in the company's laboratory. In 1879 he devised the original formula for the company's 'Ivory brand' soap – a product that was so pure that it could float on water.

James Gamble was still in charge of Procter & Gamble at this time and used the invention of Ivory soap to launch the business beyond the national borders and create the company's first iconic brand. For example, he paid for full colour advertisements to be printed in national newspapers across the country. What he did was to lay the foundations that revolutionised the world of branding, marketing and advertising by pioneering methods that are still used by businesses today.

Eventually, one of these innovative ideas would lead Procter & Gamble to sponsor serials on the radio that became extremely popular and would be known as 'soap operas'. Even though this development was long after the elder James Gamble's time, it was his creative flair that was the original driving force behind this and other brilliant ideas.

Elizabeth Gamble and her husband James had ten children, including James Jr, who became Vice President of Procter & Gamble from 1890, when his father stepped down from running the business on a daily basis.

James Gamble died of natural causes in his sleep in 1891, at the age of eighty-eight. He was buried in the Spring Grove cemetery in Cincinnati alongside his wife, who had passed away in 1888, and near to the grave of William Procter, who had died in 1884.

In 2015, Procter & Gamble is a global corporate giant with sales exceeding US\$80 billion. It employs more than 110,000 staff and its products sell in over 140 countries. It was listed by Forbes magazine as one of the Top 50 biggest companies in the world in 2015 by market capitalisation (ranked number 36). Yet Procter & Gamble still maintains its worldwide headquarters in Cincinnati and keeps the name of its two founders – one of whom came from humble origins in Ireland.

GEORGE BOOLE
(1815–64)

MATHEMATICIAN

B oole was born in Lincoln, England in 1815, the first of four children to John and Mary Boole. John Boole was a cobbler and of modest income. Even though the young Boole's education was rudimentary, he was encouraged to learn more by a father who was something of an amateur scientist and instrument maker. From an early age George displayed a gift for languages, music and mathematics and when he was sixteen he started teaching young children (part time) at local private schools to bring in extra money that the family desperately needed.

Between 1834 and 1849, Boole taught at a school he established in Lincoln. A growing number of students were attracted to his institution, which needed other members of his family to help manage it. In his spare time, Boole familiarised himself with the works of the great mathematicians of the day, such as Lacroix, Lagrange, Laplace and Poisson. There was a reason why Boole was attracted to the ideas of French mathematicians. It was because England's own great seat of mathematics – Cambridge – had fallen behind advances that were being made in the rest of the world, particularly France.

Boole was not the only person who thought that Cambridge University had lost its way in mathematics. By way of a chance encounter at Lincoln's Mechanics' Institute he met Sir Edward Bromhead, who had studied mathematics at Cambridge and was agitating for a modernisation of its curriculum. Bromhead lent Boole more books on mathematical theory and encouraged him to submit papers to the university. Boole had not studied at any university – his leaning in this discipline had been entirely self-taught – yet Bromhead considered Boole's grasp of mathematics to be equal to, or better than, anyone else then currently teaching in Britain. Bromhead's opinion of Boole's capability would soon be shared by many others.

George Boole's first paper appeared in 1841 in the *Cambridge Mathematical Journal* and the co-founder and editor of the journal, Duncan Gregory, was so impressed with the quality and clarity of Boole's work that he also encouraged him to continue submitting more material. Between 1841 and 1845, Boole obliged by submitting a total of twelve papers for consideration. All were published.

One particular paper authored by Boole drew much attention. The article was titled 'On a general method in analysis' (1844), which some historians now consider was the origin of modern algebra.

When it was published, it caused quite a sensation in the usually refined and polite world of higher education, launching a controversy between a Scottish philosopher and an English mathematics professor, which Boole had to step in and resolve personally. This article won the Royal Medal for being the most important contribution in the field of mathematics from the Royal Society in 1844.

Encouraged by the positive reception to 'On a general method in analysis', Boole continued to develop his theories in the area of algebra and in 1847 published an 82-page booklet titled, *The mathematical analysis of logic*. By now, his reputation and influence had pushed him to the very top levels of mathematics in Britain. He was only thirty-two and was just beginning to approach the most productive period of his life.

Meanwhile, the English Parliament was trying to grapple with the 'Irish Question'. The mass demonstrations against English authority, led by Daniel O'Connell at the head of the Repeal Association, shook the English establishment to its core (*see* Daniel O'Connell, p. 67). Prime Minister Peel accepted that indeed there were inequities with the way Irish Catholics and some Irish Protestants were being legally discriminated against. He instituted a raft of reforms, which included establishing well-funded, new educational colleges in Galway, Belfast and Cork.

Boole applied for the position of inaugural mathematics professor at Queen's College Cork (renamed University College Cork after 1908) and was supported in his application by one of Ireland greatest scientists, William Thomson (later Lord Kelvin, *see* p. 104). In today's world it is rare, if not impossible, for an individual to reach such an exalted academic position as professor of a faculty without having successfully completed a number of undergraduate and postgraduate degrees. But the academic world was not as rigid in the mid-1800s and Boole, with strong written testimonials from his scientific colleagues, was appointed Chair of Mathematics at Cork in 1849: a position he would hold for the rest of his life.

From his papers, which are held at University College Cork, it would seem that Boole found Ireland much to his liking. Certainly his salary of £250 per annum, plus an additional fee of £100 for tutoring was, in the standards of the day, a very handsome income indeed. The average wage at the time was less than £50 per year. It is clear he settled into a very comfortable and very intellectually stimulating part of his life. George purchased a fine house for himself at Grenville Place, Cork, overlooking the River Lee. There, he wrote the following masterpiece.

In 1854, Boole published *An Investigation of the Laws of Thought on Which are Founded the Mathematical Theories of Logic and Probabilities.* It is considered to be his most influential work and the foundation for a branch of mathematics that would become known as 'Boolean algebra', the basis for all computer computations. This was followed by two papers: 'Treaties on Differential Equations' in 1859 and then 'Treaties on the Calculus of Finite Differences' in 1860, both published in the *Cambridge Mathematical Journal.* These two works explored and further developed Boole's theories about logic and the process of thinking, as seen in mathematical terms.

Boole fell in love with Mary Everest, whose uncle would famously name the world's highest mountain after himself. In 1849, Mary had come to stay in Cork with another uncle who was Professor of Classic Languages at University College Cork. Because the young Mary had an interest in Mathematics, she was introduced to George Boole, initially on the basis of being tutored by him in the subject. They shared a lot of time in each other's company and romance blossomed, resulting in marriage in 1855.

Despite the fact that Mary was seventeen years younger than George, they had a good and happy married life. The couple had five daughters over the next nine years. However, this pleasant and dynamic period in George Boole's life was cut short in 1864 when he was caught in a heavy storm while walking on his way to the university. He had forgotten to take a raincoat with him and did not change out of his wet clothes until he had returned home at the end of the day. George Boole contracted pneumonia a few days later and died. He was only forty-nine years of age and was intellectually at the top of his profession. There were unfinished manuscripts found in his papers that have still to be fully understood today.

The couple were very happy in Cork, where their surroundings were congenial and he had ample time for research. If it were not for the untimely death of this brilliant mathematician, the family may well have stayed permanently in Ireland. In one sense, George Boole never left Ireland, for he was buried in the churchyard of St Michael's Church of Ireland, Cork.

For the next eighty years or so, Boole remained relatively unknown, except by a handful of elite mathematicians who were working at the esoteric boundaries of logic, calculus and algebra. But in the 1930s some brilliant minds, such as Turing, Shannon, Hilbert and Aiken, started working on the concept of a computing machine that could answer any question, if fed the right data. However, there was a major stumbling block that needed to be resolved before a computer could be created: this was, how would it process data?

It was at this point that George Boole's breakthrough work a century earlier provided such a perfect answer. His concept – otherwise known as Boolean algebra – has been at the heart of every computer that has ever been made. Without George Boole and his mathematical theories on thinking and logic, there simply would be no information age today. It is easy to see why so many people now regard Boole as the 'father' of the modern computer and why there has been a recent revaluation of his contribution to science.

GEORGE BOOLE (1815–64)

Even the United Nations has recognised the immeasurable impact Boole has made to computing science by designating 20 October 2015 as 'World Statistics Day' in his honour. To mark the day, the United Nations and University College Cork, issued a joint press statement in which Dr Michael Murphy, President of UCC said: 'Our objective … is to ensure that as many people as possible across the globe become familiar with the story of George Boole, his life, his genius, and his legacy.'

University College Cork, which describes itself as the academic home of George Boole, also named a building after the great man and commissioned a magnificent stained-glass window in his honour that is proudly displayed in the university's *Aula Maxima* (Great Hall), the symbolic and ceremonial heart of this tertiary education institution. One of the major initiatives the university has already committed to is the restoration of Boole's house in Cork. If Boole can have a crater on the moon named after him, then surely he should have a decent house in Cork named after him too!

CATHERINE HAYES
(1818–61)

FIRST IRISH DIVA

Catherine was born into a very humble Anglo-Irish family in Limerick. When she was still an infant, her father Arthur, a musician and bandmaster in the local militia, abandoned the family and Catherine grew up in desperate circumstances with her mother and older sister Henrietta. Catherine's mother, Mary Hayes (née Carroll), obtained work as a domestic servant in the household of the Earl of Limerick.

Like most nobles, the Lord Limerick would regularly entertain and when household staff discovered Catherine had an unusually beautiful voice, she periodically sang for the Earl's distinguished guests. By the time Catherine was a young woman, she was giving private singing performances to the Protestant elite of Limerick.

At one of her concerts, Catherine's voice attracted the attention of Reverend Edmund Knox, the Bishop of the Anglican Church of Limerick. After paying for the best voice lessons available in

Limerick, Knox raised more funds for Catherine to be sent to Dublin in 1839, to study under Señor Antonio Sapio, who at the time was regarded as the best voice coach in Ireland. Under Sapio's tutelage, Catherine's improvement was so rapid that one month later, when she gave her first public appearance in the Irish capital at the age of twenty-one, people were stunned by her voice.

Catherine continued her voice lessons in Dublin over the next few years and gave frequent performances in both the capital city and her native town of Limerick. Up to this time, she had been mainly singing popular ballads and folk songs to the delight of her growing admirers, but events occurred in 1841 that would change her musical direction and set her on a path to musical stardom.

In early 1841, Catherine shared the stage of Dublin's 'Rotunda' theatre with the renowned Hungarian pianist, Franz Liszt, who was on his first visit to Ireland. One of the pieces that Liszt played was from Donizetti's *Lucia di Lammermoor*, an opera which had premiered in Naples only six years earlier. Catherine, listening in the wings, was spellbound at the magically uplifting quality of the music and wanted to know more about opera, which was still a comparatively rare form of entertainment in Dublin.

Later that year, she got her wish when a visiting operatic company performed Vincenzo Bellini's recent opera *Norma* in Dublin for the first time. From this point on, Catherine was determined to become a soprano on the opera stages of the world. Señor Antonio Sapio arranged for her to study under the great vocal pedagogue Manuel Garcia in Paris. This man was so impressed with her ability, that after only eighteen months of tuition, he advised Catherine to go to Milan, Italy, and audition for one of the truly great opera companies in the world – The Italian Opera – which was about to embark on its usual tour of Europe.

The audition was a success and Catherine debuted at the Marseilles Opera House in 1845, playing the lead role in another of Bellini's operas, *I puritani*. The local papers said her performance was, 'a blaze of triumph', which was repeated at La Scala in Milan, and subsequently at Vienna, Venice, Florence and Genoa during the touring season.

During her early years with the opera company in Milan, another young Italian composer was beginning to make his name in the world of opera. He was Giuseppe Verdi and his first three operas – *Nabucco* (1842); *I Lombardi* (1843) and *Ernani* (1844) – had all become hugely successful. Verdi composed rousing nationalistic arias that had great patriotic appeal to the audiences of northern Italy, which was under the rigid control of the Austrians at the time.

Verdi and Hayes met several times in the early 1840s and the young composer was so impressed with the equally young soprano's singing voice that he decided to write an opera just for her. He would call it, *I masnadieri*. Catherine initially declined the role intended for her, as she considered her delicate voice would not do justice to Verdi's powerful music and orchestration. However, she was persuaded to reconsider the part of Amalia by Verdi's assistant, who trained her for the role, which she sang to great acclaim when *I masnadieri* made its Italian premier in Verona in 1847.

Season after season followed in which Catherine played the leading role in many operas at many venues. Her fame spread before her and audiences flocked to hear her extraordinary voice, which experts at the time said was the purest they had ever experienced.

Wherever she went, Catherine became the toast of the town, fêted by ambassadors, royalty and civic leaders. On one occasion in Genoa, an American warship in the harbour treated her attendance as an honoured dinner guest by erecting bunting, setting off flares and turning on all its lights, which aroused (and alarmed) the citizens of the town.

During 1848, the so-called 'Year of Revolutions' that spread across many European cities, Catherine was touring extensively. Many people were worried for her and debated whether the entire tour should be scrapped. Milan itself came to a standstill with barricades and fighting on the streets. La Scala closed for the duration of the troubles. Yet, it was Catherine's calm and positive optimism that encouraged the opera company to go ahead with the scheduled tour of engagements, which thankfully coincided with the company's stay in these European cities during times of relative calm. In any event, Catherine's mind was preoccupied with her debut in the United Kingdom, which was scheduled to take place the following year in 1849.

Catherine's first appearance on the stage of Covent Garden in London astonished local audiences, who could not get enough of her. While in London, at a royal performance before Queen Victoria and over 500 guests at Buckingham Palace, Catherine sang an Irish tune *Kathleen Mavourneen* as an encore. This was a Gaelic Irish song composed in 1837, and its title meant 'Kathleen, my beloved'. Following London, Dublin was included on the schedule at Catherine's request. It was an emotional return for Catherine, who had been away from Ireland for almost seven years. At the close of her concerts in Ireland and in many concerts elsewhere, Catherine would stand proudly on the stage and sing *Kathleen Mavourneen.* It would become her signature song for the rest of her career.

In 1851 Catherine toured America, where she was met by a wave of adulation. She performed in about fifty major cities across the country and along the way, Catherine was acclaimed by statesmen and business leaders everywhere she went. In Washington DC, she even met Millard Fillmore, the President of the United States. Catherine was billed as the 'Swan of Erin', and ex-patriot Irish flocked to hear her in their thousands. Finally in 1852 her triumphant American tour concluded in San Francisco, where the local paper wrote that her appearance on stage was greeted, 'by rapturous cheers and applause'.

Miners in the Californian gold fields paid exorbitant prices to be seated in the front rows of the theatres and some were so enthralled with Catherine's performance that they literally threw gold nuggets to her. Following on from her incredible success in the goldfields of America, the plan was to repeat this phenomenon on the goldfields of Australia.

But first Catherine was contractually obliged to tour South America and give concerts in Hawaii. When Catherine Hayes arrived in Sydney, Australia, in 1854, she was the first great European opera star to have visited the country and the reaction was amazing. One paper breathlessly wrote that her arrival in Sydney, 'caused an excitement wholly unparalleled in the theatrical annals of this colony'. She astonished audiences in most of the major cities on the continent and spent much time performing on the goldfields of New South Wales and Victoria, collecting more gold nuggets on the way.

During her stay in Australia, Catherine donated the proceeds from her final concert to build a medical facility to treat children and orphans. The Catherine Hayes Building still stands in the grounds of the Prince of Wales Hospital in Randwick, Sydney.

After two years in Australia, which included side trips to Calcutta, Jakarta and Singapore, Hayes returned to London from Sydney in 1856 as a very wealthy woman, who had incidentally circumnavigated the globe. In the following year she married her business manager, William Avery Bushnell, whom she had met in the United States in 1852 at the wedding of the daughter of P. T. Barnum, the famous American impresario. The wedding ceremony was a gala occasion, attended by London's elite.

Tragically, William died in Biarritz, France, of consumption in 1858. Three years later Catherine suffered a severe stroke at the house of a friend in Sydenham, just outside London, from which she did not recover. Catherine was only forty-two years old at the time of her death in 1861, yet she had achieved phenomenal success in such a brief career. She was the first Irish woman to sing at La Scala, Milan and at the Royal Opera, Covent Garden in London. The story of Catherine Hayes is of a young Irish woman's determination to be the best in the world at a time when women, and Irish people generally, were not encouraged to succeed.

WILLIAM THOMSON, 1ST BARON KELVIN (1824–1907)

MATHEMATICAL PHYSICIST AND ENGINEER

William was born in Belfast, the son of mathematics professor James Thomson and his wife Margaret (née Gardner). The father assumed sole responsibility for raising William and his siblings after their mother died in 1830. He was a precocious child, learning French, German, Latin and Greek, as well as having a thorough grounding in the sciences from an early age as a result of being home-tutored by his intelligent and encouraging father, who strived to challenge and stretch his son's learning.

When William was seven, his father accepted a Professorship in Mathematics at Glasgow University and the family relocated to Scotland, though the Thomsons would retain a small farm they owned in Co. Down until 1847. When William was only ten he was attending lectures at Glasgow University with the other students and competing with them for top academic grades in natural science (now referred to as physics). He demonstrated all the hallmarks of a gifted prodigy. At fourteen, he was excelling in the area of astronomy and chemistry. When he was fifteen, William won a University gold medal prize for writing 'An Essay on the Figure of Earth'.

At the age of seventeen in 1841, William continued his studies at Cambridge University, where his father hoped he would do so well that he would eventually return to Glasgow as a professor. Thomson received an all-round education at Cambridge, excelling in sport, music as well as academics, and a year after he graduated his father got his wish when in 1846 William was appointed Professor of Natural Philosophy at Glasgow University, a position he would retain for an extraordinary fifty-three years.

Thomson's scientific interests were wide-ranging: from chemistry to physics and from the practical to the theoretical. Now a professor at the age of twenty-two at one of Britain's most prestigious universities, young William began to indulge his sense of scientific curiosity. He created the first physics laboratory in Britain, stocked it with the latest scientific apparatus, and instructed his students to conduct experimental work across a range of scientific fields.

The first area he explored was in the newly emerging field of thermodynamics, dealing with heat and temperature and their relationship to energy. Thomson had been interested in this field from his days as a student, but the main problem he had come up against was that the thermometers of the day, which were filled with gas, were unreliable.

He decided to create an absolute temperature scale, which he subsequently revised and presented to the world in an article 'On the Dynamical Theory of Heat', published in 1851 in *Mathematical and Physical Papers*.

He went on the write further articles expanding on his original ideas and in the process helped to discover or confirm several Laws of Thermodynamics, including coining the expression 'Absolute Zero' in temperature.

In 1852, he married Margaret Crum. When he returned to the academic world after his honeymoon, he switched direction to explore electricity and magnetism.

From 1854 on, William provided scientific advice on the first transatlantic telegraph cable, that was eventually completed between Britain and Canada in 1858, by proving the relationship between voltage, resistance and current. Thomson was appointed to the Board of the Atlantic Telegraph Company as a reward for his scientific expertise and over the next decade continued to make further improvements and invent better devices for the company. The translatlantic cable ushered in a new era in communications across the Atlantic Ocean by slashing the transmission time of a message from ten days by ship, to ten minutes via cable. For services to this vital industry he was knighted in 1866.

Between lectures and research into intriguing areas of science, Sir William Thomson patented several of his inventions, including instruments to accurately measure electricity, such as the galvanometer. The royalties from his inventions made him wealthy and his academic work gained him increased recognition and influence around the world.

Sometimes Thomson would like to liven up his classes with hair-raising demonstrations. On one occasion, to illustrate the principle of momentum, he fired a blunderbuss across the lecture hall at a steel plate suspended on the opposite side of the room. When the smoke, smell and wadding of the discharge had dissipated the plate was swinging wildly due to being struck by the bullet, which dramatically proved Newtonian physics to the startled students.

There was one methodology in scientific research he rigidly adhered to all his life, insisting that his students should also follow it religiously. It became his dictum. He once wrote, 'when you cannot express it in numbers, your knowledge is of a meagre and unsatisfactory kind...' In other words he believed that any object or activity should be accurately measured and studied with mathematical certainty.

This scientific approach to research had been around for a century, but Thomson insisted on applying this method more rigorously than had been seen before. The result was that under his tutelage, scientific advancement in Glasgow in particular, and Britain generally, progressed faster than at any time previously in history.

Following the death of his first wife in 1870, he subsequently married Frances Blandy in 1874, whom he had met in 1873. Frances was the second daughter of Charles Blandy, the famous Madeira wine producer, and a wealthy heiress in her own right. They spent much of their time sailing on William's yacht *Lalla Rookh*, whose name is a term of endearment in the Persian language.

Time on the yacht incidentally provoked Thomson to invent the adjustable compass to compensate for magnetic deviations, as well as a new tide gauge and predictor.

Neither of his marriages produced children.

Ideas constantly came to him and he learned the habit of stopping whatever he was doing to jot them down in a notebook he always carried. It did not matter whether he was sailing, walking, lecturing to students or having an intense conversation with a colleague, if a thought popped into his head he felt obliged to capture it in a notebook he always had ready for just such an occasion.

However, not everything he touched turned to gold. Some scientific theories he held were plainly wrong, such as his thoughts on the age of the earth (which he estimated was less than 40 million years old), but the overwhelming majority of his ideas led to positive improvements to mankind.

In 1893 Queen Victoria raised him to the peerage, and he took the title of Baron Kelvin, after the river that ran near to where he lived at Glasgow University. Lord Kelvin died in 1907 at the age of eighty-three and had a state funeral, being buried near the tomb of Sir Isaac Newton in Westminster Abbey, London.

Over the course of his life Lord Kelvin wrote more than 600 scientific papers, held dozens of patents and was elected to numerous societies. He presided over the Royal Society from 1890 to 1895. He remained Professor of Natural Philosophy at Glasgow University until 1899. Many years after his death, his absolute temperature scale was renamed the Kelvin scale and is still known as such today.

The list of the areas of science Lord Kelvin achieved success in are too numerous to mention, but include: optics, elasticity, electricity, magnetism, thermodynamics, navigation, geophysics, crystallography, hydrodynamics, meteorology and telegraphy. This was a staggering achievement by one of the world's greatest scientific minds of the nineteenth century.

THOMAS D'ARCY MCGEE (1825–68)

ONE OF THE 'FATHERS' OF CANADIAN CONFEDERATION

Thomas was born in Carlingford, Co. Louth, son of James McGee of the Coast Guard service and his wife Dorcas (née Morgan). The members of the McGee family were pro-Irish sympathisers and Thomas's grandfather had been imprisoned for his involvement with the United Irishmen (*see* Wolfe Tone, p. 49). When McGee was only eight, his father was transferred to Wexford, on Ireland's south-east coast. Tragically, his mother was killed during the relocation when she was thrown from the cart containing the family possessions.

James McGee remarried in 1840, but his son Thomas could not get on with his stepmother, Margaret Dea. In 1842, Thomas, now seventeen, together with his sister, sailed from Wexford harbour bound for the United States of America, via Quebec, Canada. As a result of a passionate Fourth of July speech in Boston, Massachusetts, in which he thrilled a crowd on Boston's Common, holding the people spellbound, Thomas was offered a job with the *Boston Pilot*, the leading Catholic newspaper for the Irish community. Within two years, he had become the newspaper's editor and had published two books about Ireland, which attracted the attention of influential people back in the country of his birth.

He accepted an offer from Daniel O'Connell, Ireland's 'Liberator', to join the staff of the *Freeman's Journal* in Dublin in 1845 and became its parliamentary correspondent until he was asked to leave for writing articles under an alias for a rival publication, *The Nation*. Since his return to Ireland, the country had been afflicted with a catastrophic famine that caused widespread starvation, yet food was still being exported from Ireland, under guard by British soldiers. Seeing the plight of his fellow countrymen, Thomas became politically more radical and *The Nation* newspaper he now worked for became an extreme nationalist broadsheet advocating the use of armed insurrection against the British.

He married Mary Caffrey of Dublin in 1847 and the couple had five daughters and one son, but only two of these offspring survived to adulthood.

In 1848, a year in which revolutions and riots broke out across Europe, a group of young Irishmen, with which McGee was closely associated, launched an ill-fated rebellion against the British Crown. McGee had been sent to Scotland to drum up support, but by the time he returned to Ireland empty-handed, the rebellion had been crushed and its ringleaders imprisoned. McGee was on the run, a wanted criminal, who managed to flee to the United States by boarding a ship disguised as a priest.

Upon his arrival in New York, McGee started his own paper called *The Nation*, but ran foul of the Roman Catholic Church when he heavily criticised it for opposing the recent rebellion in

Ireland. The paper folded in 1850 when the Church placed a ban on it. Thomas moved to Boston again, where he founded another newspaper, *The American Celt and Adopted Citizen*. He moderated his stance against the Roman Catholic Church in order to see his paper survive and worked to improve the assimilation of Irish immigrants into the fabric of American society.

In the volatile world of Irish politics during the mid-nineteenth century, McGee found himself being denounced for not advocating strongly enough the cause for Irish independence, while others criticised him for being too extreme. The political atmosphere in Boston, with its high concentration of Irish settlers, became too heated for Thomas, so he relocated himself and his paper to firstly Buffalo, New York, in 1852, and finally to New York itself in 1853.

He found New York to be conducive to writing thoughtful and well-researched literature and over the next three years published four significant pieces of writing: *The History of the Irish settlers in North America*, the first book on the Irish in America; *A history of the attempts to establish the Protestant reformation in Ireland*; *The Catholic history of North America* and a biography of Dr Edward Maginn, the Catholic Bishop of Derry.

During the 1850s, McGee visited Canada several times, where he addressed sizeable Irish communities in Toronto and Montreal. His position on Canada had altered over the years. He had once advocated the idea of Canada's absorption into a pan-continental 'United States of North America', but had come to view America's democracy as deficient, even flawed. It was the mid-to-late 1850s and the USA was beginning to tear itself apart over issues such as States' rights, slavery and industrialisation. Meanwhile in Canada, Thomas McGee found a more benign political climate, where the Irish were treated as equals, unlike their treatment in Ireland itself.

McGee decided that his future was to be in Canada and in 1857 he immigrated to Montreal where he established another newspaper, called the *New Era*. In the same year he was elected to the provincial parliament for the constituency of West Montreal by that electorate's mainly Irish voters. From the start of his parliamentary career, Thomas began advocating for a 'Confederation of four provinces' to replace the existing three Canadian colonies and thus usher in a new era of limited self-government as a Dominion of the British Empire. He delivered over a thousand lectures across the eastern half of Canada during the next three years, setting out his reasons why Canada would be better off if it became a Confederation. In this regard he was ten years ahead of his time, for the Confederation he devoutly wished for would not become a reality until 1867.

Being a Catholic himself, there were times when Irish immigrants to Canada tried to involve McGee in sectarian conflict between Irish Catholics and Protestants, but he steadfastly refused to take sides. In a speech given in Quebec City in 1862 he said:

'We Irishmen, Protestants and Catholic, born and bred in a land of controversy, should never forget that we can now live and act in a land of the fullest religious and civil freedom. All we have to do … is to cultivate that true catholicity of spirit which embraces all creeds, all classes and all races, in order to make our boundless Province, so rich in known and unknown resources, a great new Northern nation.' (Speech reprinted in full by the Honourable Edward McMurray, Speaker of the Canadian Parliament in an address to The Empire Club, Toronto in 1925.)

In 1864, McGee became Minister of Agriculture, Immigration and Statistics in the provincial parliament and continued to prosecute his case for a Canadian Confederation. In 1864, he attended two conferences as a delegate to determine the make-up of the new Canadian Confederation. Throughout the 1860s he helped draft the Canadian Constitution, which would ultimately be passed by the British Parliament in London.

In the 1860s there arose in the United States a new Irish nationalistic movement called the Fenian Brotherhood, whose goal was to secure Irish independence through violent means. The Brotherhood naively thought that if they invaded Canada from the USA, the British would have to redeploy troops from across its vast empire, including Ireland. This would weaken Britain's military presence in Ireland to the point where another rebellion would finally succeed in liberating Ireland from British occupation.

The Fenian Brotherhood and Thomas McGee became avowed enemies, with the Brotherhood declaring him a 'traitor' to the cause of Irish independence. Hardly a week went by without McGee receiving a death threat in the post from one Fenian supporter or another.

There were several raids by Fenian supporters from the United States across the border into Canada, but each was repulsed without any threat to the security of Canada itself. If anything, the cross-border attacks – there were at least four raids in 1866 involving up to 2,000 armed followers in total – helped to provide impetus to the colonies to join together to form a Confederation for national security.

The British North America Act was passed by London in 1867 and Canada became a Dominion within the British Empire. McGee was elected to the first Canadian Parliament as the member for Montreal West. After a late-night session in the new Parliament in 1868, McGee was on the doorstep of his Ottawa boarding house when he was shot through the head from behind by a Fenian supporter.

Thomas McGee's death at the age of forty-three, was the first and, to date, the only political assassination in Canada's history. He was awarded a State funeral and his widowed wife, together with his two surviving daughters, were granted pensions for life from a grateful and shocked Canadian government. McGee's mausoleum, newly restored in 2000, is located at *Notre Dame des Neiges* Cemetery, Montreal. A plaque on the door reads, 'In Memory of Thomas D'Arcy McGee, The Most Eloquent Voice of The Fathers of Confederation.' He was a great Canadian patriot and yet still one of the dominant Irish Catholic figures in Canadian history.

ELIZA LYNCH (1835–86)
'QUEEN' OF PARAGUAY

Eliza was born in Charleville, Co. Cork to John Lynch and his wife Jane (some say Adelaide). The father was a physician and the family had a reasonably affluent lifestyle. Little else is known about Eliza's upbringing apart from the fact that she was raised an Anglican under the Church of Ireland.

The Great Irish Potato Famine (1845–1852), which resulted in at least 10 per cent of Ireland's population dying from starvation and disease, possibly including Eliza's father, forced the family to flee to Paris, where Eliza's older sister Corinne had been living for several years. In 1850, when Eliza was only fifteen, she married a French military surgeon who was twenty-two years her senior, Jean de Quatrefages. But Eliza was not happy in the marriage, though she stayed with him in various military barracks for three years. When her health suffered from the harsh desert heat after de Quatrefages was transferred yet again to Algiers, the union quickly ended in a permanent separation, though there was never an annulment or official divorce.

Back in Paris in 1853, Eliza started working as a high-class courtesan in expensive Parisian salons to earn a living (some biographers say she was employed as a language-teacher). There, she met a rich gentleman from South America, Francisco Solano López. It was love at first sight. He was smitten with her beauty and she was taken by his wealth and position; López was fabulously rich and heir to the dynastic presidency of Paraguay.

Shortly afterwards, Eliza became pregnant and when the López family found out about it, they informed Francisco in no uncertain terms to pay the girl off and have nothing further to do with Eliza. Francisco took no notice of his family's objections and when he returned to Paraguay in 1854, he made arrangements for her to follow. While in Europe, Francisco had already lavished gifts on Eliza and she had become his most trusted confidante and his chief advisor. Eliza was determined that this new-found status and wealth should continue.

Eliza arrived by boat in Buenos Aires in early 1855 where she gave birth to their son, Panchito. When she recovered sufficiently to travel, Eliza continued her journey via steamship up the Paraná and Paraguay rivers for the 1400 kilometre-long voyage to Asunción, the capital of land-locked Paraguay. Her appearance caused a sensation amongst the ordinary people because they had never witnessed such a display of glamour and French finery. She was exotic, cultured and elegant, with the finest white skin. The people were dazzled.

However, Francisco's father, President Carlos López, was not impressed. He forbade his son to live publicly with his lover, yet it became an open secret throughout Paraguay that the two were inseparable. People started called her, 'Madame Lynch' and seeing her almost always by Francisco's side at balls, in meetings and other official functions. Eliza quickly became part of the social scene of the Paraguayan upper classes and learned to take advantage of her elevated status. She entertained, held soirées, and introduced European music, dance, theatre, clothing and culture to the country. Eliza encouraged the Paraguayan elite to think of themselves as grander, more sophisticated and advanced than they had previously regarded themselves.

Along with encouraging the people of Paraguayan society to become more ambitious for themselves, Eliza's lover became more ambitious for Paraguay as a whole. He began to think that the country he would someday inherit should become stronger and more powerful than it was. But first he considered that the country needed to be modernised.

During the 1850s, European engineers and industrialists started pouring into Paraguy, building iron factories, railways, bridges, a telegraph system, an armaments manufacturing centre and a merchant fleet to trade directly with the outside world. To protect the vital river lifeline, Francisco López ordered the construction of one of the largest and most heavily defended fortresses in South America, overlooking the Paraguay River at Humaitá in the country's south. At every step along the way he was supported, some say encouraged, by his consort Eliza.

López continued to shower Madame Lynch with jewels, money and land. At one point during the early 1860s she became the woman who was the world's largest landowner, with property totalling over 80,000 square kilometres being transferred into her name. This area was larger than the entire island of Ireland!

Francisco succeeded to the presidency when his father died in 1862, and demanded absolute deference, for example banning people from sitting while he stood. He also wasted no time proving to the rest of the continent just how powerful he believed Paraguay had become. Brazil and Uruguay had a contested border between them, which from time-to-time was subject to incursions from Brazil. Hoping to make Uruguay an ally, President-Dictator Francisco López notified Brazil he had closed the essential and shared waterway between their two countries.

This action provoked an inevitable war between Brazil and Paraguay, which López had foreseen. To his surprise, Uruguay sided with Brazil, not Paraguay, fearing, quite correctly, that ultimately López would swallow Uruguay in his drive to become the largest and most powerful nation in South America. This setback did not seem to unduly worry the Paraguayan President-Dictator, for he believed he still had more than enough men and materiel to take care of two adversaries.

It would seem that this cavalier attitude may have led to one of his most disastrous miscalculations. In 1865, López sought permission to move his troops through Argentinian territory, but was refused. Argentina had remained neutral in the conflict up to now. López became so infuriated with Argentina's refusal that he rashly declared war on that country. Suddenly Paraguay was now at war with three of its neighbours and the ensuing conflict would be called the War of the Triple Alliance.

López believed it did not matter if Paraguay was fighting one, two or even three opponents, because his country still had a larger army than all the other countries combined! On paper that was correct; Paraguay started the war with about 70,000 soldiers, which dwarfed the 35,000 soldiers the triple alliance could collectively assemble at the beginning. Yet the raw numbers belied the fact that the Paraguayan military build-up had been too rapid. The army was poorly armed and equipped. Its military leaders were untrained and inexperienced. Finally, no decision could be made without the approval of President-Dictator López, which meant that the generals in the field were uncertain what to do for fear of upsetting their increasingly irascible ruler.

The war proved to be a complete disaster for Paraguay, from the long siege at the fortress of Humaitá (1866–1868), to the terrible retreat to the north of Paraguay (1868–1870), people died of hunger, disease and warfare in their hundreds of thousands. It is regarded by most historians as the most brutal conflict ever seen in South America. All the time this catastrophe was unfolding, Eliza was by her lover's side giving him comfort, urging him not to lose heart and taking care of the nine children he had fathered with her.

After five long years, Paraguayan resistance collapsed and President-Dictator López had lost his mind. As the dictator's family retreated into the jungles of Paraguay's north. López unleashed a bloody slaughter of his own people whom he had now come to believe were all conspiring against him. Paranoia gripped him and the remnants of his army.

President López jailed and tortured thousands of his most loyal supporters. He even flogged his own mother and had his brother killed. Yet through it all, Eliza was safe and appeared to be the only person who could control him.

Finally in March 1870 a Brazilian detachment caught up with López. When called upon to surrender he defiantly refused. As he was killed by a cavalryman's lance, he is reputed to have cried out 'Me muero con mi patria!' ('I die with my homeland!'). When Eliza and her now fifteen-year-old eldest son, Panchito, came upon the body, the son refused to surrender too, and like his father he was run through with a lance as well. A blood-soaked Eliza Lynch was permitted to dig a shallow grave to bury her lover and son.

When the final cost of the war was tallied up, the world was shocked. Out of a pre-war population of approximately 450,000, some commentators say only 200,000 had survived, of whom only 28,000 were adult males. Overall some two-thirds of the entire population died, which included the astounding statistic that up to 90 per cent of all adult males had perished!

But the consequences of the war on Paraguay were not limited to its population. The three victorious winners proceeded to annex large tracts of Paraguayan land for themselves. Some 140,000 square kilometres of territory was lost, reducing Paraguay's pre-war size by about a quarter. Furthermore, Paraguay was required to pay reparations that it was forced to continue paying well into the twentieth century (Brazil cancelled the remaining payments only in 1943!).

It was Francisco's blind ambition to become a South American Napoleon that utterly destroyed Paraguay, but what part did his lover Eliza Lynch play in this catastrophe? One group of historians argue that her involvement was inconsequential and that Francisco López was always going to take his country into a calamitous war without Eliza Lynch's backing. But a contrary view is that López would not have even started down this path if it had not been at the urging of Lynch.

Eliza's behaviour after the war may shed some light on the matter. When the war was over in 1870, Eliza was forced to forfeit her lands and jewellery, though she did manage to take a small fortune of jewels, gold and cash when she made a hasty return to Europe with her surviving offspring. There, she immediately started a campaign to retrieve properties, possessions and titles that she claimed still rightfully belonged to her and the children. She even insisted that López had assigned her all his worldly goods and that she, together with her children, intended to get what was rightfully theirs. There was no sympathy in her statements for the plight of the Paraguayan people or for the untold destruction her lover's megalomania had caused.

Her campaign for the return of untold wealth over the next dozen years or so, would prove ultimately fruitless. Paraguay did not have the capacity to pay her and if the truth be told, Paraguay did not want to pay her, for many believed she was just as responsible for all that had gone wrong as her lover was.

In 1886, Eliza Lynch died in Paris alone and ignored, of stomach cancer at the age of fifty-one, still insisting she was owed enormous sums of money and land. Here was a woman who greatly influenced the outcome of a nation through blind ambition.

JOHN PHILIP HOLLAND
(1841–1914)

INVENTOR OF THE
MODERN SUBMARINE

Holland was born the second of four boys in the small coastal village of Liscannor, Co. Clare to John Holland, of the British Coast Guard service and his wife, Mary (née Scanlon). Mary Scanlon was a native Irish speaker and the entire family spoke Gaelic at home. Son John only learned English when he attended the local English-speaking National school in Liscannor.

John would accompany his father as Holland senior patrolled the coast looking for smugglers, shipwrecks and keeping a watchful eye out for the local fishermen as they plied their trade in the wild waters of the Atlantic Ocean. During these formative years young John Holland developed an intense love of the sea, and for the men and women who sailed on it. This love of all things maritime would stay with him for the rest of his life.

Holland's son John was born just a few years before the Irish Potato Famine struck Ireland. This was one of the greatest natural disasters to ever befall the country. Mr Holland's government work continued during the crisis, which prevented the family from starving, but still one of John's brothers died of cholera, a disease that swept through the Irish population that was already weakened by malnutrition and the typically poor hygienic standards of the day. This transformative event also affected and in some cases changed the lives of others who are mentioned in this book (see contents page for: Thomas McGee, James Gamble, Daniel O'Connell, Mary Aikenhead and Michael Davitt).

John thought of a career at sea when he left school, but poor eyesight prevented that move. Being a devoted Roman Catholic, he decided instead in 1858 to join the Christian Brothers Religious Order as a priest. The Christian Brothers, founded by Edmund Rice in Ireland in 1802, was a teaching order and Holland thought that becoming a priest and educating the Irish poor would be a perfect way to achieve these two objectives together.

During his years of training to become a priest, John taught at a number of Christian Brothers' schools in Ireland, but towards the end of his training the lure of the sea began to call him again. In the late 1860s, John read an account of the battle of 'ironclad' vessels, the *Merrimack* and the *Monitor*, during the American Civil War and he reasoned that if the boats could have been submerged, rather than riding on the water's surface, then they would have been invincible.

Shortly after 1870, he read the latest book written by Jules Verne titled *20,000 Leagues under the Sea* and this fired his imagination! He drew up crude plans for a vessel that could travel underwater and even coined a new word for it: 'submarine'.

In the mid-1860s, John's brother Michael joined a small, secret, revolutionary organisation called the Irish Republican Brotherhood. He was involved in a rebellion in Limerick in 1868, which was ruthlessly put down by the British authorities. It is not known to what extent John was involved in the actions of his brother, but there is no question he was certainly sympathetic to the Brotherhood's goal of Irish freedom from British rule.

What swiftly followed in the aftermath of the failed action against British authority was that Michael fled to America to escape arrest. Shortly after in 1872, John's only remaining sibling in Ireland, Alfred, also departed for America, taking their mother with him. With no family left in Ireland, John received dispensation to leave the Christian Brothers Order in 1873. He then joined his siblings and mother in the USA where he would remain for the rest of his life.

Soon after his arrival in America, John started teaching in a Christian Brothers' school in Paterson, New Jersey, while he continued to refine his submarine designs. John submitted his latest plans to the US Navy in 1875, but they were rejected on the grounds that they were 'a fantastic scheme of a civilian landsman'.

The United States might not have been interested in Holland's submarine design, but the Irish independence movement certainly was. Michael Holland had continued his membership with the American branch of the Irish Republican Brotherhood (known commonly as the Fenians) and introduced John, together with his ideas for a submarine, to the head of the Fenians in the USA.

In an extraordinary turn of events in John Holland's life, the Fenians became intensely interested in how an underwater device might be able to wreak havoc on the all-powerful British Navy. They commissioned Holland to build a prototype and even bankrolled the cost of production. In 1878, in front of an audience of eager leaders of the Fenians, John Holland launched his first submarine into the waters of the Passaic River, New Jersey. It sank immediately.

But Holland convinced his backers that the concept was still sound and had the prototype raised, modified and demonstrated again. This time it successfully dived to a depth of four metres and remained underwater for an hour. The next model was larger and wider and could carry a crew of three. When tested off the waters of New York harbour in 1881 the more advanced model was capable of making nine knots and could dive to a depth of twenty metres. It was a significant improvement on Holland's previous model and was dubbed the 'Fenian Ram' by the onlookers from the Press.

However, all was not right with his relationship with his Fenian financial backers. When John asked for more money to develop yet another, larger and improved submarine, the Fenian leaders decided they had already waited long enough and spent too much money. They cut their losses and towed the prototype vessels away, never to use them again. Decades later the 'Fenian Ram' was found hidden in a boatyard and is now proudly on display at the Paterson Museum, New Jersey.

John Holland continued improving his designs and worked on several experimental boats over the next decade, during which he was married in New York in 1887 to Margaret Foley of Paterson, New Jersey. They had five children, four of whom survived to adulthood.

In 1893, the US Navy Department announced a competition for a submarine torpedo boat and Holland responded enthusiastically. He started the John Holland Torpedo Boat Company to obtain sufficient public money to construct what would be the largest submarine ever built at the time. The John Holland Torpedo Company later became the Electric Boat Company and ultimately, after Holland's death, General Dynamics Corporation, one of the largest defence contractors in the world.

And in 1897, Holland produced what is regarded as the world's first true modern submarine. His breakthrough innovation was the use of electric battery power when the sub was submerged and petrol engines when it was travelling on the surface, the latter simultaneously recharging the electric batteries. This hybrid propulsion method allowed the vessel to stay underwater much longer and travel much further than any of its competitors. The submarine also had a tube for launching torpedoes underwater, a deck gun and diving planes that allowed it to dive and surface, much like a fish. The improved design features that Holland incorporated into his latest submarine would become standard in all submarines for the next century.

After stringent tests, the US Navy finally purchased Holland's new type of submarine in 1900 and named it the *USS Holland*. Impressed with the submarine's attack capabilities, for which there was no defence at the time, the US Navy ordered six more 'Holland' class submarines, each of them for the then considerable price of about $150,000.

Orders started flooding in from the Japanese, Russian and British navies. It is said that Holland initially wanted to reject the British order, but was outvoted by his fellow directors, who considered that the contract was too lucrative to ignore.

In 1904 Holland split from the Electric Boat Company and went his own way, continuing to improve submarine designs. For example, he invented a respirator that people could use underwater if it became necessary to escape from their submarines.

John Holland died in 1914 in Newark, New Jersey, having spent three-quarters of his seventy-four years working on submarines. He was survived by his widow and four of his children. The First World War was only one week old when Holland passed away, yet only weeks later a German submarine *U-9* (loosely based on Holland's design) sank three British heavily armed cruisers in the North Sea in a battle that lasted less than one hour. The British cruisers could do nothing against the German submarine and in the one-sided contest almost 1,500 British sailors lost their lives. John Holland's submarine had changed naval warfare forever.

THOMAS JOHN BARNARDO
(1845–1905)

PHILANTHROPIST

Thomas was born in Dublin, the fourth of five children to John Barnardo, a furrier, and his second wife, Abigail. The Prussian-born father had arrived in Dublin in 1823 and married Elizabeth O'Brien, the elder sister of Abigail. Elizabeth died in childbirth in 1836 leaving five children under nine. At a time when no public or private assistance was offered to a single parent trying to raise young children, John Barnardo felt obliged to quickly find another wife. Within a year John had married Elizabeth's younger sister Abigail, who would go on to have five children of her own, fathered by John Barnardo.

Thomas's birth was difficult and he was not expected to survive, but the intense care of one of his older stepsisters managed to see him grow into a lively, intelligent young boy. Thomas received a decent, if strict, education in Dublin at two Protestant church-based schools. When it was time to follow his brothers into Trinity College, Dublin, it was felt that Thomas was not good enough to enter the university and he was apprenticed to a wine merchant instead.

In the mid-nineteenth century there was a great worldwide revival in the Protestant churches of a renewal in Christian faith through being 'born again' and doing 'good deeds'. One day in 1862, when Thomas was seventeen, he attended a revivalist evangelical meeting. He was so moved by the preacher's oratory that he felt he had undergone a spiritual awakening. The experience changed his whole outlook and from that point on he dedicated the rest of his life to God.

At first he performed mission work in the backstreets of Dublin, helping to bring the word of God to the mainly Catholic poor, but he found this experience unfulfilling. Then he heard that there were vacancies to work as a missionary doctor in China, and Thomas felt compelled to apply. The applications needed to be made in person with the China Inland Mission based in London, so in 1866 he set sail for London, against his father's wishes.

The Mission was in its infancy (it had started the year before) and only wanted the most capable men qualified in medicine for the arduous and dangerous task of proselyting millions through administering health to the people in the interior of China. Despite his undoubted enthusiasm, Thomas was told his candidacy would be deferred until he gained medical experience and a little more physical strength.

Thomas enrolled as a student at the London Hospital in 1868 and began preaching on the streets. He managed to find cottages in Hope Place (now Ben Jonson Road) Limehouse, London, where he intended to both teach and preach. London's East End might be an attractive, sought-after property location today, but in the mid-

1800s it was a fetid, rundown slum area, crammed to overflowing with the poor, the sick and the homeless.

Originally concerned with the spiritual well-being of the people around him, Thomas watched helplessly as a cholera epidemic swept through the East End, leaving 3,000 Londoners dead and many more destitute. He quickly realised that the poor – and in particular the children of the poor – desperately needed their physical well-being attended to as a priority.

Barnardo gave up the idea of missionary work in China to pursue local missionary work in London and in 1867, he opened his first 'ragged school' (the name for charity schools for the poor). Ragged schools had started in the 1840s in the working-class districts of some rapidly expanding industrial towns of Britain and often provided food, clothing and sometimes even lodgings, along with a basic education. In the early days it was explained that the schools offered the 'ragged people' of the slums an opportunity to improve and the name stuck. By the mid-1860s there were an estimated 250 ragged schools across Britain, looking after some 25,000 young destitute people.

The ragged school that Barnardo established in 1867 is considered to be the true beginning of his lifelong work and the building in London has been preserved as the Ragged School Museum.

Barnardo had a gift for telling the story of the poor in such a way that donors felt their financial contributions materially improved the lives of destitute children. He wrote many articles and gave numerous speeches in which 'success stories' abounded. Barnardo even set up his own photographic studio in London to take photographs of destitute children in heavily stage-managed 'before' and 'after' images.

Thomas Barnardo stood at just 160cm high (5 foot 3 inches)

and had weak eyesight: he was not a figure to install confidence. But he was so full of vision and enthusiasm to save the children that many thousands of pounds poured money into the coffers of Thomas Barnardo's charity. Some of his most ardent and generous supporters included Lord Shaftesbury and the banker Robert Barclay. The organisation he named after himself quickly spread into the more industrialised cities of England, Ireland, Scotland and Wales. Barnardo established separate homes for boys and girls with the slogan: 'No destitute child ever refused admittance'.

This truly decent man married Sarah (Syrie) Elmslie in 1873, someone whom he had met through their joint interest in the ragged schools. The couple would have seven children, four of whom would live to adulthood. One daughter was to later marry the great writer Somerset Maugham in 1917.

Barnardo's philosophy was that once 'rescued' from a life of impoverishment, the young person would be educated and trained into becoming a productive member of society. Girls were taught to become good domestic servants and future wives, and boys learned a trade. For those children with little or no prospects for the future, Barnardo encouraged the idea that emigration was good for the person as well as for the empire. From 1882 until Barnardo's death, 11,000 children were sent to Canada, with another 8,000 in total going to Australia, New Zealand and South Africa.

Thomas Barnardo's capacity for work was phenomenal. His ability to raise funds was unquestioned and his organisational skills exceptional. But there was another side to Thomas Barnardo, one that even caused his many supporters concerns from time to time. Without completing a medical degree he insisted on using the title 'Doctor' and when challenged to prove this claim in the mid-1870s he produced a supporting document from the University of Geissen in Germany. This document was later proven in court to be false and the person many suspected of being the forger was Barnardo himself. Eventually, he did complete his medical training at Edinburgh University and Thomas became a registered medical practitioner in 1880.

Barnardo worked prodigiously for most of his adult life, filled with religious zeal to take care of the children of the desperate poor, but all this effort came at the cost of weakening an already frail body. In 1905, he died from a heart attack at his home on the outskirts of London at the age of sixty. A national memorial was launched to pay off the organisation's considerable debts. Thousands of people filed past his coffin, condolences were received from royalty and hundreds of boys and girls from Barnardo's homes escorted the hearse through the streets, which were packed with people wanting to pay their respects.

It was Dr Barnardo's Christian faith that led him to start the organisation which became one of the largest in the world for the care of deprived children. At his death Barnardo had founded ninety-six of his homes across Britain, admitted 60,000 children to them, and helped up to a quarter of million more in various minor ways.

Unfortunately, it must be acknowledged that some children within the walls of his homes were abused, both sexually and emotionally. There is further evidence that some of Barnardo's homes became factories where child labour was exploited to make profits. But it is important to stress that these abuses occurred without Thomas Barnardo's knowledge or long after he had passed away. None of these terrible practices were Barnardo's doing. He only wanted to save the children, not harm them. And in the case of the vast majority of children under his care, this is exactly what he did.

MICHAEL DAVITT (1846–1906)

FOUNDER OF THE IRISH LAND LEAGUE

Michael was born in Straide, Co. Mayo, the second of five children to Martin Davitt and his wife Catherine (née Kielty), who were small-time farmers on rented land. The family was Catholic and were staunch supporters of Irish independence. These beliefs would continue to influence Michael all his life.

When Michael was born, Ireland was entering the grips of a great famine, caused by the collapse of the potato crop through disease (*see* contents for pages for: Thomas McGee, James Gamble, Daniel O'Connell and Mary Aikenhead). At first the Davitt family appeared to survive the worst of the famine when the father managed to secure a low-paying position in road construction on a famine-relief scheme.

Nevertheless, the Davitts still fell behind in rent for the small three-hectare landholding. And in 1850, the family was summarily evicted from their cottage and the building burnt down as they departed. The forced eviction from the only home he knew, seared an indelible memory in the four-and-a-half-year-old Michael that would result in his passionate campaign for land reform later in his life.

Rather than accept an unknown future in a land still ravaged by malnutrition and starvation, the Davitts joined a long queue of people fleeing Ireland through emigration. They journeyed by ship to the small textile town of Haslingden, about twenty kilometres north of Manchester.

When Michael was nine, he was put to work in one of the textile mills. In 1857, while attempting to clear a blockage in a cotton-carding engine, his arm was caught and mangled in the exposed teeth of the machine. As a result, what was left of his arm was amputated just below the shoulder. This life-changing incident could have severely limited his opportunities at a time when society did not treat disabled people fairly, but Michael learned how to be a competent one-handed typesetter at the local Post Office. This indirectly led him to attend a public meeting in 1861 of an English radical (Ernest Jones), who was calling for electoral and land reform.

The public lecture by Ernest Jones awakened a dormant political awareness in Davitt and over the next few years he found himself drawn ever closer to the beliefs and activities of the Irish Republican Brotherhood, also known as Fenians (*see* John Philip Holland, p. 122).

The Fenians believed in using violence to achieve Irish Independence and by 1865, Michael Davitt had become a fully paid-up member. In 1867, he took part in a failed Fenian raid on Chester Castle in Lancashire, their objective being to obtain a large cache of weapons and explosives in preparation of a planned uprising in

Ireland the following year. Davitt's participation in the abortive raid was not detected at the time, but in 1868 police surveillance identified him as a full-time organiser who was now playing a leading role in the Irish Republican Brotherhood. The British authorities decided to keep him under close observation.

In 1870, Michael Davitt was arrested at Paddington Railway Station as he waited to take possession of guns he intended to transfer to Ireland. He was convicted of treason and sentenced to fifteen years' hard labour, spending most of his time behind the high stone walls of bleak Dartmoor prison, breaking rocks and tending gardens.

He was not the only Irish revolutionary figure behind bars though. There were another twenty prisoners languishing in English gaols convicted of similar offences against the British Crown. In part because of pressure by prominent Irish dignitaries asking for amnesty for these men, Michael Davitt was conditionally released from prison in 1877 on a 'ticket-of-leave'. Davitt went straight to Dublin, where he and the other released prisoners were hailed as returning heroes. He was elected to the supreme council of the Irish Republican Brotherhood and sent on a worldwide lecture tour drumming up support and money for the cause of Irish independence.

During his years in prison, Davitt had pondered the question of how the Irish, who had been deeply divided down religious lines for centuries, could unite to achieve independence from Britain. He concluded that the answer was land ownership, in that many Catholic and some Protestant Irish over centuries had been legally prevented from owning land. This gave rise to the absurd situation where in 1870, just 3,000 of England's wealthy elite owned 81 per cent of Ireland! Whereas the vast majority of Ireland's population of 5 million owned no land at all, ending up paying rent to rich landlords and remaining poor.

Armed with an unshakeable belief that land reform was the key to an independent and prosperous Ireland, Davitt would often finish his speeches with the following call to action: 'The soil of Ireland for the people of Ireland!' In 1878 he founded The Land League in his home county of Mayo, whose principles were based on fair rents, fixity of tenure and freedom of sale.

The organisation quickly spread across several more Irish counties as tenant farmers in particular flocked to an association that offered them an alternative to a lifetime of back-breaking poverty. Watching in the wings while The Land League grew into a phenomenon was a dynamic and up-and-coming politician by the name of Charles Stewart Parnell (*see* p. 142). Parnell decided to join forces with Davitt and the two founded the Irish National Land League in 1879. Davitt had now been thrust onto the centre stage of Irish politics.

Parnell convinced Davitt that political change could be achieved constitutionally without resorting to violence and this caused Davitt to move away from the more extreme methods of armed struggle advocated by the Irish Republican Brotherhood. His stance brought him into conflict with other members of the Supreme Council of the IRB and in 1880 he was effectively expelled from the Brotherhood.

Davitt was gaoled several times over the next few years for his agitation on land reform, though he was never convicted. Each arrest became a political triumph for Davitt, who was ably assisted by the voice of Parnell in parliament. The Irish Land League used the court system to stall evictions and with each delay the popularity of the movement continued to grow.

Lord Erne was a peer of the United Kingdom and sat in the

House of Lords in London. He owned over 16,000 hectares of prime agricultural land in Ireland across a number of counties. In 1880, The Irish Land League withdrew the local labour required to harvest the grain on one of Lord Erne's estate next to Lough Mask in Co. Mayo, and systematically ostracised his local land agent, Captain Charles Boycott. Boycott was a retired army officer who faced the entire local community turning its back on him, including refusing to serve him in shops and delivering his mail.

The action against Boycott gained much attention around the English-speaking world and became a 'David and Goliath' story, with Michael Davitt playing the part of David. The Lord's harvest of 1880 could only be saved through outside workers being brought in from Ulster, escorted by over 1,000 soldiers. In the end, it cost the government many times more money to harvest the crop than the collected grain was worth. Since then, the word 'boycott' has become synonymous for withdrawing services or custom as a form of protest.

Unfortunately, the harvesting of the Lord Erne's crops by outside agricultural workers opened a dark rift in Davitt's campaign for land reform. The men from Ulster were Protestant and once again in Ireland's long struggle for independence, the ugly religious divide between Catholics and Protestants started to raise itself again. Encouraged by agitators in England, Protestants began to characterise the Irish Land League as a Catholic takeover of Ireland that would ultimately threaten the livelihoods of any Protestants living in that country.

In 1880, the newly-elected Prime Minister of the UK, W. E Gladstone, was sympathetic to the Irish Land League objectives. He introduced the 'Land Act' of 1881, which went some way to appease the desires of Davitt and his followers. But Gladstone also matched his sympathy for the Irish with repression. He passed the 'Coercion Act' of 1881, giving powers to arrest and imprison men in Ireland without trial.

It was Parnell's contention to test the new act in court, but before the process started Davitt, Parnell and other leading members of the Irish Land League were arrested. While Davitt languished in gaol yet again, he found out that the British government had reconsidered the issue of tenants in arrears and as a gesture of goodwill had decided to quash all outstanding amounts, thereby financially freeing up 100,000 farmers, and allowing them to buy their own property through government long-term, low-interest loans.

This was a significant victory for Davitt, Parnell and the Irish Land League. Further, the government decided it served no practical purpose keeping Irish leaders in prison and released them all without delay. From this point on, the campaign for land reform would gradually be replaced with another campaign for 'Home Rule' (limited Irish independence).

On the very day that Davitt was released from prison in 1881, the Chief Secretary for Ireland and his Under-Secretary were stabbed to death in Dublin by radical extremists of the Irish Republican Brotherhood. This was the last straw for Michael Davitt, who vowed to have nothing to do with the organisation ever again and he completely repudiated the use of violence to achieve Irish nationhood. He now despised terrorism.

As a result of continuing poor harvests in the 1880s, Michael Davitt worked tirelessly to complete the agenda he had set himself on Land Reform, because forced evictions were still occurring in their thousands each year. He also continued to tour abroad. During what was his fourth tour of America in 1886, Michael married Mary Yore of Michigan. The couple had five children, one of whom (Cahir Davitt) would become the President of the High Court of Ireland.

During the 1880s there developed a growing difference of opinion between Davitt and Parnell. Both men wanted Home Rule (self-government) for Ireland, but Davitt's ultimate goal was Irish independence from the United Kingdom, whereas Parnell wanted Ireland to become a Dominion within a British Empire, much like Australia, New Zealand, Canada and South Africa.

The matter came to a head over Parnell's affair with a married, though separated, woman with whom he had fathered three children. When the movement for Home Rule stalled with the Parnell scandal, Davitt decided it was time he entered politics to move the agenda forward. He was successful on his third attempt in 1893 when he was elected to the seat of North-East Cork in the Westminster Parliament, London.

For the next seven years he continued to vigorously agitate for Irish Home rule against a sea of resistance in the British Parliament. Finally, in disgust at Britain's declaration of war against the Boers in South Africa, he resigned from parliament, but not before he uttered these prophetic words:

'I have been some five years in this House and the conclusion with which I leave it, is that no cause, however just, will find support; no wrong, however pressing or apparent, will find redress here unless backed up by force. This is the message I shall take back from this assembly to my sons.'

For a man who had repudiated violence as a means of achieving a form of independence for Ireland, it was a strong portent indeed of what was to lay ahead, after Michael Davitt had died.

And for the next seven years, Michael Davitt wrote books,

travelled the world and submitted thoughtful articles to newspapers that were widely read and appreciated. His political influence in Ireland, though still respected, had waned. In 1906, while preparing to write a piece in favour of state-run schools in Ireland, Michael Davitt died of an infection after a dental operation. He was sixty years of age and in accordance with his Will, was buried in a simple grave in his home town of Straide, Co. Mayo. Nevertheless, over 200,000 people turned out to pay their last respects.

Michael Davitt lived such an extraordinary life that it is difficult to pigeonhole him into one category. He was at times a child labourer, victim of an industrial accident, revolutionary, land reformer, convicted felon, activist, politician, journalist and commentator. But one major theme ran through his entire life and drove him to perform many great deeds. That was his profound love of Ireland and its people, and his unquenchable desire to see his beloved Ireland free and independent.

CHARLES STEWART PARNELL
(1846–91)

POLITICIAN AND NATIONALIST

Parnell was born at the Parnell family estate in Avondale, Co. Wicklow, the third son and seventh child of John Parnell and his American wife Delia (née Stewart). The Parnells were descended from a Protestant English family that had relocated to Ireland on the promise of land in the 1600s and two centuries later, had become a wealthy, influential 'Anglo-Irish' family.

John Parnell was known for his Liberal politics and for being a good landlord. Delia was the daughter of an American commodore who had fought and captured two British naval vessels off the coast of Spain during the 1812 war between Britain and the USA. As the young Charles Stewart Parnell grew up, he was fed a constant diet of not only the positive aspects of a liberal British democracy, but also the limits of British military power.

Charles Parnell's education was a mix of private colleges and home-schooling, where he did not apply himself and did not subsequently go on to university. For most of his youth there was no indication he was interested in politics, so it came as a surprise that when he was twenty-eight, Charles helped his brother win a seat in the British Parliament in the 1874 election, representing Wicklow. This appears to have been the catalyst for Charles's desire to enter politics himself, for the following year (1875) at a by-election, Charles contested and won the seat of Meath in the Westminster Parliament.

The latest Parnell to enter the world of politics started his career with only a vague idea of what he stood for, but within months he was beginning to articulate a political philosophy that would continue to drive him for the rest of his life. One of the major issues that faced the London Parliament was the question of what to do with Ireland? It was part of the United Kingdom, which was comprised of England, Ireland, Scotland and Wales; and like Scotland and Wales was administered directly from London. Yet the people of Ireland were clamouring for some form of freedom, which manifested itself in calls ranging from limited self-government through to complete separation as a sovereign independent nation.

Charles stunned most of his Irish colleagues in the Westminster Parliament (there were 101 Irish members in the 1874 UK House of Commons) when he said in his maiden speech: 'Why should Ireland be treated as a geographical fragment of England...? Ireland was not a geographical fragment but a nation.'

In short measure he became adroit at using parliamentary practice and procedure to score points of order against speakers who rose to attack Ireland. From someone who, just twelve months earlier, appeared not to have a purpose in life, his behaviour and performance in parliament showed drive, conviction and direction. He had become a champion for Irish Home Rule – a form of self-government – and this gained him many supporters back in Ireland.

The next year, he and others used parliamentary practice to object or propose amendments to almost every bill that came before the house. This 'obstructionism' created much frustration within the house and much admiration outside it, for the practice had the effect of constantly highlighting the issue of Home Rule for Ireland. By now Parnell was seen as the new leader of the Home Rule movement, which was confirmed when Charles became the movement's president at the annual conference in 1877. Charles Parnell now set about modernising and invigorating the movement on his own terms.

In 1878, Parnell met Michael Davitt, who had just been released from Dartmoor prison for his part in supplying firearms to the revolutionary organisation the Irish Republican Brotherhood (*see* Davitt, p. 134). Davitt had founded the Land League to bring about land reform in Ireland, which Davitt believed was at the root cause of much of Ireland's economic impoverishment. Davitt wanted Parnell to join the Brotherhood, but the latter declined, as he believed that obtaining Irish independence through violent revolutionary means was not a goal he could agree with. Nevertheless, he agreed to continue working with Davitt, in whom he saw a fellow Irishman who was genuinely concerned for the future well-being of their mutual homeland.

In 1879, Parnell was elected Leader of the Irish Parliamentary Party, as it had become known, and under his guidance, it was turned into a major political force. He now threw his party's support behind Davitt's land reform movement too, since Parnell saw the movement's growing popular support as another way to pressure London into granting Home Rule.

And in the 1880 UK elections, Parnell managed to increase the number of Home Rule candidates from Ireland represented in Westminster, which reinforced his political position within the corridors of powers of the UK government. It was also during the 1880 campaign that he formed a relationship with a married woman, Katherine ('Kitty') O'Shea, which would ultimately bring about his political downfall a decade later.

Parnell threw his considerable political influence behind Davitt's Land League movement, delivering many powerful speeches at massed meetings across Ireland and gave voice to a new form of protest to the Irish people, called 'boycott' (*see* p. 138). Parnell spoke at one meeting saying, 'When a man takes a farm from which another has been evicted, you must shun him on the roadside when you meet him, you must shun him in the streets of the town, you must shun him at the shop-counter, you must shun him in the fair and at the marketplace, and even in the house of worship, by leaving him severely alone, by putting him into a sort of moral Coventry, by isolating him from the rest of his kind as if he were a leper of old.' (from Pelling, *Anglo-Irish Relations*, p. 53).

Events moved rapidly in both Ireland and England. Unrest in the countryside of Ireland led, initially, to repression from the London government in the form of arrest and imprisonment without trial. Parnell was arrested under this act, as was Michael Davitt and other leaders of the Land League movement, which only increased acts of civil unrest throughout Ireland. The situation became so volatile that the Prime Minister, Gladstone, fearing an Irish uprising, gave ground and enacted some degree of land reform in order to calm the situation. He further announced that the emergency arrest and imprisonment powers would be removed.

While these concessions were appreciated by the Land League

movement, it demonstrated to Parnell that given a sufficient amount of agitation, significant political changes were now possible. Parnell realised the critically important role Prime Minister Gladstone had played in pushing some degree of Irish agrarian reform through parliament against significant opposition from Gladstone's own party. From this point on Parnell would cultivate a personal friendship with the Prime Minister in order to achieve the ultimate goal of Home Rule.

Shortly after the murder of the new Irish Chief Secretary, Lord Frederick Cavendish, and his Under-Secretary in Phoenix Park in 1882, Parnell felt compelled to denounce terrorism. This caused a rift between Parnell and the Irish Republican Brotherhood, but made him an ally of Gladstone. By 1885, under constant pressure from Parnell and the Irish lobby in parliament, Prime Minister Gladstone had been converted to the idea of Home Rule for Ireland. It was the breakthrough that Parnell had been waiting for, and was desperately hoping might happen.

Gladstone and Parnell worked on the details of a Home Rule Bill together and then jointly brought the legislation before the Westminster Parliament in 1886. If passed, it would have made Ireland a Dominion within the British Empire, on equal status with Canada, South Africa, New Zealand and Australia. But so deeply unpopular was the proposed legislation among the English upper classes that a large section of Gladstone's own party crossed the floor of the House to defeat it.

Gladstone was so humiliated by the defeat of the bill and the undermining of his authority by members of his own party, that he took the unprecedented step of resigning as Prime Minister. Gladstone would continue to advocate for the Home Rule cause in parliament over the following years and during this time he would maintain his partnership with Parnell, until a scandal of colossal proportions erupted on the political scene. It involved Charles Parnell.

There had been rumours for some time about the relationship between Parnell and Kitty O'Shea, the wife of one of his parliamentary colleagues, Captain William O'Shea. But the matter came to a head when Captain O'Shea filed for divorce in 1889 on the grounds of adultery and named Parnell as the 'co-respondent' (the adulterous third person). Katherine O'Shea did not contest the grounds for divorce and Parnell never challenged his role as the adulterer, which meant that the divorce was granted without much fuss. In 1891, a newly divorced Kitty O'Shea married Charles Parnell, as they had unquestionably loved each other since their first meeting in 1880. In the preceding ten years, Kitty had often lived with Parnell and had given birth to three of his children.

There was an outpouring of moral indignation across Ireland and England. The Protestants were outraged at the adultery. The Irish Catholics were offended at Parnell's marriage to a woman who had been divorced, which at the time was prohibited by the Roman Catholic Church. Even members of the Irish Parliamentary Party deserted Parnell on moral grounds, which caused an irreparable split within the ranks of those supporting Irish Home Rule. Gladstone, still hoping to pass an Irish Home Rule Bill even after several false starts and a failed attempt, knew he could not continue his political partnership with Parnell, who was now a liability, so he cut him adrift.

As a result of his relationship with Kitty O'Shea, Parnell was also broken politically. In Ireland he was still loved by the town folk, who cared little for his personal life. But he no longer held any influence over the majority of the Irish population, who lived in the small villages and farms across Ireland and went to Mass every Sunday. Physically, he was not a well man either.

In 1891, Parnell set out once more to a meeting in Brighton, England, to salvage what he could from the parlous situation that his own actions had instigated, but by the time he arrived he was in a dreadful state. He died at the age of forty-five of pneumonia in the arms of Kitty, his wife of just four months. Parnell's body was returned to Ireland, where an estimated crowd of over 200,000 attended his funeral.

To some he was a 'failed' man who had never achieved the one thing he wanted to accomplish more than anything else: Home Rule for Ireland. However, for others, Charles Stewart Parnell was absolutely the right person to try and attain Home Rule. More to the point, he almost achieved the impossible against formidable English political opposition.

An apt footnote to Parnell's biography was that Gladstone never gave up on the idea of Home Rule for Ireland and in 1892, in extreme old age, he was called upon to form yet another government in Westminster. By virtue of sheer personality he managed to get the Home Rule Bill passed in the lower house, only to see it crushed in the House of Lords. Gladstone died before he could resubmit the bill through the House of Lords again and the opportunity for a political solution for the status of Ireland was lost.

The men who came after Parnell believed that a political solution was impossible in late Victorian and early Edwardian Britain. Based on what happened to Parnell, it was clear to them that the English establishment would stop at nothing to undermine the cause of the Irish. With the death of Parnell (and Gladstone) the last chance for a peaceful solution to Ireland's aspirations was lost. A generation later, in frustration, the Irish would turn to guns and violence.

MICHAEL CUSACK (1847–1906)

FOUNDER OF THE GAELIC ATHLETIC ASSOCIATION

Cusack was born in the small village of Carron, Co. Clare, the third of five children to Matthew Cusack, herdsman and his wife Bridget (née Fleming). The family was poor, uneducated and spoke their native Gaelic. Young Michael was educated at the local State-run primary school, where he leant English.

When he was in his teens, Michael decided that his future lay in the profession of teaching. He completed his teacher training in Dublin in 1866. After he qualified, Cusack took on a number of teaching jobs within government schools throughout Ireland. He married Margaret Woods, the sister of a Dublin barrister, in 1876 and decided to settle down in Ireland's capital to raise a family and establish his own educational business. In 1877 he started an academy to help prepare students taking examinations for the army, police and civil service. The business thrived and elevated Cusack into the middle class.

The ancient Greek philosopher, Plato, believed that the educational ideal was to produce an all-round individual, where physical exercise was just as important as classroom learning. This classical Greco-Roman philosophy was summed up in the writing of Juvenal, a 2nd Century AD commentator, who wrote, 'A sound mind in a sound body' (Juvenal, *Satire X*, line 356). This concept had been rediscovered by the educators of the nineteenth century and had permeated its way through most private educational establishments in the English-speaking world, including Cusack's school in Dublin.

Cusack, who was physically strong, enjoyed taking his students out of the classroom and onto the playing fields of Dublin, where they played cricket, rugby, soccer (football) and other athletic pursuits. These sports, all imported from England, had grown in popularity in the main cities of Ireland during the latter half of the 1800s. However, there were other sporting activities which were native to Ireland that had existed for centuries, such as hurling, weight-throwing and Gaelic football, but these sports were mainly played by the Irish poor and confined to the rural regions of Ireland.

In his spare time, Michael Cusack joined amateur athletic clubs in Dublin, and he also played rugby for a local side when time permitted. In the late 1870s, he became Irish National Champion at the sport of shotput. He regularly attended athletics meetings as an official and participant, but he became disillusioned with the direction these organising bodies had taken. Cusack was ashamed that many working-class people were excluded from attending because they could not afford the subscription fees or were regarded as too 'uncouth'.

Initially, he tried reforming these organisations, but gave up in

1881, when repeated attempts over the previous three years had fallen on deaf ears. It was during this period when Cusack was trying – but failing – to reform sport from within, which he began to think about reviving Ireland's own indigenous sports and making them accessible to everyone.

He discussed his plan with fellow athletes, some of whom were secretly members of various nationalist political organisations, and was encouraged to take the idea forward. Ireland was going through a strong pro-independence phase in the mid-to-late 1800s, with political campaigns by Fenians, Irish Republicans and proponents of Home Rule (*see* Parnell, p. 142). Together with a new-found sense of Irish nationalism came a resurgence in Irish culture, literature, music and art. It was Cusack who added sport to this heady mix of Gaelic Revivalism, by strenuously arguing that English games such as rugby and cricket were corrupting alien influences and should be banned. To underscore the point, Michael Cusack never played these sports again.

Cusack wrote in one of the papers he edited and regularly contributed to: 'It [is] imperative, therefore, that the Irish people should found their own sporting organisation to encourage and promote in every way, every form of athletics which is peculiarly Irish, and to remove with one sweep everything foreign and iniquitous in the present system' (*United Ireland* newspaper, 1884).

In late 1884, Cusack called a public meeting at a hotel in Tipperary in order to form this new Irish sports body he had written so passionately about. Only eight people attended, though Cusack was in possession of many more dozens of letters of support. Undaunted by the low turnout Michael Cusack declared the creation of a new national sporting body, called the Gaelic Athletic Association (GAA), which was open to Irishmen of all classes, creeds, and political persuasions, that was to be committed to cultivating and promoting indigenous games.

When word got out about the new organisation and people read its rules, the GAA spread rapidly across the land. By 1886, over 600 new and existing athletic clubs had become affiliated to the association. The main focus for the GAA was in the two sports of Gaelic football and hurling, with the association deciding to develop Croke Park in Dublin to showcase both these sports to the general public. It has since become one of the largest stadia in Europe for sporting events, with seating for over 82,000 people.

In 1885, the GAA under Cusack's leadership placed a ban on GAA members playing or watching 'foreign' games, such as soccer, rugby, field hockey and cricket. This ban lasted for almost one hundred years, and in a hugely historic and significant act of reconciliation, Croke Park played host to its first games of rugby and soccer in 2009. Both games were well attended and free of incidents. Since then, many 'foreign' games have been played at the association's home oval of Croke Park, without impacting on the games of Gaelic football or hurling at all.

Creating an indigenous sporting association rivalling the English-speaking establishment was a stunning feat and this period in his life should have been the very best of times for Michael Cusack, but they were not. The organisation founded by Cusack was growing strongly and interest in the almost forgotten sports of Gaelic football and hurling was enjoying a healthy recovery, but Cusack's autocratic management style was causing rifts in the executive of the Association. Michael Cusack was a combative, vain person and at the height of his power in the mid-1880s his heavy drinking became so excessive that it caused his working relationships to break down. At the end of 1886, Michael Cusack was formally dismissed as Secretary (Chief Executive Officer) of the Gaelic Athletic Association.

From this point on, Cusack's fortunes and health declined. His once-profitable academy closed through bankruptcy in 1887 and his wife, Margaret, died in 1890. Being in no fit state to care for all his seven children, some had to be placed in an orphanage. Now dependent on private tutoring, Cusack met the young James Joyce several times to discuss academic matters over a pint or two in the local hotels of Dublin. Michael Cusack had by this time become a familiar figure around Dublin, dressed in a frock coat, sporting an unkempt bushy beard and carrying a blackthorn walking stick. Cusack became the model for 'Citizen' – one of the central characters in Joyce's *Ulysses* – as a larger-than-life, aggressive person who dominates the boisterous gathering in Kiernan's pub near Green Street Courthouse.

In the two decades following Cusack's dismissal from the GAA, his relationship with the association gradually went from outright hostility to a sort of acceptance by Cusack of his part in his own downfall. In recognition of this improved relationship, the association publicly acknowledged the central role Cusack played in the foundation of the GAA. Even so, Michael Cusack died penniless in Dublin in 1906 and was buried in a simple grave in Dublin's Glasnevin cemetery. As a sign of the future rehabilitation of Cusack's reputation that was in its infancy, his funeral was attended by many members of the Gaelic Athletic Association and various nationalist organisations.

Today, Michael Cusack is remembered as one of the few Irishmen who not only stopped the decline of native Irish sports, but turned their fortunes around. According to attendance figures, Gaelic football and hurling are by far the two most popular sports in Ireland today. Michael Cusack was intensely interested in supporting other aspects of Irish culture too, including the restoration of the original Irish language.

Following in Cusack's footsteps, today the Gaelic Athletic Association financially supports Irish music, dance and language. It has grown from its humble beginnings in 1884 when Michael Cusack addressed an audience of eight, to have over 500,000 members worldwide and revenue in excess of €100bn. Thanks to Michael Cusack, the organisation he founded over 130 years ago, has become one of the most significant influences over Ireland's sporting and cultural life.

OSCAR WILDE
(1854–1900)

MAN OF LETTERS

Oscar's full name was Oscar Fingal O'Flahertie Wills Wilde, yet he mainly used only his first name. Oscar was born the second of three children to Sir Robert Wills Wilde and Lady Jane (née Elgee) in Dublin, Ireland. Sir Robert was Ireland's leading ear and eye surgeon, a descendant from Dutch Protestants who went to Ireland with the invading army of King William of Orange in 1690. The Wilde family was entrenched as part of Ireland's 'Anglo-Irish', yet Sir Robert was a liberal philanthropist. He had established at considerable expense his own eye hospital in Dublin, where he treated the poor for free.

Oscar's mother, Lady Wilde, wrote poetry and was a gifted linguist. She submitted poems for the revolutionary paper *Young Irelanders* in the 1840s and was a lifelong Irish nationalist. Wilde grew up in an atmosphere of learning, letters and liberalism and it influenced him for the rest of his life.

Oscar attended Portora Royal School in Enniskillen from 1862 to 1872, which was, then as now, known for its superior academic performance. He excelled, winning several prizes for studying the classics and art. Oscar received a scholarship to study at Trinity College in Dublin, where he continued to show his brilliance during his undergraduate studies by winning a further scholarship to continue his education at Magdalen College, Oxford University.

Oscar's talent continued to shine at Oxford, where he won yet more prizes and even found time to write his first poem *Ravenna* in 1878. The composition won him additional acclaim and First Class Honours upon graduation. While at Oxford he came under the influence of Professor Walter Pater, who introduced Oscar to the 'aesthetic movement', a theory of art that emphasised the pursuit of beauty for its own sake, rather than the principle of art being used to promote any political or social viewpoint. Wilde was captivated by this philosophy and would go on to become its leading practitioner in the artist community of Europe.

After graduating, Oscar moved to London and published his first collection of poetry in 1881 called, naturally enough, *Poems*. Although it received only modest praise by the critics, it reassured Oscar that he was heading in the right direction with his writing and his pursuits of aesthetics.

Wilde embarked on a lecture tour of the United States in 1882. It was supposed to be a tour of four months only, but lasted almost a year because his audiences were so taken by his wit, charm and eloquence. During his tour he met some of the great luminaries of the American literature scene, such as Henry Longfellow, Oliver Wendell Holmes and Walt Whitman. By all accounts, these acknowledged leaders of American literature were as much impressed by this up-and-coming Irishman as Wilde was of them.

When he returned to the United Kingdom in 1883, Wilde immediately set out on another lecture tour of England and Ireland, establishing himself as the leading proponent of the 'aesthetic movement'. In 1884, Wilde married Constance Lloyd, the wealthy daughter of a prominent barrister and they had two children together. After settling into marriage (which some now say was a sham) and having a young family to support, he was invited to revitalise *Lady's World*, a women's magazine that had fallen out of favour. In the two years that he was the magazine's editor (1887–1889), circulation rose strongly when Wilde insisted that the paper should not only report about what women wore, but also about what they thought and how they felt about a range of issues.

Starting in 1888, Wilde entered a seven-year period that would be the most creative of his life. Oscar published a collection of children's stories in *The Happy Prince and Other Tales* (1888). In 1891, he published *Intentions*, a collection of essays outlining the principles of aestheticism, and in the same year published his first and only novel, *The Picture of Dorian Gray*. The novel is a cautionary tale about a beautiful young man who wished to remain forever youthful so that could continue to pursue an indulgent, hedonistic lifestyle indefinitely. It had a homo-erotic theme which scandalised puritanical Victorian sensibilities and would go on to feature predominantly in later legal trials involving Wilde.

Wilde's first play, *Lady Windermere's Fan* opened in 1892 to much popular and critical acclaim. It also proved to be rather lucrative for Oscar, encouraging him to focus on writing more plays for the theatre. His subsequent plays included *A Woman of No Importance* (1893), *An Ideal Husband* (1895), and his most famous play *The Importance of Being Earnest* (1895). A further play, *Salome* (1893), written expressly for the great actress Sarah Bernhardt, would not be performed until 1896. The culmination of so much success at the box-office was that by the mid-1890s, Oscar Wilde had become Britain's most acclaimed playwright.

A few years earlier in 1891, Wilde had met Lord Alfred 'Bosie' Douglas, the third son of the Marquis of Queensberry. Wilde had become instantly attracted to the handsome young man, who was sixteen years his junior. Over the next few years the two were inseparable and it became an open secret around London that the two had a homosexual relationship. The Marquis of Queensberry had tried discreetly to end the affair between his son and Wilde on several occasions, but each attempt had failed. Finally in 1895, when Wilde was at the height of his success, the Marquis had had enough of the affair and publicly accused Wilde of homosexuality. In retaliation and against all advice, Oscar sued the Marquis for libel (making false statements). It was the biggest mistake of his life.

At the trial, Wilde's case against the Marquis quickly collapsed when passages of Wilde's book *Dorian Gray* were read out and love letters from Wilde to 'Bosie' were presented. But worse was to come when the Marquis's defence counsel indicated he was about to bring several low-class male prostitutes to court who would testify that they each had had sex with Wilde. The latter tried to withdraw the case, but it was too late. The judge found in favour of the Marquis and ordered costs against Wilde, which bankrupted him.

Within days Wilde was arrested for 'gross indecency' under the Crimes Act, an offence which carried the penalty of two years' imprisonment. Wilde was remanded in custody to await his trial. Justice was swift in this particular case and Oscar Wilde was convicted in 1895 and sentenced to the maximum of two years.

Constance Wilde knew of her husband's affair with Bosie and it was widely suspected that she was even aware that Oscar may have had homosexual relationships with several male prostitutes. But the enormous publicity generated by two sensational trials within months of each other shocked her deeply. She took her two young children to live in Switzerland, where she changed her surname to avoid public scrutiny. She died in 1898, from complications caused from spinal surgery, but some said that she also died from shame.

When Oscar Wilde was released from Reading prison in 1897, he was a man broken in spirit and body. He wrote a lengthy poem based on his harrowing experiences in gaol, called *The Ballad of Reading Gaol*, but even though it was a commercial success his creative genius had left him.

For many in Britain he was a social pariah tainted with a conviction for one of the most 'unnatural crimes' a man could commit in Victorian times. Wilde went into self-imposed exile in France where he lived in cheap hotels or with the few remaining friends he had. He briefly reunited with Bosie but the relationship did not work out. In 1900, a chronic ear infection flared up again and meningitis set in.

Oscar died lonely and penniless in a dingy hotel room in Paris, having been unable to rekindle the flame of his once stellar creativity. For the last three years of his life he was legally prevented from contacting his wife or his two sons.

Throughout his adult life, this talented writer remained faithful to the principles of aestheticism and for some this pursuit meant that Oscar Wilde was decadent, vacuous, foppish and a dandy. But he was also highly intelligent, literate and extremely witty. He was a man of letters. His poems and plays are still read and performed today. His novel, *The Picture of Dorian Gray* and his play *The Importance of Being Earnest* are considered by many to be literary masterpieces of the late Victorian period.

One unexpected development concerning the life of Oscar Wilde has only evolved over the last few decades. Wilde has become an icon for the Gay, Lesbian, Bisexual, Transgender and Intersex (GLBTI) community worldwide and for Ireland in particular. In the country of his birth, a country which at times has been known for its conservativism, Wilde has become a martyr for gay liberation and social freedom.

In 2015, the Republic of Ireland became the first nation in the world to legalise same-sex marriage by popular vote. During the many months of campaigning leading up to the historic referendum, in which 62 per cent of those who cast a ballot voted in favour of the change, the past figure of Oscar Wilde loomed large in people's minds. The legalisation of same-sex marriage in Ireland may have come more than a century too late for Oscar Wilde, but as one campaigner put it, 'The Irish people have voted for love and equality. Oscar Wilde would be so proud.'

GEORGE BERNARD SHAW
(1856–1950)

PLAYWRIGHT AND
NOBEL LAUREATE

This future famous playwright and author was born in Dublin, the youngest of three children to George Shaw and Lucinda (née Gurly). George senior was a failed grain merchant with an alcohol problem and the family was kept solvent by the mother, who was a professional singer. Technically, the Shaw family should have belonged to the Protestant 'ascendancy' (Ireland's ruling elite), but the father's unsuccessful business and alcohol dependency meant they financially lived a very uncertain existence.

Young George was initially educated at Wesley College, a Methodist establishment, in Dublin and then at two other schools that were also in Dublin, but never did well at any of them. By the time he was sixteen, he had developed a disdain for formal education and had secured a job in a land agent's office. His considerable talent for art, music and literature that he would display later in life came from the influence of his mother, who regularly took him to visit the National Gallery of Ireland and personally encouraged him to read.

In 1872, Lucinda Shaw made the decision to finally leave her husband and relocate herself and her two daughters to London, where there were better prospects for her as a singer. Shaw was sixteen and had just started work, so he stayed to look after his father. Four years later in 1876, Shaw decided that he wanted to be a writer and joined his mother and elder sister in London (the younger one had died of tuberculosis). There, he was financially supported by his mother and sister while he wrote five novels over the next decade, only to have all of them rejected by publishers for being outmoded and substandard.

It was during these ten years of personal development for George (1876–1885) that his viewpoint on life became increasingly 'socialist'. In 1884, he joined the newly founded Fabian Society as one of its early members and started writing articles expounding the Society's principles of greater equality of power, wealth and opportunity for everyone, drawing positive attention to himself and much critical acclaim. The Fabian Society was a middle-class movement designed to create a socialist utopia by peaceful means. During this period, Shaw also became a skilled orator, known for marshalling his points succinctly and arguing them convincingly. On a personal note, he became a vegetarian.

From 1885, Shaw started writing reviews and critiques of newly released books and plays, earning a reputation for his insight, wit and fearless opinions. At the suggestion of a good friend, Shaw began writing plays inspired by the works of Norwegian playwright, Henrik Ibsen, whose plays had recently been translated into English. The style of English theatre at the time was contrived and highly artificial, with plots bordering on the ridiculous played by a narrow spectrum of characters. But Ibsen's plays injected realism into the plots, which were believable and played by characters who were entirely normal. The first Ibsen play performed on the London stage was *A Doll's House* (1890) and was met with a hugely positive audience reaction.

Shaw wrote *The Quintessence of Ibsenism*, a brilliant essay on the Norwegian playwright that instantly promoted Shaw as an expert on Ibsen. In his haste to get a play of his own onto the stage that reflected a more realistic tone, Shaw rewrote a script he was already working on. When performed in 1892, *Widowers' Houses* dealt with the touchy subject of slum landlords in London getting rich off the backs of the poor. It was a shock to the audience, but they loved it.

The young writer then penned *Mrs. Warren's Profession* (1893) on the theme of prostitution, and *Arms and the Man* (1894), a satire about the military establishment. *Candida* followed in 1895, which not only presented a woman in the central role as the wife of a clergyman, but dealt with the drama of her having to choose between her husband and another man who had fallen wildly in love with her.

The pace of his writing came at a cost. Small ailments were ignored and turned into larger medical issues. In 1898, while recuperating from an illness, he married his unofficial nurse: Charlotte Payne-Townshend, an Irish heiress whom he had known for several years, as they were both committed Fabians. The marriage was unusual, to say the least, in that Payne-Townshend supposedly declined to ever have sex with Shaw, but accepted his numerous affairs with other women.

Shaw kept producing plays, essays, and writing personal correspondence at a prodigious rate. Throughout a career spanning more than six decades, George Bernard Shaw wrote an unprecedented total of sixty-three plays. The pages of his last, *Why She Would Not*, were left unfinished on his deathbed. As well as plays, for which Shaw is most remembered, he also wrote many essays, critiques, five novels, short stories and a staggering number of personal letters, estimated at 250,000 individual items of correspondence.

The comprehensive list of his plays and publications are too numerous to list in this biography, but there are a few standout items that are worthy of individual mention. In 1903, Shaw wrote *Man and Superman*, which was and continues to be regarded as one of his greatest plays. It is an epic four-act play in which the audience follows the main character, Don Juan, into hell for a debate with the devil on evolution. The play was not performed in its entirety until 1915 and is considered so powerful, so draining on both the lead players as well as the audience, that it is still performed sparingly to this day.

By the first decade of the twentieth century, George Bernard Shaw had established himself as a world-class playwright and his works were being performed regularly on European, British and American stages. One play in particular enjoyed such a long run in theatres worldwide that years later it would be turned into a musical and win Shaw even more fame posthumously. The play was *Pygmalion* (written 1912) about a Professor of Phonetics being able to coach a poorly-bred, uneducated and atrociously spoken London flower girl into passing herself off as a duchess among London's aristocratic elite. *Pygmalion* won Shaw an Oscar for best screenplay in 1938.

Of course the play was a satire of the rigid class system in late Victorian Britain, but it was written so brilliantly that audiences everywhere loved it then and still do today. After Shaw's death, *Pygmalion* was turned into the musical *My Fair Lady* (1956). A film by the same name followed in 1964 that won a staggering eight Oscars, including: Best Picture, Best Actor and Best Director.

Shaw was horrified with Britain's involvement in World War One and virtually stopped writing for commercial purposes to concentrate on writing anti-war essays and peace entreaties to anyone who would listen. But no one did and it was to Shaw's profound regret that the war ground on for four long horrible years, slaughtering the best and the brightest of the world's young men.

During the 1920s, Shaw went on to write many ground-breaking plays in which he deftly blended social issues with a comic technique that constantly placed him at the vanguard of progressive theatre in the United Kingdom. In 1919 he published *Heartbreak House*, about the decline of Edwardian England. Then in 1922, he finished *Back to Methuselah* which was an ambitious series of five linked plays viewing the history of mankind from its very beginning to the distant future.

In 1924, Shaw published what many regard as his masterpiece, *Saint Joan*, in which he rewrote the well-known story of the French heroine transposed from the middle ages to the modern period. It intelligently, yet forcefully, examined the nature of religious belief. *Saint Joan* stunned audiences when it was performed and attracted the attention of the members of the Swedish Academy, the body that awards the Nobel Prize for Literature.

In 1925, George Bernard Shaw was awarded the Nobel Prize for his significant body of work up to that date. Incidentally, Shaw would only accept the prize on the basis that it was a tribute to

Ireland. The citation read: 'for his work which is marked by both idealism and humanity, its stimulating satire often being infused with a singular poetic beauty'.

His wife, Charlotte, died of a lingering illness in 1943, in the midst of World War II. Shaw was eighty-seven years of age and somewhat frail himself. He left London to retire permanently to a rural retreat the couple had purchased decades previously in the small village of Lawrence, Herefordshire. He died there in 1950, of renal failure sustained from a fall. He was ninety-four years of age.

What is not so well known about George Bernard Shaw is that he, together with three other members of the Fabian Society, founded the world famous London School of Economics in 1895. It was established 'for the betterment of society' to focus on social sciences, with a substantial bequest of £20,000 (the equivalent of almost £3 million today). Its location in the heart of London was no accident. Covent Garden and the main theatre district were close by, allowing Shaw to visit both areas easily in one trip.

The London School of Economics (LSE) was a comparatively small institution when it opened its doors in 1895, with less than two dozen students enrolled, but it attracted the best teachers and set the most rigorous and intellectual standards of academia for the students from the start. In its 120-year history, the LSE has produced sixteen Nobel prize-winners and over thirty-five presidents and prime ministers have, at one stage in their lives, studied there. Today, the university has almost 10,000 students and is consistently ranked as one of the Top 25 universities in the world (*The Times* Higher Education World University Rankings, 2015).

George Bernard Shaw is one of only four Irish writers to have won a Nobel Prize for Literature, the others being W. B. Yeats (*see*

p. 168), Samuel Beckett and Seamus Heaney. However, Shaw is the only person to have ever won both an Oscar and a Nobel Prize to date. No one else on the planet has that unique distinction.

WILLIAM BUTLER YEATS (1865–1939)

POET, PLAYWRIGHT AND IRELAND'S FIRST NOBEL LAUREATE

Yeats was born in Dublin, the eldest son of six children to John Yeats and his wife Susan (née Pollexfen). John Yeats had given up a career at the Irish bar to become a painter and also forsaken his family's traditional Protestant faith to follow the philosophy of Positivism (a belief in rational human morality), as expressed by its founder Auguste Compte.

In William's youth, the family moved between the west and east coasts of Ireland, as well as between Ireland and England, to further the father's career as an artist. This put a strain on the marriage and for lengthy periods of time the parental couple remained separated. Also, the father's pursuit of a radical philosophy fascinated the young William as he grew up, and the future poet saw mystery in the myths and legends of Ireland's past, as well as in religion, spiritualism and even the occult. William's curiosity in the irrational world would become a lifelong interest.

WILLIAM BUTLER YEATS (1865–1939)

When William was in his teens, he started spending more time in his father's artistic studio in Dublin. Many of the city's up-and-coming painters and writers visited this place and William spent a lot of time in their company. This was the awakening of William's own artistic qualities. Yeats started writing poetry in 1882, when he was seventeen years of age. This was fairly unremarkable material that did not signal the outstanding quality of poetry that Yeats would later produce.

During his teenage years, William became increasingly attracted to the cause of independence for Ireland and by the time he joined the Irish Republican Brotherhood in his late teens, he had become a committed Fenian. He believed that through his pen he might contribute to a spiritual and cultural revival of Irish nationalism, thereby making the actual achievement to nationhood a physically easier task.

In 1887, the Yeats family took up residence once again in London, where William Yeats was determined to establish himself as a poet and a man of letters. In the early period of his artistic career, poems such as *The Wanderings of Oisin* (1889), *Poems* (1895), *The Secret Rose* (1897) and *The Wind Among the Reeds* (1899) started becoming noticed by the general public and the young man began slowly building a reputation for himself as a poet of some note. Yeats felt his skill and artistic capability improved with the release of each new work and that he was on the cusp of becoming a poet of some importance.

Throughout the 1890s, Yeats continued to publish poems (and one novella) about myths, legends and fairies, such as *The Countess Kathleen and Various Legends and Lyrics* (1892), but the events that were transpiring in Ireland were having a profound effect on him. For example, Charles Stewart Parnell (*see* p. 142), whom Yeats greatly admired and who stood for Irish Home Rule, died in 1891.

In the early 1890s, Yeats returned to Ireland and there met Lady Augusta Gregory of Coole Park in Co. Galway, who became his patron and encouraged him to pursue Irish nationalism with ardour. Together with Lady Gregory and a small number of fellow artists, Yeats, in 1899, became a founding member of the Irish Literary Theatre – the precursor of the Abbey Theatre in Dublin (now known as the National Theatre of Ireland). The theatre attracted a growing number of dramatists and playwrights, whose collective efforts became known as the 'Irish Literary Revival' movement; this was a force that was determined to showcase Ireland's independent past and possible future. Yeats found himself at the forefront of the Irish Literary Revival and from this point in his life onwards his writing would reflect a strong sense of Irish nationalism that had developed over the preceding decade.

Yeats continued his involvement with the Abbey Theatre for decades as a playwright, producer and finally as a Board member, guiding the theatre's choices of productions over the course of his long involvement. One of the little known areas over which his influence was felt was the development of ballet in Ireland. Yeats formed a collaborative partnership with Ireland's first prima ballerina and together they helped nurture the development of the Abbey Theatre School of Ballet (*see* Ninette de Valois, p. 253).

Apart from writing poems and plays that were stridently patriotic, Yeats also established two publishing houses for the express purpose of publishing nationalistic works by other Irish writers. By the end of the first decade of the twentieth Century, W. B. Yeats (as his name was often written) was at the vanguard of a new-found sense of Irish pride.

WILLIAM BUTLER YEATS (1865–1939)

Yeats was deeply moved by the 1916 abortive uprising (known as the Easter Rising) in Ireland during the First World War (1914–18) and penned a melancholy poem *Easter 1916*, in which he lamented the dead, yet suggested the sacrifice was worth it. In the swirling tumult of politics, war and nationalism that existed in Ireland during these turbulent times, Yeats had moved to firmly back the independence movement. He wrote other poems about the uprising, the Great War and its aftermath, including *The Second Coming*, *A Prayer for My Daughter* and *Sixteen Dead Men*, which he released as a collection in 1920.

One of the men executed for his part in the 1916 uprising was John MacBride, the husband of Maude Gonne since 1903. Yeats, who was fifty-one years of age, sensed an opportunity to look after the recently widowed Maude and her son, Seán (*see* MacBride, p. 265). Yeats had first met her decades earlier in 1889 and had fallen hopelessly in love at that time, yet multiple advances to her had been rejected. Yeats then proposed to Maude for the fifth time and like every occasion in the past, she rejected this final approach. With surprising swiftness, William turned his attention to the twenty-five-year old Georgie Hyde-Lees, whom he had known for a number of years. She accepted his proposal of marriage and the two were wed in 1917. The couple had two children.

Georgie Hyde-Lees believed in the occult, and specifically, a practice called 'automatic writing', a psychic ability in which a person can write unconsciously from a spiritual or supernatural source. Yeats was fascinated by this phenomenon and wrote a poem about it called *A Vision* in 1925. The early years of William's marriage were particularly productive and the combination of poet and the occult bore fruit in what many regard as Yeats's finest single volume of poetry, *The Tower* (1928).

Yeats served as senator in the Republic of Ireland from 1922 until 1928. In 1923, he was awarded the most prestigious prize of his career, the Nobel Prize for Literature, becoming the first ever Nobel laureate from Ireland. Upon receiving the prize, Yeats said, 'I consider that this honour has come to me less as an individual than as a representative of Irish literature. It is part of Europe's welcome to the Free State [of Ireland]' (Foster, *W. B. Yeats: A Life*, p. 245).

Yet the man did not stand on his laurels. He continued to produce a prolific amount of prose and poetry for the rest of his life. Some even say that the quality of his work actually got better after he was awarded the Nobel Prize. As the times changed, so did Yeats's writing. For instance in the 1930s he fought against a tide of growing conservatism in the Republic of Ireland caused, in part, by the imposition of fundamental Catholic values on society. Yeats believed that conservativism crushed innovation, creativity and entrepreneurship, an outcome to be avoided if Ireland's creative arts were to flourish.

Towards the end of his life, illness forced him to move to the warmer climate of southern France, where his work continued unabated. As the competing political forces of Democracy, Fascism and Communism began to play out across continental Europe, Yeats wrote his most ambitious work. Unfortunately *Last Poems and Two Plays* would also prove to be his last compilation and was published posthumously in 1939.

Yeats produced a staggering quantity of work in his fifty-seven years of writing: one novella, nine plays, sixteen short stories, fifty essays and almost four hundred poems. It is the sheer volume of his work, together with his evolving style of writing, that makes it impossible to categorise the style of literature of William Butler

Yeats. His poetry and plays changed from being romantic to realistic in nature. His political sense evolved over time to become stridently in favour of Irish independence. His fascination with the occult world of spiritualism and supernatural forces became more pronounced after his marriage in 1917.

Even though Yeats adopted different styles and themes in his writing over his life, three dominant forces could be felt throughout all of his literature: Yeats was authentic, he wrote with indisputable power, and he wrote with unquestionable passion.

Many years after his death, his body was brought back from France and reburied in Drumcliff churchyard, in Yeats's spiritual homeland of Co. Sligo. William Butler Yeats had chosen this final resting place for himself in one of his last poems *Under Ben Bulben* (1939). The epitaph on his headstone was taken from the last three lines of this poem and reads:

Cast a cold eye
On life, on death
Horseman, pass by.

CONSTANCE, COUNTESS MARKIEVICZ (1868–1927)

REVOLUTIONARY AND POLITICIAN

Constance Gore-Booth was born in London, the oldest of three daughters and two sons to a family who had a considerable estate in Sligo, Ireland. The Gore-Booths were Anglo-Irish, having been part of the Protestant ascendancy in Ireland since the original family was given land there in the seventeenth century. Successive generations had been Lord Lieutenants, High Sheriffs, soldiers, sailors and civil servants. The sons were educated in the best English schools and often served in the elite Irish regiments of the British Army.

Constance's father was Sir Henry Gore-Booth, philanthropist and explorer, and also the 5th Baronet of Artarman who married Georgina Hill of Tickwell Castle in Yorkshire. The family's ancestral home was Lissadell House, Co. Sligo on Ireland's west coast and Constance, along with her younger four siblings, was raised there from infancy.

CONSTANCE, COUNTESS MARKIEVICZ (1868–1927)

It was a huge estate of some 13,000 hectares, which had comfortably provided the Gore-Booths with sufficient income to enjoy a lavish lifestyle. Unlike many Anglo-Irish landlords who treated their Irish tenant-farmers poorly, Constance's father looked after the welfare of his tenants and spent much of his life ploughing a considerable portion of the family's fortune back into developing the estate.

It was this liberal, considerate and sympathetic attitude to his tenants displayed by Sir Henry, which extended also to the Irish people in general, that significantly influenced the development of each of his children, but did so with Constance and her sister Eva in particular (*see* Eva Gore-Booth, p. 183).

Constance had a happy, privileged and unremarkable upbringing on the family's estate. When she was old enough she was introduced to high society in London to find a husband, but she persuaded her father to indulge her desire to become an artist instead. Constance enrolled in the exclusive Slade School of Art in London (now part of University College, London) where she took classes for a year. In 1893, when Constance was twenty-five, she went to Paris to continue her education. Several years into her studies, she met a tall, handsome Polish count by the name of Casimir Dunin-Markievicz, and he was also studying art in Paris; they married in 1900. Their only child, Maeve Allys de Markievicz, was born at Lissadell House in 1901.

The couple settled in Dublin in 1903, but a life of painting and pleasure was not enough for Constance. Dublin was undergoing a cultural revival at the time and the couple with the 'unspellable last name' (as a friend said) naturally began to move in the circle of talented artists, writers and poets who were at its forefront, including W. B. Yeats, George Bernard Shaw, Oscar Wilde and

James Joyce. But the people she mixed with included not just artists, but also Irish nationalists and avowed revolutionaries, including Michael Davitt and Padraig Pearse (refer to contents for relevant chapters). The more time she spent in this stimulating company, the more her own thoughts and motivations turned to radical politics.

At first many people were suspicious that one of Ireland's Protestant ruling elite would be genuinely in favour of any form of Irish independence, but gradually Constance won them over by her commitment to the cause. Before her marriage, Constance and her sister Eva had agitated for the women's vote in Sligo. Now in Dublin, she resumed her campaign for women's suffrage, to which she then added Irish nationalism and socialism to the list of political objectives that she was prepared to fight for.

As Constance became more extreme in her politics, the more her husband started to pull away from her. He was a Polish noble with a large estate of his own in present-day Ukraine. He was definitely not a radical political revolutionary, and by 1912 the marriage was virtually over. The couple separated amicably and Count Markievicz left Ireland in 1913 to reside permanently on his hereditary estate. Although they corresponded, the couple only ever met once again, when Constance was dying, fourteen years later.

In 1908, Constance publicly declared her support for an independent Ireland by joining the recently formed Sinn Féin (We Ourselves) organisation, one of the fastest-growing patriotic movements in Ireland. The following year, she founded Na Fianna Éireann (The Warriors of Ireland), an Irish nationalist version of the Boy Scouts that cultivated militant patriotism. Under the firm control of Constance Markievicz, this organisation was to play a vital role in the ill-fated Easter Rising of 1916, by providing a large number of paramilitary personnel to fight, supply food and equipment, and run messages.

Constance Markievicz was arrested in 1911 while protesting against the visit to Dublin of King George V. It was to be the first of many arrests and prison sentences she would receive during the rest of her life. She joined the 'Daughters of Ireland' to further her campaign for female suffrage and wrote many articles for newspapers and magazines.

During the 'Great Lockout' of 1913, in which thousands of Dublin's workers were locked out of their workplaces for simply wanting to join a trade union, Markievicz established a soup kitchen to feed the unemployed and organised transport to bring food and fuel into the city from the countryside. She was everywhere, addressing meetings and organising demonstrations in support of the workers. During one particularly large gathering, Constance and others were set upon by a sizeable contingent of police, resulting in two demonstrators being killed and more than 450 suffering injury, including Constance. The dispute dragged on for months, with several more instances of police brutality towards the demonstrators until finally the men, hungry and defeated, were forced back to work on the bosses' terms.

The labour unrest may have been brutally crushed but having witnessed and experienced ferocious repression by the authorities first hand, Constance Markievicz now believed that the only way Ireland would be free of Britain was through a violent armed struggle. In her mind, Markievicz had crossed a line and had become a committed militant revolutionary.

Constance became a commissioned officer in the volunteer Irish Citizen Army and started planning for the overthrow of British control in Ireland by organising gunrunners to bring weapons and munitions into Ireland. Another organisation, the Irish Republican Brotherhood (IRB), convinced other groups – including the Irish Citizen Army – that the time was right for a general uprising. The date was set for Easter 1916.

It was the height of the First World War and the IRB hoped that British forces would be too stretched elsewhere to counter any insurrection. They were wrong. The British authorities had planted spies among the ranks of the IRB and knew exactly what was about to take place. When the day for action came, the armed revolution was woefully unprepared and under-strength.

The idea was that a quick takeover of government buildings in Dublin would rapidly lead to a general uprising across Ireland and the country would then be in the hands of the Irish before the British could react. It never happened. A few key buildings in Dublin were seized, but the anticipated massed uprising by the Irish citizenry never eventuated. Most of the Irish people watched on bemused, as the British army swiftly and powerfully crushed the rebellion in a matter of days, with about 450 people killed and over 1,000 taken prisoner. Under emergency provisions, another 1,000 Republican sympathisers across Ireland were arrested and deported to internment camps in England and Wales.

One of the prisoners was Constance Markievicz who, dressed in a dark green military uniform and armed with a rifle and pistol, held out in the College of Surgeons building in Dublin for a week, leading a small detachment of rebels under her command. She only surrendered when food and water had run low and the British artillery had pounded her position to bits. The sixteen ringleaders were put on trial for insurrection, including Constance, who was the only woman. After an expeditious hearing by a military court, all sixteen rebels were sentenced to death. Because of her gender, the sentence for Markievicz was commuted to life imprisonment, and she thereby became the only leader of the insurrection to avoid being shot by firing squad.

While Constance was in Kilmainham Gaol in Dublin and present during the executions of her fellow convicted revolutionaries, she decided to convert to Catholicism. One of the prisoners who was executed was James Connolly, a firebrand leader of the rebellion to whom Constance was particularly loyal. He was so badly wounded in the failed rebellion that he was shot while strapped to a chair, instead of standing in the usual manner when facing a firing squad. On his death, Constance wrote the following poem:

> You died for your Country my Hero-love
> In the first grey dawn of spring;
> On your lips was a prayer to God above
> That your death would have helped to bring
> Freedom and Peace to the land you love,
> Love above everything.
> (www.html://lissadellhouse.com/countess.html)

Constance Markievicz served only thirteen months of her life sentence when she was released during a general amnesty offered as an olive branch to the Irish people by Prime Minister Lloyd George, who at the time was struggling to win the bloodiest war in world history. In a strange twist of fate she was immediately elected to the Dublin seat of St Patrick's in the UK general elections of 1918, thereby becoming the first woman ever returned to the lower house at Westminster in London. However, still a member of Sinn Féin, she refused to take her seat in protest.

Instead she served as Minister of Labour (1919–1921) in the

newly created alternate parliament of Ireland, called the Assembly of Ireland (Dáil Éireann). Markievicz had become a strident radical by this time, and when it was proposed to sign a Treaty elevating Ireland to Dominion status within the British Empire, with the northern province of Ulster given the choice of remaining directly controlled from Britain, she was bitterly opposed. For her, all of Ireland must become independent, not 80 per cent of it.

Countess Markievicz sided with the anti-Treaty forces of Éamon de Valera (*see* p. 224) and was determined to stop the Irish representatives, led by Michael Collins, from signing the Anglo-Irish Treaty. Michael Collins realised that unless a treaty was signed with Britain, Ireland would quickly descend into a bloody civil war between the mainly Protestant north and the overwhelmingly Catholic south. This likely war would drag Britain back into the conflict and with it any chance of Irish independence would be lost forever.

It is said that politics is the art of compromise. For Collins and other supporters of the proposed Treaty, this was a once-in-a-lifetime opportunity for Ireland to become Britain's equal, not her colony. With a stroke of the pen he hoped to erase the shame and humiliation of four hundred years of subjugation.

When the treaty was eventually signed in late 1921, a civil war did in fact break out, not between Ireland's north and south, but wholly between supporters and opponents of the Anglo-Irish Treaty in the Irish Free State. Markievicz took up arms against the Irish Free State Government and spent most of the next two years in an Irish gaol, charged and convicted of sedition. Shortly after her release in 1923, Constance was arrested for the fifth and last time in her life for campaigning for the release of republican prisoners and went on a hunger strike.

CONSTANCE, COUNTESS MARKIEVICZ (1868–1927)

Constance had by now become a fundamental, radical revolutionary, determined to achieve full independence from Britain at any cost. She was also dedicated to achieving total equality between the sexes and the implementation of an extreme form of Socialism that bordered on Communism. Though Markievicz was still much loved by the people for her previous ardour and commitment, many felt that her causes had become too extreme and futile. Support fell away.

In 1927 Constance fell seriously ill with peritonitis following an emergency appendectomy, but could not be saved. She was attended by her immediate family and her estranged husband, who had urgently returned from Europe. Knowing that she was dying, Constance gave away all her possessions to the poor of Dublin. Ironically, one of the daughters of Ireland's wealthiest family, died penniless in an open ward of a public hospital. She was fifty-nine years of age.

Although her contribution to the cause of Ireland's independence was immeasurable, the politicians in the Irish Free State – still smarting at Constance's armed opposition in the Civil War – refused to give her a State funeral. Nevertheless, an estimated 300,000 citizens turned out to pay their respects at the funeral of one of Ireland's greatest revolutionary heroes.

Standing beside the graveside, Constance's great friend and mentor Éamon de Valera delivered the following funeral oration:

Madame Markievicz is gone from us. Madame, the friend of the toiler, the lover of the poor. Sacrifice, misunderstanding and scorn lay on the road she adopted, but she trod it unflinchingly ... We knew the friendliness, the great woman's heart of her, the great Irish soul of her, and we know the loss

EVA GORE-BOOTH (1870–1926)

LABOUR REFORMER, POET AND SUFFRAGIST

Eva was born the second of three daughters and the third of five children to Sir Henry Gore-Booth, fifth baronet and his wife Georgina (née Hill). The Gore-Booth family were Anglo-Irish nobility having lived on the same large estate – Lissadell – in Co. Sligo since the seventeenth century.

Young Eva was raised by enlightened, liberal parents who did much to foster good relations with the local Irish citizenry, especially the tenant farmers on the estate. During a time of significant food shortages in 1879–80, the family provided free meals to needy people in the district. Acts of charity and compassion like these influenced the children to become pro-Irish nationalists with a strong sense of equality and fairness for all. The eldest son became the first landlord in Ireland to sell large parts of the estate to his tenants. Eva's older sister, Constance, became a radical feminist and nationalist, who would be the first woman elected to the UK Parliament (*see* Constance Markievicz, p. 174).

The whole family lived a life of luxury and privilege compared to the ordinary people of Ireland. The Gore-Booths entertained a great deal at Lissadell, with nobles, writers, poets and smart-looking men in military uniforms being frequent guests. On one occasion in the 1890s, the poet W. B. Yeats (*see* p. 168) was so moved by the beauty of the young Eva and her sister Constance, that he later penned the following poem:

> The light of evening, Lissadell,
> Great windows open to the south,
> Two girls in silk kimonos, both
> Beautiful, one a gazelle.
> ('In Memory of Eva Gore-Booth and Con Markievicz', 1927)

In 1895, Eva became ill with what appeared to be tuberculosis and was advised to spend time in a warmer climate to recuperate. The following year, while convalescing in Italy, she met and fell in love with Esther Roper, a social activist and suffragist from England, who was also in Italy recuperating from an illness. The two had an instant connection and would remain inseparable for the next thirty years, until Eva's death in 1926. Esther was from a working class background in England's industrial north and within months Eva had rejected her own privileged lifestyle to go and live with Esther in a modest terrace house in a tough, working-class suburb of Manchester.

Eva Gore-Booth threw herself into the world of politics, trade unionism and the women's suffrage movement. In the early 1900s, she was elected Secretary to the Women's Trade and Labour

Council and successfully campaigned over many years for improved pay and conditions for working women. She addressed meetings and organised workers across England and regularly joined Trade Union deputations to cabinet ministers and members of parliament. On separate occasions Gore-Booth represented the interests of barmaids, female coal miners, textile workers and women florists in her untiring efforts to improve their industrial conditions. Gore-Booth's successes in Manchester influenced the formation of dozens of other female unions across England.

In 1908, Eva campaigned on behalf of an opposition candidate against the sitting member of Parliament, the Right Honourable Winston Churchill. Churchill looked as if he would easily retain his seat of Manchester Northwest in the by-election, but he grossly underestimated the power of the suffrage movement. Churchill supported proposed legislation to severely restrict the employment of barmaids and as a result the women's movement was up in arms. Thanks in part to Eva's brilliant campaign, Churchill was roundly defeated and the proposed piece of legislation was never passed.

In Eva's opinion, industrial action for women was closely aligned with political action for women, so it was natural for Gore-Booth to find herself at the centre of the Women's suffrage movement. In the decade leading up to WWI, she campaigned ceaselessly for women to be given the vote. In the early 1900s Eva was introduced to Christabel Pankhurst, the daughter of Emmeline Pankhurst, the undisputed leader of the Women's suffrage movement in England at the time. Unfortunately, Christabel grew increasingly militant in the methods she was prepared to use to achieve votes for women, so that in the end both Gore-Booth and her lifelong companion, Esther Roper, pulled away from the young Pankhurst's organisation. However, Gore-Booth and Roper would never waver in their campaign to see women given the vote throughout the United Kingdom.

In 1913, even though she had recovered from her earlier bout of TB, Eva's general health declined, forcing the couple to move to London, which was also the location of the headquarters of the National Union of Women's Suffrage Societies (NUWSS). Eva and Esther found themselves playing a crucial role in this organisation, arranging many high-profile demonstrations.

When war was declared by Britain on Germany and her allies in 1914, the NUWSS declared it was suspending all political activity for the Women's vote in support of Britain's participation in the war. Eva and Esther left the organisation in disgust.

Both women were committed pacifists and for the rest of the war became actively involved in the Women's Peace Crusade and travelled the country speaking in support of a negotiated peace to end the bloody conflict. The two women also joined the No-Conscription Fellowship to convince young men to conscientiously object to being conscripted for military service. The campaign itself was an abject failure, barely 16,000 publicly declared their conscientious objection to fighting compared to the almost 5½ million who either voluntarily or compulsorily enlisted. Yet, the campaigns led by Eva Gore-Booth and others to consider human life sacred did strike a chord with many people across the United Kingdom and laid the groundwork for the introduction of the idealistic League of Nations which would be implemented after the war.

Following the Easter 1916 uprising in Dublin, in which her sister Constance Markievicz played such a prominent role, Eva returned to Ireland and tirelessly campaigned for improvements to the living conditions of the prisoners and the reprieve of the death sentence against a number of prisoners, especially her sister, Constance. But her health continued to decline and soon after Eva returned to London, she withdrew from active politics and concentrated on writing.

Since her youth, Eva had written the occasional poem and when she had accumulated enough material they were shown to W. B. Yeats on one of his many visits to Lissadell. Yeats was so impressed, he encouraged Gore-Booth to publish them. When *Poems* was released as a volume in 1898, it was met with critical acclaim and sufficient sales to warrant Eva's continued interest and involvement in writing.

Another volume of poetry, *The One and the Many*, was released in 1904 and included possibly her best known work 'The Little Waves of Breffny', which has become proudly listed in many anthologies of Irish verse. Other publications followed regularly, such as *The Egyptian Pillar* (1907), *The Agate Lamp* (1912), *Brocken Glory* (1918) and *The Shepherd of Eternity* (1925). Eva even found time in her busy schedule to write a small number of plays that were performed on the stages in Ireland. More than a dozen volumes of her poems and plays were published during her lifetime and the main themes she wrote about involved mysticism, theosophy, romance, as well as Irish and Celtic myths and legends.

After a prolonged struggle with bowel cancer, Eva Gore-Booth passed away in 1926 and was buried in St John's churchyard, Hampstead. London. She was fifty-six years of age. After her death, her lifelong companion Esther Roper published a large collection of her work in *Poems of Eva Gore-Booth* (1929) containing many pieces not previously seen before. Esther died of heart failure in 1938 and was buried in the same grave as Eva. A quote from Gore-Booth's poem *In Praise of Life*, which was about lesbian icon Sappho, was carved on their joint headstone ('Life that is Love is God') together with conjoined Celtic circles.

Eva Gore-Booth was a gentle, spiritual and sympathetic person who was well-respected and admired during her lifetime, yet she was always in the shadow of her more dynamic and militant older sister, Constance. Since her death in 1929, Eva Gore-Booth's place in Irish history has largely been forgotten, but thankfully a very recent reappraisal of her contribution has gone a long way to resuscitate her reputation.

Eva Gore-Booth was a labour reformer, women's suffragist, pacifist and successful writer. She was at the vanguard of the women's movement and contributed significantly to the revival of the Irish literature. Most families would consider themselves lucky to produce one famous offspring, the Gore-Booth family were blessed with two!

KATHLEEN LYNN (1874–1955)

MEDICAL DOCTOR AND POLITICAL ACTIVIST

Kathleen Lynn was born near Killala in Co. Mayo, the second child of Robert Lynn, a Protestant clergyman, and his wife Catherine (née Wynne). The Lynn family had aristocratic connections through the mother to the powerful Maxwells, nobles of Ireland. The family was part of the so-called Protestant ascendancy in Ireland that was already in the process of breaking down when she was born.

Robert Lynn's second child grew up on the west coast of Ireland, one of the most beautiful areas of the country, but it was also one of the poorest, having not fully recovered from the Great Famine of a generation before. It is thought that the obvious poverty and destitution of so many people in her district may have influenced Kathleen to spend the rest of her life trying to alleviate these conditions wherever she went.

The young woman was educated at Alexandra College, a private

Protestant girl's school in Dublin, where she performed so well that Kathleen was encouraged to continue her studies at university. The Royal University of Ireland (National University of Ireland since 1909) had only opened its doors to women in 1890 and was still not fully accepting of females even when Kathleen enrolled on a course for Medicine in 1893. Her studies included classes at the Royal College of Surgeons in Dublin where she performed so brilliantly that Kathleen came first in her class and was awarded a prize.

Lynn graduated with honours in 1899, but faced entrenched prejudice when she tried to secure employment. The all-male staff at Adelaide Hospital in Dublin (part of Tallaght Hospital since 1998), opposed her appointment and for a while the best that Kathleen could do was obtain short term appointments only at various hospitals around Dublin. After completing a post-graduate course in the United States, Kathleen returned to Dublin in the early 1900s to establish herself as a General Practitioner in the inner-city suburb of Rathmines, Dublin.

From the moment Kathleen Lynn set up her practice, she was shocked by the poor conditions of the ordinary working class people she treated. Families lived crammed together in unsanitary tenement buildings, where diseases such as smallpox, tuberculosis, typhus and cholera were rampant at the time. She also observed the plight of women, who were crushed under the impossible burden of raising a family with little or no amenities, money or hope. Over the next few years Kathleen gradually became involved in agitating for better living conditions and the suffrage movement that she believed would give women a voice to change their oppressed lives.

Dr Lynn treated gaoled and hunger-striking suffragettes in 1912 and became friends of fellow activist Constance Markievicz, (*see* p. 174), with whom she discovered she had a distant family connection. Then in 1913, Kathleen became more involved in industrial unrest, when during the Dublin 'Lock Out', she helped the Irish Citizen Army (a workers' militia) to organise ambulance and first-aid assistance to the workers and their families. She also worked in the soup kitchen, serving meals to Dublin's poor. These acts politicised Lynn and drew her closer to the aim of the Irish Citizen Army, which was to bring about an independent Irish republic. Lynn became Chief Medical Officer of the organisation and was given the rank of captain, just in time to assist in the planning that was being put in place for a rebellion.

During the Easter Rising of 1916, Dr Lynn led small parties of medics about Dublin tending to the dying and the wounded who were valiantly defending civic buildings against overwhelming British counter-attacks. At Dublin's City Hall, Sean Connolly, the commander of the small brigade defending the building, was shot and Kathleen Lynn, being the next highest-ranking officer present, assumed command. But the task was hopeless and after several days, the small garrison surrendered.

Lynn was arrested and imprisoned in Kilmainham gaol, Dublin, along with other ringleaders of the failed rebellion, including three other women – Markievicz, Malony and Madeleine ffrench-Mullen, who had become her closest friend. Released in 1917 under a general amnesty, Lynn was immediately made honorary vice-president of the Irish Women Workers' Union and voted onto the Sinn Féin national executive as the women's representative.

Madeleine ffrench-Mullen came to live with Kathleen in Rathmines and the house became a gathering place for republicans and revolutionaries. It was watched constantly by the police, who arrested Dr Lynn again in 1919 for spreading seditious material, but she was released almost immediately, as her professional services were urgently required to combat the influenza epidemic of 1919–1920. In just a few months the epidemic had already killed 18,000 people in Dublin alone and authorities could not cope. Every medical doctor was desperately needed.

While fighting the epidemic, Lynn realised that there were not enough facilities to treat the poor. She and ffrench-Mullen founded the St Ultan's Hospital for Infants. St Ultan's was the first hospital in Ireland to be completely staffed by women and was named after an Irish saint who was reputed to care for children.

On the political side of matters, in 1921 Lynn was elected to her local council in Dublin and remained a councillor until she retired from politics completely in 1930. At the urgings of others, Kathleen was successfully elected to the new Irish Free State Parliament, the Dáil in 1923, but she was bitterly opposed to the Anglo-Irish treaty signed into power the same year, and refused to take her place in the Parliament in protest. Lynn took no part in the bitter and divisive civil war that followed the signing of the Anglo-Irish Treaty and progressively withdrew from politics to concentrate on her work in children's healthcare.

Part of the reason for Lynn's withdrawal from politics was her growing disillusionment at the way the young Irish Republic was heading. According to Lynn, the republic had become too insular, too conservative and lacked any commitment to badly needed social reform. She was most unsettled by the rising influence of the Catholic Church, which in the 1920s and 1930s seemed to be determined to reassert a fundamental moral code over the young republic.

At one point in the 1930s, the Catholic Church even wanted the multi-denominational St Ultan's Hospital to be shut down and replaced with a Catholic children's hospital. But there may have been a darker reason for the Catholic Church's desire to shut St

Ultan's: Kathleen Lynn and ffrench-Mullen had been lovers since they had first met in 1913, and although the relationship between the two was discreet, it was an open secret to many people. It is not confirmed in any documentation, but nevertheless there is a strong assumption that the Catholic Church wanted St Ultan's shut down simply for no other reason than its two founders were lesbians: a relationship that they viewed to be sinful.

It was not just the Church from which Lynn faced opposition, it was the State itself. In 1929, Kathleen founded the world-famous Irish Sweepstakes (Hospital) lottery as a secure source of revenue for St Ultan's and three other voluntary hospitals. Soon, revenues from the sweepstakes rose into the millions and the Irish Republican Government insisted it should be put through its own accounts for safekeeping. By 1943 almost all the money collected had been redirected to the government's own purposes. After paying commissions, taxes, subsidies and sundry other administrative costs, less than one tenth of collected revenue went to the hospitals.

Dr Lynn never lost sight of her cherished dream of a united, independent and compassionate Ireland. She also never wavered in her desire to see her beloved St Ultan's Children's Hospital prosper, but at about the time of her death a large children's hospital had indeed been built in Dublin by money from the State and St Ultan's' role slowly declined.

Lynn's lifelong companion passed away in 1944, leaving Kathleen to live alone. In 1955, at the age of eighty-one, Kathleen Lynn died in a Dublin nursing home. There was a military funeral for her and a small number of nurses from St Ultan's attended, but by this time her contribution to Ireland's recent history had already been largely ignored and forgotten.

One sad aspect of her funeral showed that the sectarian fissures which had divided Ireland for centuries were still dominating life in 1955. One of Lynn's best friends, Éamon de Valera (*see* p. 224) wanted to pay his respects at Kathleen's funeral. Even though he was Ireland's most significant politician at the time, he stood outside the Protestant church during the funeral service for fear of being excommunicated by the Catholic Church if he entered.

Today, Kathleen's hospital is gone (having finally closed its doors in 1975), but during her lifetime Lynn saved and changed the lives of countless Irish people. There have been plans recently to construct a new and expanded children's hospital in Dublin. It would be right and fitting for the new hospital to be named, 'The Kathleen Lynn National Children's Hospital'.

SIR ERNEST SHACKLETON
(1874–1922)

ANTARCTIC EXPLORER

Shackleton was born near Kilkea, Co. Kildare, the second child and eldest son of Henry Shackleton, gentleman farmer and his wife, Henrietta (née Gavan). On his father's side, the Shackletons had lived in Co. Kildare since the 1720s. On his mother's side, the Gavans had lived in Ireland since the twelfth century. By the late eighteenth century the family had become Protestant Quakers and part of the Anglo-Irish ascendancy.

In 1884, when Ernest was ten years of age, the family moved to London, where his father completed his training to become a medical practitioner. The family settled into a successful practice in the London suburb of Sydenham and there Ernest had a normal and unremarkable education at Dulwich College. (The school continues to honour the memory of one of its most revered students by proudly displaying in the centre of its new science building the small boat, the *James Caird*, that Shackleton used to make his most epic journey in the Antarctic.)

Then in 1890, when he was sixteen, Ernest rejected his father's wish for him to follow in his footsteps and become a doctor. Instead, Ernest joined the merchant navy. He applied himself diligently to his studies as he plied the oceans and qualified as a master mariner in 1898. A few years later when Ernest heard about an opportunity to join Robert Falcon Scott's expedition to Antarctica in 1901, he jumped at the chance. Ernest's application was successful and he was appointed 3rd Officer of the expedition's vessel *Discovery*.

The expedition was not a personal triumph for Shackleton. He disagreed with Scott's authoritarian management style and strong words were exchanged between them on more than one occasion. He was present when many new milestones of exploration were achieved in Antarctica, but recurring bouts of ill health meant he had to be returned to England as an invalid in 1903.

Some say that it was during this voyage that Shackleton fell in love with the idea of exploring the Antarctic, the last continent on earth waiting to be traversed by man. As soon as he was back in England, he started making preparations to return to the Antarctic, but this time he wanted to go in command of his own expedition. He was appointed secretary of the Royal Geographical Society in 1904 and unsuccessfully tried to raise money through investing in a failed Glasgow engineering business.

This period in world affairs (roughly 1900–1920) was dubbed the 'Great Age of Antarctic Exploration'. Heroic explorers including Robert Falcon Scott (UK), Roald Amundsen (Norway), Douglas Mawson (Australia) and Ernest Shackleton, fought their way through the ice and freezing conditions in a race to be the first to reach the South Pole. Governments and their citizens were all willing to fund these costly voyages and in Shackleton's case, even though his own personal attempts at raising money had failed, donations from other sources continued to accumulate.

By 1907, Shackleton had managed to raise sufficient private funds to launch and be in charge of his first expedition to Antarctica. This particular project lacked government support and was not equipped with the very best men and materials, but Shackleton still believed their resources were more than adequate to last the two years or more it would take to reach the South Pole and to return safely.

The exploration party established a base camp in McMurdo Sound, Antarctica, from which they climbed the summit of Mount Erebus and surveyed parts of the coast. In early 1909, Shackleton, leading a party of three others, made a valiant attempt to reach the South Pole, only to be forced back by a freak accident. The party was only 150 kilometres short of their goal when one of the pack-horses carrying a large amount of their food suddenly fell through a crevasse, and could not be rescued. One of his party was injured trying to save the provisions that the horse was carrying, and as a result there were insufficient rations to feed everyone, plus there was an injured man to tend to.

Shackleton could have forged on with just one assistant to reach the South Pole, but he knew his duty was to the entire party and he could not risk their lives just to satisfy his selfish ego. For everyone's sake Shackleton turned the party around and brought his party safely back to the base camp.

When Shackleton's party arrived back in Britain, he was greeted as a national hero. The King knighted him and the government awarded him £20,000 to defray the costs of the expedition. A financially rewarding lecture tour of Europe and America followed in which more awards and accolades were heaped upon him.

But Sir Ernest had unfinished business waiting for him back in Antarctica, so while he continued receiving praise as an intrepid explorer, his burning desire still remained to be the first person to get to the South Pole.

One of the greatest disappointments of his life occurred when he learned that Roald Amundsen from Norway had achieved this aim in 1911. Amundsen even planted the Norwegian flag there. But there was no time to wallow in self-pity, because within months Shackleton and the rest of the world heard that Robert Falcon Scott and his party of explorers had perished on their way back after having reached the South Pole, just thirty-three days after Amundsen's party had done so.

All eyes now fell on Shackleton to redeem Britain's status. He commenced to plan another expedition immediately, complete with a new and even bolder objective: to achieve the first crossing of the huge Antarctic continent from one side to the other. Shackleton had finished his preparations when war broke out in 1914. He offered his two ships *Endurance* and *Aurora* to the Royal Navy, but the Admiralty insisted that national pride would be best served with him completing the very first transpolar crossing of Antarctica, and so ordered him to proceed with the expedition.

Sir Ernest Shackleton's Trans-Antarctica expedition of 1914– 1917 remains one of the most incredible adventure stories of all time. And the heroic part Shackleton played in it has become the stuff of legends.

The *Endurance* was the main ship that carried most of the provisions and expedition personnel. The *Aurora* was the supply vessel, whose purpose was to wait on the opposite side of the continent for the transpolar party to emerge. However, the expedition became critically threatened before it had really begun. In 1915, the *Endurance* became trapped in pack-ice prior to reaching the shores of Antarctica, and over the next several months the wooden sailing ship was slowly crushed. It finally sank under the weight of ice, with the crew having to abandon her as well as most of the valuable equipment that they needed to survive.

With the expedition running dangerously low on food, the crew ate any penguins and seals they could capture. Finally, they started eating the dogs they had brought along to pull their sleds. Shackleton realised that their only hope was to reach one of the few whaling stations operating thousands of kilometres away in the South Atlantic Ocean. The twenty-eight-crew complement of the *Endurance* took to small lifeboats and reached the small, uninhabited Elephant Island, planning to rest there. But they were in no fit state to continue as a group. Shackleton then took the five fittest men with him and made a desperate 1,300 km open-boat journey in treacherous conditions to reach South Georgia Island. It was a miracle of navigation and seamanship that the small boat found the tiny island at all in the huge expanse of the Southern Ocean.

But on arrival at South Georgia, Sir Ernest was faced with yet another seemingly insurmountable problem. They had landed on the opposite side of the island to where the whaling station was located and the prevailing winds and currents prevented them from sailing around the coast. There was no choice but to cross overland, but a huge mountain range lay between them and their destination, and they had no climbing equipment with them.

Two days later, six half-frozen men stumbled out of the mountains down to the whaling station below. From there, Shackleton was able to mount a rescue of the men waiting on Elephant Island, and to bring everyone back to the United Kingdom without any loss of life.

His fame was now assured and an adoring public flocked to his lectures and public speaking engagements. In 1919, Shackleton was asked if he would ever return to the Antarctic. Shackleton admitted that he felt the faraway 'voices' of the vast, frozen continent calling him again. He then quoted from a recently published Canadian poem, written by Robert William Service:

They're wanting me, they are calling me, the awful lonely
    places;
They are whining, they are whimpering, as if each had a soul;
They are calling from the wilderness, the vast and God-like
    spaces,
The stern, and sullen solitudes that sentinel the Pole.
    (Service, *The Spell of the Yukon and Other Verses*, pp. 38–9.)

After a short period of service in Russia, working with the North Russia Expeditionary Force after the Great War, Shackleton departed for Antarctica once again in 1921. As the research vessel was approaching the Southern Ocean, Sir Ernest suffered a massive heart attack and died. He was buried at the whaling station on South Georgia Island in 1922, the personnel of which had saved him and his crew in the near fatal 1914–17 expedition.

Sir Ernest Shackleton never lost his deep love for Ireland and the people among whom he grew up – indeed on several occasions in later life he had no hesitation at all in describing himself as an Irishman. To emphasise the point, a recent biography written by a family relative was titled *Shackleton: An Irishman in Antarctica* (by

Jonathan Shackleton & John MacKenna, first published in 2003). In more recent times, his name has become a synonym for courageous leadership and eventual triumph over adversity.

HANNA SHEEHY-SKEFFINGTON
(1877–1946)

FEMINIST AND NATIONALIST

anna Sheehy was born in Kanturk, Co. Cork as the first daughter of seven children to David Sheehy and Elizabeth (née McCoy). David Sheehy was a long-term politician who was sitting as a member of parliament in Westminster. The Sheehys were part of a new wave of Irish nationalists vigorously asserting their Catholicism and politics against a declining Protestant ascendancy in Ireland.

The Sheehy family moved to Dublin in 1887 and the children grew up in a household filled with the comings and goings of interesting people as well as the voices of many, many discussions about politics. It was a stimulating environment and the children grew up bright, intelligent and politically active.

Hanna finished her secondary schooling in 1896 as a prize-winning student, but her choices were limited when it came to continuing her education at a university. At the time, women were prevented from attending lectures at the two leading colleges in Ireland (University College, Dublin and Trinity College). However, Catholic women of 'good standing' could receive tuition at the newly-opened St Mary's College from 1896 and were permitted to sit exams at either of the other two universities.

Following this rather complicated method, Hanna succeeded in obtaining a Bachelor's degree in Arts (1899) followed by a Master's degree in Arts with First Class Honours (1902). Sheehy went on to teach part time at her old secondary school.

While she was a student, Hanna met Francis (Frank) Skeffington, son of a medical practitioner who was attending University College, Dublin. He was an eccentric individual: a committed supporter of women's suffrage and active in student politics. Hanna and Frank had similar views and were drawn to each other. They were engaged in 1900 and married in 1903.

Together, the two advocated for women to be admitted to male-only universities in Ireland, a campaign that cost Frank his job as Registrar of University College, Dublin. Over the course of the next half dozen years, both became progressively politicised in their activism for social reform. The couple moved house to the Dublin suburb of Rathmines in 1908 and Hanna gave birth to their first and only child, Owen, in 1909.

In 1908, Hanna founded the Irish Women's Franchise League (IWFL), a group aiming to secure women's voting rights, and they took the campaign to the streets. During one demonstration in 1912, Hanna was arrested and convicted of breaking the windows at public buildings in Dublin. She was sentenced to a month's imprisonment and as a consequence lost her part-time teaching position. But Hanna was undaunted by this setback and attended a large rally for women's rights in London, which was addressed by

Emmeline Pankhurst. In the same year as her arrest, she established *The Irish Citizen*, a weekly newspaper to promote the views of the IWFL, which had rapidly grown to become the largest suffrage group in Ireland.

During the Great Lockout of 1913, Hanna and Frank spent much of their time serving food to the undernourished families of unemployed workers in Dublin. By now, both had become borderline radicals, heavily influenced by the ideals of nationalists and republicans from Sinn Féin and the Irish Republican Brotherhood – the difference in their approach was that Hanna and her husband wanted to achieve these outcomes through peaceful means.

At the outbreak of war in 1914, Hanna and Frank became committed pacifists and strongly campaigned against participation in the First World War. Frank was arrested and sentenced to six months' imprisonment in 1915 for distributing leaflets against recruiting. He immediately went on a hunger strike, however a subsequent public outcry led to his release a week later.

Frank went on a lecture tour of America, which was still a neutral country, while Hanna edited *The Irish Citizen* and looked after their son Owen in his absence. Within months of Frank's return, the two found themselves in the centre of the uprising, known as the 'Easter Rising' in 1916. As mentioned earlier, the couple were opposed to violence, yet both supported the objectives that the insurgents were fighting for. Hanna began bringing food to the rebels and Frank organised a 'citizen militia' to prevent looting.

One evening during the week-long struggle, Frank and two journalists were arrested and summarily shot on the orders of Captain Bowen-Colthurst (of the Royal Irish Rifles). Bowen-Colthurst was charged with three counts of murder. He was found guilty, but suffering from temporary insanity at the time of the crime. After being detained in Broadmoor Criminal Lunatic Asylum for two years, Bowen-Colthurst was conditionally released and in 1921 immigrated to Canada.

Hanna was devastated by her husband's murder and never accepted the insanity verdict handed down at Bowen-Colhurst's trial. She kept calling for a full judicial inquiry. She even refused a substantial offer of compensation, something which strengthened her demands. Later in 1916, the British Government held an inquiry, which uncovered more detail, but they steadfastly refused to alter the previous outcome of the trial. At the time the British were fighting the most devastating war in its history and wanted no further bad publicity.

However, to keep up the pressure on the UK Government, Hanna and her young son left Ireland for a lecture tour of America during 1916–17. The tour was a triumph, with a highlight being a personal audience with President Wilson. Hanna spoke at 250 venues during the months she was away and returned with over US$40,000 in donations, which was handed over to Michael Collins (*see* p. XXX), a man who was now a key player in Irish politics. The British authorities had refused to issue a passport for Hanna's American tour, so she travelled under a false identity, which led to many complications when she returned to London. The main restriction placed on her was that she could never return to Ireland.

However, Hanna ignored the order and journeyed to Ireland disguised as a workman, but was arrested and returned to England, this time to spend time in Holloway Prison, London. There she joined other Irish women prisoners, including Constance Markievicz (*see* p. 174) and immediately went on a hunger strike. Her stay in prison on this occasion lasted only two days, though her exile from Ireland was to remain in place for the duration of the war.

When she was allowed to return to Ireland in late 1918, Hanna became an executive member of Sinn Féin and committed herself to continue the struggle for an independent Ireland. She entered local politics when she was elected to Dublin's city council in 1920, but her decade-long campaign for the rights of women and those of Ireland increasingly came under the attention of paramilitary groups who were determined to stop the march towards Irish independence. In 1920, one group called the 'Black and Tans' raided the offices of *The Irish Citizen*, beating up staff and smashing the printing presses.

Still, Hanna continued to crusade for matters that she was passionate about. In 1918, women throughout the United Kingdom had been given the vote, but only if they were over thirty years of age and owned property. Hanna wanted the age lowered to twenty-one, without any property qualifications, which were the same conditions applying to men at the time. Her campaigning finally brought the matter to a head in the alternative Irish Parliament (Dáil Éireann), and in a great victory for women's rights, suffrage for women on the same terms as men was granted subject to independence from the United Kingdom.

At the outbreak of the Irish Civil War (1922–3), Hanna sided with the anti-treaty Republicans and was sent by Éamon de Valera (*see* p. 224) to America to raise funds to continue the fight against pro-treaty supporters. By the time Mrs Sheehy-Skeffington returned to Ireland in mid-1923, the civil war had run its course with the pro-treaty side eventual winners. Ireland was now a deeply divided and traumatised country in which Irish nationalists had fought and killed each other.

Hanna continued to be a member of Sinn Féin and participated in public life. She attended the International Women's Suffrage Conference in Paris in 1925, the Women's International League for Peace and Freedom Congress in Dublin (1926) and again in Prague (1929).

In 1926, Hanna was served with an order from the Northern Ireland government, forbidding her to enter its territory. However, her feisty and determined personality could not be silenced for ever and in 1933 she defied the order to attend a meeting across the border. Sheehy-Skeffington was arrested in Armagh and imprisoned there for a short time. At her trial she said, 'I recognise no partition. I recognise it as no crime to be in my own country. I would be ashamed of my own name and my murdered husband's name if I did ... Long live the Republic!'

From the moment she crossed the border back into the Irish Free State, she was applauded by cheering crowds of supporters who came out to greet her on her way back to Dublin. In the capital, there was a civic reception, and a torchlight parade was organised at which bands played and the Irish Free State flag was flown. Hanna Sheehy-Skeffington had become a celebrity, much loved by the people and regarded as a symbol of dogged determination for the things she believed in.

But during the 1930s Hanna became disillusioned at what she saw was the growing conservatism of politics in the Irish Free State that coincided with a gradual erosion of women's rights. In 1927, legislation was enacted preventing women from sitting on juries and married women were barred from working in the public sector (1933); these laws were followed by a ban of contraception in 1934. Abortion remained illegal, and still does today. As Ireland felt the lingering effects of the Great Depression grind the economy to a halt, creating massive unemployment, the Irish Free State enacted legislation imposing even further restrictions on women. In order to save jobs for men, the government gave itself power to limit the number of women in any industry.

In response, Sheehy-Skeffington wrote an article detailing the declining status of women in the Irish Free State that had occurred in the previous twenty years and concluded that the Irish Free State had in fact turned its back on women. Hanna's assessment was correct and the government of the Irish Free State in 1936, led by one-time friend Éamon de Valera, was about to go even further by enshrining the concept of gender inequality in the new constitution it was working on.

When the wording of the proposed new Irish Constitution was published in 1936, every women's group opposed it. Some of the proposed phrases included stating that the women had 'inadequate strength' and admonishing them '[not] to neglect their duties at home'. Once more, Hanna felt compelled to lead the fight against what she felt were real injustices against women, but this time it was against her own government.

Hanna was perplexed that while the status of women had improved around the world and particularly in the United Kingdom, the conditions of Irish women had declined. After much campaigning and strenuous objections, the best that Sheehy-Skeffington and other women could achieve were only cosmetic changes to the draft constitution.

It would seem that the Irish Government, as it transitioned from the Irish Free State into effectively an undeclared Republic in 1937, was no longer interested in women's issues and in Hanna Sheehy-Skeffington in particular. She had become a thorn in the government's side and it ignored her.

For the next ten years, Hanna continued working as a part-time teacher and journalist, but she had little income and no pension. In 1945, she became ill and was confined to bed where she slowly declined over several months. Hanna Sheehy-Skeffington passed away in 1946 at the age of sixty-nine years.

Her funeral was simple and did not attract much attention, yet in recent years there had been a reassessment of her role, and indeed the role of women in general, in Ireland in the early years of the twentieth century. It is now clear that a number of women, including Sheehy-Skeffington, played a prominent part in Ireland's independence. In the case of Hanna Sheehy-Skeffington, the twin forces of feminism and nationalism entwined their way through her entire adult life and drove her to be at the vanguard of improvements for not only Irish women, but for Ireland itself.

MARGARET COUSINS (1878–1954)

SUFFRAGIST, EDUCATOR
AND THEOSOPHIST

Margaret was born Margaret Elizabeth Gillespie in Boyle, Co. Roscommon, the eldest of twelve children to Joseph Gillespie, a lawyer's clerk and his wife, Margaret Ann. Margaret spent her youth in Boyle, growing up in a Protestant, Unionist (pro-Britain), middle-class family. However, Margaret's experiences while growing up shaped her in a profoundly different way than might have been expected. Margaret's mother had little say in the running of the household and had to constantly ask for money for everyday expenses. This was typical in many families at the time, but Margaret saw this as inherently unfair and would later champion the cause of women's equality.

Young Margaret also witnessed the growing divide between Protestants and Catholics, Unionists and Nationalists, and much to the surprise of her family and friends began sympathising with the Catholics and Nationalists. But there was an emerging common theme: Margaret was supporting the weaker, the oppressed and the disenfranchised people in every case.

In 1898 she moved to Dublin to study music at the Royal Irish Academy and there quickly fell in with a circle of intellectuals and artists who were reinvigorating Irish culture, music and language. She was befriended by James Joyce, W. B. Yeats, and George Russell. Margaret was also introduced to nationalists such as Hanna Sheehy-Skeffington, Constance Markievicz and Padraig Pearse and her dream for an independent Ireland was formed (refer to contents for relevant chapters relating to these people).

She met a rising poet named James Cousins in 1902 and fell in love with him. They had common interests in poetry, music, literature, politics and women's suffrage. They were also both vegetarian, socialists and fascinated in theosophy (an Eastern mystical philosophy). They were married in 1903 and would remain inseparable for the rest of their lives. For all of Margaret's unconventional ideas and lifestyle, she adopted the surname Cousins when she married James.

In 1906, Margaret joined the Irish Women's Suffrage and Local Government Association (IWSLGA), but became disillusioned with the organisation's avowed pacifist stance. She co-founded the Irish Women's Franchise League (IWFL) with Hanna Sheehy-Skeffington in 1906, in order to militantly agitate for the right of women to vote. Margaret Cousins (as she was now called) was not a great public speaker, but fired with the righteousness of her cause, she took to speaking at parks, street corners and halls. In fact she would give a speech anywhere where she came across a gathering of people.

In 1910, Margaret was invited to London to attend a meeting organised by Emmeline Pankhurst, to learn tactics for winning the women's vote that could be applied back in Ireland. While in London she marched with some 300 demonstrators to the House of Commons in response to Prime Minister Asquith's declaration that women should never get the vote. They were met by a wall of police who proceeded to punch, kick and beat the women brutally with their truncheons. The Press and public were appalled at the violence which required the hospitalisation of over fifty women. The incident was dubbed 'Black Friday'. In Margaret's case the beatings only strengthened her resolve.

A few days later, she was apprehended smashing windows of the Prime Minister's residence at No. 10 Downing Street, London, and was sentenced to a month's imprisonment in Holloway gaol. Back in Ireland, she continued to give speeches, wrote articles for publications such as *The Irish Citizen* and attended demonstrations. In 1913, Margaret was one of several women arrested and convicted for breaking windows at Dublin Castle, but all of them managed to have their prison terms shortened by going on hunger strike.

At this time, James and Margaret were close to bankruptcy, but were financially rescued when James was offered a well-paid job in Liverpool, England, by a fellow vegetarian. The couple moved to England, where Margaret continued her spiritual journey by founding the Church of the New Idea in 1914 that merged her interests in both Feminism and Theosophy. But the new church never resonated with the general public because its inception coincided with the sufferings of WWI. While men were fighting and dying on the battlefields of France everything else was a distraction, especially a new religion.

The couple had been corresponding for some years with Annie Besant who was a long-time resident of India since arriving there in 1893, and was Head of the Theosophical Society in Madras (now

Chennai). Annie Besant believed there were great similarities between Ireland's struggle for independence and India's own nascent independence movement. In 1915, she invited James and Margaret to India to help achieve this goal, and they jumped at the chance.

As soon as they arrived in that country, James established and ran a pro-independence newspaper, *New India*, and Margaret busied herself with earning a living and campaigning for women's affairs. Margaret became the first non-Indian teacher employed at the Indian Women's University in Poona, in 1916. In the following year, she established the Women's India Association (WIA), the first women's organisation in India, and worked tirelessly to promote its goals of equality, and to increase its membership across the country.

Through the growing influence of the WIA, Margaret was able to exert pressure on the colonial administration of India to achieve a quick victory for women. In 1917, Chennai became the first region in India to grant women full suffrage rights and within ten years most of the rest of India had followed. This was a staggering achievement and Margaret would proudly point out for the rest of her life that Indian women achieved full voting rights in India a decade before women in the United Kingdom did.

Bolstered by these victories, the WIA continued to grow and by the late 1920s, more than forty branches had been created with membership in the tens of thousands. Margaret felt it was time to take the movement to the next level and organised the first All India Women's Conference in 1927, which concentrated on educational reform. Another conference was held in 1936, which Margaret Cousins presided over.

With her reputation growing and her community services widely recognised, the colonial administration appointed Margaret

Cousins as the first female magistrate in India as early as 1922. She met and became friends with Mahatma Gandhi and was invited by him to speak at several meetings arranged by his organisation, the Indian National Congress. While Gandhi was serving one of his many sentences for sedition in 1932, Margaret Cousins went to New York to address mass meetings on his behalf.

As India's independence movement became more influential during the 1930s, the Indian colonial administration became more repressive. Margaret Cousins decided to deliberately flout new laws against public speaking and addressed a large crowd in Chennai. As was expected, Margaret was duly arrested, which provided her with a perfect forum to make another public address, this time in court.

Margaret Cousins said, 'If this is British justice and democracy, then I am proud of free speech and Indian national freedom, and I am ashamed that English idealism has fallen to the present depths of oppression' (from Cousins & Cousins, *We Two Together*, 1950, pp. 582–583).

Margaret was stripped of her magistrate's position and gaoled for almost eleven months, during which time she started classes for her fellow prisoners to improve their conditions. She also organised small recitals and concerts to lift the spirits of those imprisoned. But on one occasion during Margaret's incarceration the entire gaol fell silent and depressed when one of the prisoners was executed by hanging. The young woman was taken from a nearby cell and had always maintained her innocence of the crime. As a result of the execution, Margaret added capital punishment to the already substantial list of matters she would ban in some idyllic world.

During the rest of the 1930s and into the 1940s, Margaret and James Cousins continued campaigning for women's education, and for the prevention of child marriage and inheritance rights for women. She wrote many letters and articles that were published in Ireland, Britain and India. Somehow they also found time to write their joint autobiography, which has become one of the major primary resources for studying the early feminist movements of Ireland and India.

The Chennai government awarded a substantial pension to the couple in 1949 in recognition of their courageous contribution to nationhood. Later in 1953, Shri Jawaharlal Nehru, the Prime Minister of India, personally gave the Cousins a cash reward as a thank you from a grateful nation. Margaret suffered from high blood pressure for most of her life and a severe stroke in 1943 left her paralysed and partially disabled. James lovingly cared for her until she passed away in 1954 at seventy-six years of age.

Margaret was a gifted musician with a degree in music from the Royal Irish Academy. She will always be immortalised by the fact that she composed the tune for the Indian National Anthem: *Jana Gana Mana*. The original words had been written in Bengali by Nobel laureate and legendary Indian poet Rabindranath Tagore. When Margaret met Tagore in 1919, the Bengali version of the anthem had just been translated into English and Cousins was asked if she could arrange some music that would suit the translation. Her efforts have resulted in an anthem that is rated as one of the best in the world and is sung by over 1.2 billion people.

Cousins is commemorated in her birthplace of Boyle, Ireland with a plaque unveiled by Irish President, Mary Robinson in 1994 (*see* Robinson, p. 283). Margaret had lived long enough to see the independence of the two countries she loved – Ireland and India, yet she grieved that both had been partitioned in the process.

PATRICK PEARSE (PÁDRAIG MACPIARAIS) (1879–1916)

WRITER, EDUCATOR AND REVOLUTIONARY

Patrick was born the eldest son and second of four children in Dublin to James Pearse, a stonemason and his second wife Margaret (née Brady). His father was Protestant English and his mother was Catholic Irish who had Gaelic-speaking friends and relatives. From a very young age, the twin forces of Irish and English culture and language influenced Patrick. The young man was very adept at languages and he learned to speak English, Irish and later at university, French, with considerable ease.

Pearse was raised a Catholic and received his education at a private school and later by the Christian Brothers, where he became convinced that the Irish language was central to the cultural identity of Ireland. In 1896, at the age of seventeen, he joined the Gaelic League (an organisation founded only three years earlier to foster the Irish language), which had a loose association with other Irish revival groups, including the Gaelic Athletic Association founded by Michael Cusack (*see* p. 149).

In order to promote his work with the Gaelic League, he changed his anglicised name to its equivalent in Irish, but he would continue to use both names interchangeably for the rest of his life. His father managed to afford a university education for Patrick and he graduated from Royal University, Dublin, in 1901 with a degree in Arts and Law.

He edited the bi-weekly newspaper of the Gaelic League – *An Claidheamh Soluis* (Sword of Light) – from 1903–1909. Through his personal exhortations in just a few short years, the Gaelic League became the largest and most influential organisation in the country to be promoting Irish culture. Pearse wrote and spoke passionately about his dream of a resurgent Irish culture. He called on people not to forget heroes from Ireland's past and evoked a noble cause for preserving Irish language and culture. In an address to the New Ireland Literary Society, of which he was president, he delivered the following speech:

> The Gael is not like other men; the spade, and the loom, and the sword are not for him. But a destiny more glorious than that of Rome, more glorious than that of Britain awaits him: to become the saviour of idealism in modern intellectual and social life, the regenerator and rejuvenator of the literature of the world, the instructor of the nations, the preacher of the gospel of nature-worship, hero-worship, God-worship. (Pearse, *Three Lectures on Gaelic Topics*, p. 49.)

He secured a position at University College, Dublin where he lectured in Irish, but Pearse realised that introducing Gaelic to children of a young age was key to the language's long-term survival. In 1908, he established his own bilingual boy's school in Dublin, St Enda's, named after a fifth-century Irish warrior saint. Lessons were taught in English as well as in Gaelic. He pioneered innovative educational concepts, such as inviting guest speakers, including W. B. Yeats (*see* p. 168) to address the students. The school proved to be popular with many like-minded Irish, who were also keen to preserve their country's native tongue, causing enrolments in the school to flourish.

Pearse followed up his experience with St Enda's by founding St Ita's school for girls in 1910, named after a fifth-century Irish nun and saint. Although popular with staff, students and parents alike, both St Enda's and St Ita's struggled financially and in 1914 Pearse journeyed to America for both financial and political reasons. Somehow, during this very busy period, Pearse found time to write two plays in the Irish language that were to receive greater acclaim after his death than during his life.

Through the first decade of the twentieth century, Pearse was a keen supporter of Home Rule for Ireland, as he saw a limited form of self-government as the best option for his country. However, he became increasing disillusioned with the Westminster parliament's failure to twice pass the enabling legislation. To Pearse it seemed that Westminster was determined to stall the process, if not to kill off the idea altogether.

In 1912, up to a half a million citizens in Northern Ireland signed a solemn covenant pledging their opposition to Home Rule, by rebellion if necessary. This represented over 40 per cent of the population of Ulster (Northern Island). This was a turning point in the life of Patrick Pearse; he went from being an idealist to a realist regarding Ireland's political future. As the prospects for a third attempt at a Home Rule Bill gathered momentum, there was a strong likelihood of violence on the streets of Ireland, no matter what the result. If the bill was passed, then the Ulster unionists swore they would rebel. If it was not passed, then it was just as likely that a large percentage of southern Ireland would rise up in an armed revolutionary struggle.

Then in late 1913, Pearse joined the Irish Volunteers, a paramilitary nationalist group who presented themselves as an alternative to the British Army, without actually challenging British authority at that moment. A few months later in 1913, Pearse took the final step along his path of conversion to militancy by joining the Irish Republican Brotherhood (IRB), an outlawed, secret, ultra-nationalistic organisation determined to win independence through armed struggle.

The IRB welcomed such a gifted and zealous writer into their midst, someone who was also part of the executive of the Irish Volunteers. The IRB dispatched Pearse to America in early 1914 on a lecture tour, which also had the not-so-hidden objective of raising funds for the inevitable revolt against Britain. Pearse willingly went, for it offered him the opportunity of also raising some funds for his own schools.

The tour was a triumph. Pearse spoke to packed halls and convinced large numbers of Americans that Ireland was justified to throw off British authority, by arms if necessary. He evinced a parallel between Ireland's impending struggle and the American Revolution. Pearse passionately said: 'There are many things more horrible than bloodshed; and slavery [for the Irish, like the American blacks] is one of them.'

Not only did he convince more Americans than ever before that the cause of Irish independence was right, he managed to return with sufficient money pledged to the IRB to enable that organisation to set about immediately purchasing arms and ammunition for the forthcoming revolution. Pearse also managed to have private meetings with several wealthy donors, who separately gave him considerable funds to keep his own schools financially viable for years.

The declaration of war by the British Empire on the German Empire in 1914 presented the IRB executive with mixed feelings. So many Irishmen volunteered for service in the rapidly expanding British Army (about 125,000 in the first year of the war), that the IRB was forced to internally concede there was still a high degree of loyalty towards the British crown. However, several crack British battalions were shipped from Ireland to the front in France, leaving fewer British troops in Ireland, meaning less opposition if the IRB launched an armed insurrection.

In 1915, Pearse was invited to deliver the oration at the funeral of one of the IRB's most beloved past leaders, Jeremiah O'Donovan Rossa. It would become the most important speech of Pearse's life and one of the most significant in Ireland's history. Rossa had been forcefully exiled to the USA for his leadership of a failed rebellion in 1865. He died in America of old age in 1915, and the IRB was quick in realising the enormous propaganda value that a funeral service in Ireland could achieve.

His body was returned and given a hero's welcome. The funeral was an elaborate piece of stage-managed theatre, with military bands and soldiers from the Irish Volunteers forming a cortège that stretched for hundreds of metres. As the procession slowly marched through the streets of Dublin, an enormous crowd of onlookers gathered to pay their respects.

At the graveside in Dublin's Glasnevin cemetery, Pearse delivered a stirring call to arms, challenging Ireland to rise up and throw off British oppression. The seven-minute' speech ended with the lines:

> They think they have pacified Ireland. They think they have purchased half of us and intimidated the other half. They think they have foreseen everything, think they have provided against everything; but, the fools, the fools, the fools! – They have left us our Fenian dead, and while Ireland holds these graves, **Ireland unfree shall never be at peace** [Pearse's emphasis].

Following his oration, Pearse was admitted into the seven-member IRB Military Council, which was already in the process of planning an insurrection for the very near future. Patrick became central to the planning of this, which included him making arrangements for the landing of German arms and ammunition. Pearse fervently believed that once the Irish saw the 'blood sacrifice' of the revolutionaries, it would ignite the goal of nationalism and they would join in the fight. It is clear today that Patrick Pearse was unrealistic in his expectation of a general uprising.

On the eve of the scheduled start date, the British Navy intercepted the shipment of 20,000 guns the Germans had sent and at that point the planned insurrection should have been called off. But Pearse argued successfully that the rebellion should still go ahead as a demonstration of the IRB's commitment to independence. As Director of Operations, he now involved the under-prepared and under-armed Irish Volunteers to rise up in rebellion.

In Easter 1916, Pearse was appointed Commander-in-Chief of the nationalist forces. He led a column of rebels to the General Post Office where he read aloud the Proclamation of the Irish Republic, which he had drafted. He then declared that he was the 'first President of this new Republic of Ireland'. Over the next week a number of rebels held out in various locations throughout Dublin against overwhelming British retaliation. But the IRB had grossly underestimated the military strength of the British and were woefully outnumbered and outgunned.

Further, to the great disappointment of Pearse and the other leaders of the IRB, they had completely misread the mood of the general public. The Irish people did not spontaneously rise up. Many were prepared to wait for the promised Home Rule after it was finally passed on the third attempt by parliament in 1914. Then there were others who were deeply offended that while their sons were fighting *for* the British in the carnage that was France, a small group of their fellow countrymen were fighting *against* the British.

The 'Easter Rising', as it was called, collapsed and its leaders were taken into custody, including Patrick Pearse, who was court-martialled and found guilty of insurrection. In the days before he was shot by firing squad in 1916, he wrote a poem about natural beauty and farewell letters to his brother. He was composed and resigned to his fate. On the morning he was escorted out of his cell to the courtyard where a detachment of armed soldiers were waiting, one of his guards recorded in his dairy that Pearse whistled a tune. He was thirty-seven years of age and unmarried.

Although Patrick Pearse grew more realistic the more he became involved in the notion of an Irish revolution, the truth was that a part of him remained a romantic idealist. By taking a prominent leadership role in its planning, by publicly proclaiming a republic and declaring himself to be its first president, Pearse knew that he was drawing attention to himself in this doomed venture. He did not throw his live away needlessly on some fruitless attempt to overthrow Britain's authority over Ireland. He knew exactly what he was doing. He was deliberately martyring himself so that his blood sacrifice would spur others to take up the cause of nationalism in the near future.

At his trial Pearse exclaimed to the British Presiding Officer: 'You cannot conquer Ireland. You cannot extinguish the Irish passion of freedom. If our deed has not been sufficient to win freedom, then our children will win it by a better deed.' In that regard, he was proven correct. Less than a decade later five-sixths of Ireland had indeed gained some form of independence.

ÉAMON DE VALERA (1882–1975)

DOMINANT IRISH POLITICIAN OF THE TWENTIETH CENTURY

De Valera was born in New York, USA to Juan de Valera, a Spanish sculptor and Catherine Coll, an Irish domestic servant. Three years later, following the death of Juan, his mother sent Éamon to live with his grandparents in a small cottage near Bruree, in Co. Limerick.

Éamon excelled at school and won a scholarship to the prestigious Blackrock College, a Catholic secondary school in Dublin. From there he went to the Royal University, Dublin where he graduated in 1905 with an arts degree. For a time while at university, he had thought of becoming a priest, but de Valera became attracted to the growing nationalist movement and decided to become a teacher instead. Over the next few years, while he taught mathematics, French and Latin at various schools around Dublin, Éamon confirmed his commitment to the Irish nationalist cause by becoming a member of the Gaelic League in 1908.

ÉAMON DE VALERA (1882–1975)

While learning the Irish language through classes offered by the Gaelic League, he became smitten by his Irish teacher, Sinéad (Jane) Flanagan and they married in 1910. By 1913, the married couple had three children under three years of age (the couple would go on to have seven children altogether). To further his commitment to the nationalist cause Éamon joined the paramilitary group, the Irish Volunteers in the belief that if necessary, he would be prepared to fight to bring about an independent Ireland. Due to his commitment, intelligence and organisational ability, he quickly rose through the ranks of the Irish Volunteers to become a commander.

During the 1916 Easter Rising, de Valera's battalion of a hundred troops or so occupied the strategically important site of Boland's Bakery near the Grand Canal, but were quickly isolated and took very little part in the week-long struggle. When he was directed by Patrick Pearse (*see* p. 216) to surrender, Éamon was taken into custody. As a ringleader he was court-martialled for his part in the uprising and sentenced to death. But he was the only commandant of the rebellion not to be executed. His birth in New York made him an American citizen and the United States made strenuous representations on his behalf.

Éamon de Valera, lucky not to have been executed by firing squad, was nevertheless sentenced to life imprisonment. While in Dartmoor prison in England, he found himself the beneficiary of another piece of extraordinary luck when a general amnesty was granted in 1917 for all participants in the Easter Rising. This was a genuine attempt by the British government to pacify an Irish population that had hardened its opposition to British rule.

De Valera returned to Ireland a hero and was immediately elected to the seat of East Clare in a by-election to the House of Commons in 1917. As the last male leader left alive from the Easter

Rising, Éamon was elected unopposed to the Presidency of both Sinn Féin and its military wing, the Irish Volunteers, in 1918. Sinn Féin had previously proposed that Ireland should have a degree of autonomy within the British Empire and was therefore a strong supporter of Home Rule, championed by Parnell and others for decades (*see* Parnell, p. 142). But under de Valera, Sinn Féin rebranded itself as a political party now wanting full independence from Britain.

Sinn Féin won the majority of Irish electorates in the 1918 general election for the UK Houses of Parliament but, in protest, chose to abstain from attending Westminster Parliament. Instead, de Valera created an alternative parliament in Dublin, called the Dáil Éireann (Assembly of Ireland) and de Valera was acclaimed as the president of this provocative, revolutionary parliament. In 1919, de Valera declared Ireland to be a free and democratic country in direct defiance of British authority.

Shortly after, de Valera left for America on a desperate mission to raise much-needed funds. In the USA, he was greeted as a modern-day George Washington and over the next eighteen months he managed to raise millions of dollars to continue the struggle against the British. Back in Ireland, Michael Collins (*see* p. 238) and others put the money to good use by waging an effective, low-level guerrilla war that drained the resolve of the British.

In 1921, shortly after de Valera returned to Ireland, the British authorities called a truce and began meetings for a negotiated settlement of the conflict. De Valera did not attend these important discussions. Instead he sent Michael Collins, his Minister of Finance, to lead the Irish delegation. Some have since speculated that de Valera knew any settlement falling short of full Irish independence would never be acceptable to the hard-line Irish nationalists, and by sending Collins, de Valera could conveniently distance himself from any inevitable treaty compromise.

What seems to give this theory credence is that the final settlement agreed to partition Ireland into an independent southern part, while the Protestant north would remain under direct British sovereignty. Further, the independent southern part would not be fully independent, but have limited autonomy instead. The Irish Free State, as it was to be called, would continue to be part of the British Empire, though elevated in status to that of a Dominion such as New Zealand, Canada, South Africa and Australia. When this treaty came before the Dáil Éireann, de Valera himself opposed it!

Most of Ireland was tired of the fighting. In 1918, the Great War had ended in which more than 35,000 Irish soldiers had died, yet a guerrilla war with more deaths had continued for another four years. Michael Collins managed to get the majority of the Dáil Éireann behind the treaty and it was narrowly ratified.

De Valera and a significant minority of Sinn Féin members left Dáil Éireann and started campaigning against the treaty. Éamon had a charismatic personality and soon the people of southern Ireland were divided into pro- and anti-treaty supporters. In 1922, anti-treaty republicans occupied public buildings in the centre of Dublin and civil war broke out between these two forces.

For the next year both sides fought each other in one of the worst episodes of internecine feuding ever witnessed in Ireland. Brother fought brother, father fought son in a dispute essentially over what degree of independence was acceptable. In the end the legitimate government had more guns and soldiers than the anti-treaty combatants. In 1923, de Valera ordered a ceasefire. He was arrested by the Irish Free State authorities and interned in prison until 1924.

It was at about this time that de Valera decided he should try and change the status of the Irish Free State by constitutional means, not by revolution. He tried unsuccessfully to get members of Sinn Féin to see his point of view, but the majority of his party had turned their backs on him. Still the dominant and most influential personality in Irish politics, in 1926 de Valera founded a new party, Fianna Fáil (Warriors of Destiny), which included many former Sinn Féin members such as Seán Lemass, Seán T. O'Kelly, P. J. Ruttledge and Constance Markievicz (*see* p. 174).

The new party made swift electoral gains and in the 1927 election won many more seats than Sinn Féin, only narrowly failing to form a coalition government in the Irish parliament. De Valera had reinvented himself again and in the process had created a new political party that would come to dominate Irish politics for decades to come. By the time of the 1932 elections, Fianna Fáil had garnered enough seats to rule on their own. De Valera set about remodelling the Irish Free State from within, just as he had sworn to do when founding the Fianna Fáil party six years earlier.

De Valera abolished the controversial oath of allegiance to the British Crown and introduced a series of constitutional changes that effectively reduced Westminster's authority over the young state. Then he refused to make obligatory payments to Britain and raised tariffs on British imports, citing the Great Depression as extenuating circumstances. As a result, Britain half-heartedly instituted economic reprisals on the Irish Free State, but these did little harm and were soon shelved. The so-called 'Economic War' was over by 1938.

During the 1930s Ireland was not immune from the major political movements sweeping Europe at the time. The Irish Republican Brotherhood, which had dominated Irish politics for half a century, had moved to the far left and rebranded itself as the Irish Republic Army (IRA). On the extreme right, organisations such as the 'Blueshirts' roamed the streets looking for opportunities to bring about a fascist state in Ireland. Éamon de Valera, as President of the Executive Council (1932–1937) and then Taoiseach (Prime Minister) from 1937, expertly navigated Ireland through the conflicting forces of Communism and Fascism that could have easily caused the young country to spiral out of control.

From the early days of his control over Ireland, de Valera sought international recognition for the Irish Free State. He addressed the League of Nations in 1932 (forerunner of the United Nations) and by 1938 had been elected the 19th President of the Assembly of the League in acknowledgement of the valiant job he had done to champion the cause of young and emerging countries.

Éamon de Valera was a devout Catholic and in 1937, he introduced a new constitution which entrenched the Catholic Church's position at the centre of Irish nationhood. Also, 'Catholic' values became enshrined in the new constitution and the treatment of women, divorce, education, health and the family were seen as retrograde steps to appease the all-powerful Catholic Church. As a result, Protestants in Northern Ireland became even more convinced that there was no place for them in an Ireland dominated by the Catholic Church. The status of women and children as second-class citizens in a male-dominated society would not be corrected for decades. Whether intentionally or not, the net effect of de Valera's new constitution was that Ireland entered a conservative, patriarchal and introspective phase in its development as a nation.

De Valera declared Ireland officially neutral during WWII, but used the opportunity to enact a state of emergency to clamp down on any unrest and opposition. For the duration of the war, the de

Valera government strengthened its hold over Irish politics and Irish life. By 1946, Ireland was even more conservative than it had been a decade earlier and this touched every aspect of daily life in the country. For example, conservative politics drove protectionist trade policies and this meant that the Irish economy significantly underperformed well into the 1960s.

De Valera lost power after sixteen years in government in 1948 and had to sit on the opposition benches while the new Taoiseach of Ireland, John Costello, did something that de Valera was never prepared to announce. In 1949, Costello declared Ireland was now a republic. In response, British warships did not bomb the Irish coastline. British troops did not march down Dublin's main street. In fact the British, who were preoccupied by post-war austerity and reconstruction, barely registered the loss of one more of its former possessions.

Éamon de Valera's party was in and out of government several times over the next decade, during which the IRA launched its bombing campaign in Northern Island. When back in power as Taoiseach, de Valera acted decisively against the IRA and enacted emergency powers that allowed the Irish government to round up and incarcerate IRA ringleaders indefinitely without trial. Extreme measures such as these meant that the IRA terrorist campaign never grew out of control under de Valera's administration, even if he was never able to eliminate the threat completely.

In 1959, de Valera's eyesight deteriorated so badly that he was forced to undergo six operations overseas to save his sight. The procedure was only partially successful and at the urgings of his family and friends de Valera left active politics in 1959 at the age of seventy-five. But he did not quit the political stage altogether. The same year he stepped down as Taoiseach, de Valera was appointed to the largely ceremonial, but still immensely prestigious role of President of the Republic of Ireland. Despite his age and virtual blindness, de Valera would remain president until he finally retired from all aspects of public life in 1973. When de Valera retired he was the oldest head of state in the world, at ninety years of age.

And in 1975, two years after his retirement from public office, de Valera died after a brief illness. He was given a State funeral by a grateful nation, but at his insistence was buried in a simple grave in Glasnevin cemetery, Dublin. His wife Sinéad had predeceased him in 1974 after sixty-five years of marriage. He was survived by six of his seven children, who all went on to take high positons in law, medicine and politics.

Éamon de Valera's greatest legacy is that he navigated a very small and fragile country from its birth to the point where it was politically stable. This was no mean feat, when forces from within and without were regularly threatening to tear Ireland apart. However, for all his greatness and dominance of Irish politics over half a century, he had also steered Ireland into a bleaker, more conservative social and economic state.

The conscious decision to enshrine 'Catholic' values in the constitution was particularly lamentable in that it led directly to women being treated as second-class citizens for the next fifty years. Ireland, which had started off as a nation of innovation, intellectual brilliance and high ideals, became grim, closed and economically poorer under de Valera.

HARRY FERGUSON (1884–1960)

ENGINEER AND DEVELOPER OF THE MODERN AGRICULTURAL TRACTOR

Henry George (Harry) Ferguson was born in 'Lake House', a farm near Dromore, Co. Down in Ireland. He was the fourth of ten children born to James, a farmer, and his wife Mary (née Bell). The Fergusons were strict Protestants with Scottish ancestry and owned the small forty-hectare farm they lived on. Young Harry grew up knowing how important it was to earn a living off the land and the principle of finding ways to improve the productivity of the farm.

Harry left school at the age of fourteen to help out about the farm and only left when his older brother offered him an apprenticeship as a motor mechanic in Belfast. Together, the Ferguson brothers established a motor repair business of their own, which by the early 1900s had become one of the best in Belfast.

It was the early days of the automotive industry, and it was mainly the affluent who brought their cars in to be tuned or repaired.

Harry was soon on speaking terms with a number of his clients, as many shared a mutual love of cars and the seemingly limitless opportunities the internal combustion engine could deliver. Harry began racing motorcycles and motor cars to publicise the business and because he took so many risks, he became known locally as 'the mad mechanic'.

Ferguson also experimented with aviation and became the first man to build his own aeroplane from designs he copied from overseas. In 1909 he also became the first person to make a successful powered flight in Ireland. It was at about this time that Harry set up his own business, declared he was an agnostic and married the local grocer's daughter, Maureen Watson. They had one child together, Elizabeth Mary Ferguson, in 1920.

In his new mechanics' shop, Harry repaired not only the latest models of cars, but also the most recent examples of motorised farm machinery that were beginning to come onto the market. His trained hand in mechanics and his experience from growing up on a farm showed him that many of these new machines were cumbersome, difficult to use and prone to break down. But it would be the advent of WWI that provided Ferguson with the spur to actually do something about these defects.

From the advent of war in 1914, farms across Ireland were rapidly stripped of men and horses and this resulted in a drop in food production. What was desperately needed was for farms across the UK to produce more of everything with less to start with, and the perfect solution was obviously the use of farm tractors.

Ferguson turned his considerable talents to design a plough that could be attached securely to the rear of any of the first generation of primitive model tractors. It was a breakthrough because it hitched the plough to the tractor (as opposed to towing the implement on chains), effectively making them one unit, leading to greater control and productivity.

During the 1920s, Ferguson continued to improve his hitching designs and even took a mechanical version to America, where he demonstrated the device to Henry Ford, who at the time produced the largest number of tractors in the world, about 3,000 units per month, which were called the 'Fordson'. However, Ford was not interested in the device, so Ferguson returned to Ireland and continued to make further modifications until in 1926, he invented a hydraulic 'three-point linkage' that could, with adjustments, connect any implement to any tractor. Ferguson patented this device, which would go on to be eventually incorporated in more than 85 per cent of all the tractors in the world.

For the next several years, Ferguson concentrated on manufacturing his hitching device and ploughs in his works in Belfast and attaching them to tractors manufactured by the leading companies at the time, such as Ford, John Deere and International Harvester. During this period he harboured the dream of one day manufacturing his own tractor. This finally became a reality in 1936.

Ferguson joined forces with David Browne Engineering Ltd, a Yorkshire-based tank manufacturer in 1936, to produce the Ferguson 'Model A' tractor. Today, one of the first tractors produced at the Yorkshire plant is on display at the Science Museum in London. It is regarded as the forerunner of all tractors that were to follow and the reason why so many regard Harry Ferguson as the inventor of the modern farm tractor.

Sales of the Model A increased strongly and Ferguson realised he had designed a tractor that was superior to anything else on the market at the time. If he could convince Ford to manufacture the

Model A under licence in the United Sates, then he could jump to being a leading global manufacturer in one move.

In 1938, he met with Henry Ford again (now a seventy-five-year-old billionaire) and the two agreed to a partnership, sealed famously with a handshake. This led to the introduction of the Ford-Ferguson 'Model 9N' tractor in 1939, which was a quantum leap in technology ahead of its competitors. The relationship between the two companies was never perfect, but as long as the two original owners were in charge it seemed that the 'handshake agreement' between the two men remained generally adhered to.

Then in 1947, Ford's grandson Henry Ford II took over the running of the corporation and ended the 'handshake deal', but continued producing the latest model of the Ford-Ferguson tractor without any remuneration being paid to Ferguson. Henry Ferguson immediately launched a lawsuit to obtain damages, but had to wait until 1952 when Ford eventually offered US$9 million in an out-of-court settlement.

When Ford reneged on its manufacturing agreement in 1947, Ferguson had to look for another manufacturer and this time Ferguson wanted one to come from the United Kingdom. Harry Ferguson made a deal with the Coventry-based Standard Motor Company to refit its armaments factory to produce the latest Ferguson tractor (the Model TE20).

The agreement was a huge commercial success in 1949 and within two years of starting production Ferguson Tractors held 78 per cent of the new tractor market in the UK. The reliable Model TE20, became known as the little 'Fergie' tractor, and it spread in its hundreds of thousands across the farms of Great Britain and Ireland. It kick-started a revolutionary increase in farm productivity.

Reinvigorated with the success of his 'Fergie' tractor, Harry established a manufacturing plant on his own in America in 1948 and started producing his Model TE20 to supply the North American market. In 1953 Ferguson merged with Ontario-based farm equipment manufacturer Massey Harris and in 1958 when the name Harris was dropped, the famous Massey Ferguson brand name was born. Even Sir Edmund Hilary of New Zealand and Vivian Fuchs (of the UK) chose modified Massey Ferguson tractors when they became the first to successfully traverse the frozen continent of Antarctica in 1958.

By the mid-1950s, Harry Ferguson was wealthy, successful, but also aging. He sold his interest in the company back to Massey Ferguson and concentrated on pursuing other automotive manufacturing. It was his intention to improve the motor car as successfully as he had done for the tractor. The first car he produced (the R5) was incredibly advanced and possibly decades ahead of its time. Only 350 of these vehicles were ever produced, as the technical expertise and sophisticated machinery needed to make the car was at the limits of what was available at the time.

He then drew plans to produce a performance-enhanced motor vehicle, but it was never built in his lifetime. When the car was finally produced in 1966, the Jensen Interceptor, as it was known, was the most technically advanced car in the world and is still regarded as truly remarkable today.

Ferguson's final project was to produce a Formula 1 racing car. Without any experience in the world of car racing he managed to design a four-wheel drive motor vehicle that he was certain would be competitive. Harry Ferguson died before his racing car was ever produced but a model, called P99, was manufactured and raced in 1962. The vehicle was not only competitive on the track, but in the skilled hands of famous racing driver Stirling Moss, was driven to victory at Oulton Park racetrack in 1962. Over the next two years it was modified and competed successfully in the Tasman Series of open single-seater races held in Australia and New Zealand.

Harry Ferguson died at his country home in Stow-on-the-Wold, Gloucestershire, England in 1960 from a barbiturate overdose. He was ninety-seven years of age and many believed that he may have accidentally overdosed on his medication, but no one was certain, so the coroner had no choice but to record an 'Open' finding.

Today, Massey Ferguson tractors and the numerous implements they haul are built in Brazil, Italy, Japan, China and the USA. Over the course of its long history, it has been estimated that more 'Fergie' brand tractors have been sold worldwide than any other brand.

From the primitive shed of an Irish inventor and engineer, Harry Ferguson's genius produced simple, reliable and robust farm tractors that turned wasteland into productive farmland and increased crop yields exponentially. Ferguson's genius also found an outlet in aeroplanes, motor cars and Formula 1 racers, but it is the ubiquitous 'Fergie' tractor for which he will be best remembered. It is not an unreasonable claim to say that Harry Ferguson, the Irishman, invented a machine that has helped feed the world!

MICHAEL COLLINS (1890–1922)

REVOLUTIONARY LEADER AND MILITARY COMMANDER

Michael was born on a small farm near Clonakilty, in Co. Cork, the youngest of eight children to Michael Collins, a tenant farmer and his wife, Mary (née O'Brien). His childhood was normal, but shaped by the environment around him, which was filled with a rising sense of Irish nationalism and a feeling of injustice caused by absentee British landlords.

He left school at fifteen years of age to secure employment in London, working in the banking industry. In 1909, while still working and living in London, Collins became an enthusiastic participant in the Gaelic Athletic Association, a sporting organisation founded by Michael Cusack in 1884 (*see* Cusack, p. 149). He also joined the Gaelic League, a cultural organisation founded in 1893 and championed by Patrick Pearse (*see* p. 216). As his enthusiastic support for an Irish revival in sport and culture grew, it was only a matter of time before his involvement became political. In 1914 he joined the Irish Republican Brotherhood (IRB) as one of its London members and began cultivating contacts within the large expatriate Irish community that would serve him well in the future.

Collins returned to Ireland in early 1916 and only took a peripheral part in the abortive Easter Rising of the same year. His administrative and organisational abilities learnt in the finance industry, taught Collins that the insurrection was destined to fail from the start, because it was poorly led and executed. Collins admired the wild, romantic and reckless ideals of the IRB leaders, but he saw through the bravado and passion and realised that lack of planning, lack of clear objectives and lack of decisive leadership were the critical factors in the rebellion's failure.

Although Collins played a relatively minor role in the Easter Rising, he was arrested along with thousands of other IRB members under martial law and incarcerated in a prison camp in Wales. There, he made a name for himself for clear thinking, organisational abilities within the Irish prison population and leading discussions on military tactics that should be employed in the inevitable event that another rebellion should occur.

At the end of 1916, Collins and the other IRB internees were released under a general amnesty and Collins returned to Ireland, where he immediately started putting into practice many of the strategies and policies he had discussed in prison. He took up a senior position in the Irish National Aid and Volunteer Dependents' Fund (INAAVDF), ostensibly a charitable organisation offering financially support to the families of men and women who had participated in the Easter Rising. He used this association to shape the popular memory of the event from a failed revolution to a glorious, heroic attempt at throwing off the shackles of British oppression. The changed narrative struck an accord with the Irish people. Those who had been largely indifferent to the insurrection in 1916, began to support radical Irish nationalism.

One more very significant activity Michael Collins used the INAAVDF for, was to reorganise the entire republican movement into one coherent body with a military as well as a political wing. He encouraged recently released prisoners, such as Joe McGuiness and others, to run for parliament in the House of Commons. In 1917, Collins was elected onto the executive committee of Sinn Féin, allowing him to play a more central role in the restructuring of this organisation and its affiliated groups.

Collins reorganised the Irish Volunteers, which was a remnant of the military wing of the Sinn Féin. He was promoted to adjutant-general of the Irish Volunteers, which allowed him to create a revitalised intelligence section, a role to which he was well suited. Public servants, disaffected and disillusioned with an increasingly tenuous British authority over Ireland, started passing vital intelligence over to Collins and his network in the nationalist movement. At one point in 1918, he received advanced notice of pending arrests of Sinn Féin leaders in a so-called 'German plot'. The information allowed Collins to foil the arrests of several leaders and thereby cause the British government some degree of embarrassment at their purported ineptitude.

In the UK parliamentary elections of 1918, Collins got himself elected unopposed to the seat of Cork South, but along with all the other seventy-three Sinn Féin elected members, refused to take his seat in Westminster. Instead, Sinn Féin established an illegitimate alternative government of Ireland in Dublin in 1919, called the Dáil Éireann (Assembly of Ireland). Michael Collins became its first Minister of Finance.

His first task was to raise enough money for the alternative government to function and this he successfully achieved through many of his old contacts in the London finance industry. A staggering sum of £380,000 was raised. Behind the scenes, Collins was expanding his intelligence network in what would soon become the Irish Republican Army (IRA). Being driven by efficiency and purposeful organisational structures, Collins strode through the corridors of the Dáil demanding improved administration across a number of ministries, which led to many clashes of personalities.

When guerrilla war broke out in 1919 between Irish nationalists, led by the now reformed and renamed IRA, and British authorities, Michael Collins was at the forefront of directing operations. It was a low-level, but nevertheless bloody campaign that lasted for two years and thoroughly demoralised the British government. Collins used his intelligence network wisely to eliminate targeted individuals within the Dublin Metropolitan Police, where half a dozen officers were killed in that force's political division. Next, he targeted selected leaders of the Royal Irish Constabulary and started ambushing British Army patrols. Towards the end of 1920, around 300 people on both sides of the conflict had been killed and the political situation in Ireland was extremely tense. Yet thanks to Michael Collins's judicious use of guerrilla tactics, the situation had not blown out of control into open warfare.

The British authorities retaliated by bringing undisciplined and unregulated 'volunteers' from Britain, called the 'Black and Tans'. These groups quickly escalated the fight into a major conflict. In November 1920, Collins's operatives assassinated fourteen British spies who had infiltrated the IRA. In retaliation, that same afternoon the Royal Irish Constabulary opened fire on a crowd at a football match, killing fourteen civilians and wounding sixty-five others.

More tit-for-tat killings followed and as the violence threatened to get out of control, the British authorities declared martial law. Nevertheless, more than 1,000 people were killed over the next half year. Towards the end of 1921, it was obvious to all that the conflict was dividing Ireland along religious lines. In southern Ireland many Protestants were being killed, while in Ulster the victims were in the main Catholics.

Throughout the conflict, Collins was able to maintain a constant supply of arms, military equipment and most importantly money flowing into Ireland, mainly from America. For a while, he became the most wanted man in Ireland, yet he could still cycle around Dublin and drink with friends in pubs with apparent impunity. Such was the growing reputation and legend of the man that no one was prepared to inform on him.

By mid-1921, both sides in the conflict had had enough. The British saw their involvement in terms of being stuck in a perpetual cycle of violence without end and without a winner. For the Irish nationalists and Collins in particular, he coldly observed that the British forces were gaining the upper hand. A shipment of guns had been recently intercepted and one or two of his chief intelligence operators had been arrested. He felt that the British authorities were closing in on him and the leadership of the IRA. The two parties reached out to each other and a truce was called in July 1921.

Éamon de Valera had returned to Ireland by now and was allowed by the British to conduct initial discussions on a proposed peace treaty. But when it came to finalising the agreement and formally signing it, de Valera declined to attend. Instead, Collins was delegated to represent Ireland's interests in the final negotiations in London. Collins was furious and believed he was being 'set up' by de Valera to take responsibility if the treaty turned out badly.

Collins did attend the conference and in his opinion did

negotiate the best possible deal for his country. The British would leave Ireland altogether, giving the people of Ireland the freedom to determine its own form of government. There were two items that were not negotiable for the British. First, the Protestant north of Ireland would be given the choice of remaining part of the United Kingdom or becoming part of a new independent Ireland. Second, Ireland itself would remain part of the British Empire, but with the newly-elevated status of a Dominion. This last point would place Ireland on the same legal footing as Canada, New Zealand, South Africa and Australia.

It was not everything the IRA and other hard-lined nationalists wanted, but it was more than the realistic Collins could have hoped for. He knew he needed the support of the IRA to approve the treaty back in Ireland, but he sincerely believed that *realpolitik* would win out in the end. At the end of 1921, Collins signed the Anglo-Irish Treaty on behalf of Ireland and returned to Dublin to do everything in his power to convince others that this was the only practical course available. In a letter to a friend, Collins speculated that by signing the Anglo-Irish Treaty, he might have also signed his own death warrant.

Under the terms of the treaty, Collins became chairman of the provisional government. In Dublin, he had to use all of his considerable and growing communication skills to persuade others in the Dáil they should approve the treaty. Many saw the practical imperatives and sided with Collins, but there were also many strident critics such as Countess Markievicz and de Valera (*see* pp. 174, 224). After days of debate, some of it being quite venomous towards Collins, the matter came to a vote in early 1922 and the pro-treaty side led by Collins won a narrow victory.

Almost immediately, those against the treaty declared their

opposition. Éamon de Valera, who had become the *de facto* leader of the anti-treaty block, decided to boycott parliament. Collins called for fresh elections to judge the mood of the people (it was also a requirement of the treaty itself) and in the June 1922 elections he and other candidates that supported him won a slim majority of the popular vote. As a percentage of first preferences, Collins and his pro-treaty supporters won 38 per cent, while de Valera and his anti-treaty faction won only 21 per cent.

But it was not just parliamentary approval that Collins needed. He knew that the IRA was the ultimate key to the success or not of the treaty. He had worked assiduously to bring the rank and file membership over to his point of view, but it is estimated that by the elections of 1922, only a third of the IRA agreed with him. Discontent had been simmering for months and was about to explode.

Within days of the election being declared, Collins ordered the bombardment of government buildings in Dublin that anti-treaty members of the IRA had occupied for two months. He was under intense pressure from the British who informed him that if he, as the leader of the newly elected government of the Irish Free State, would not remove the armed protestors, the British Army would. Fearing a return to all-out war, he ordered the shelling of the buildings, even though the IRA were more committed and better trained than the recently-recruited Irish Free State Army that had only come into existence weeks earlier.

The fighting quickly got out of control and spread across the Irish Free State. Anti and Pro factions of the Anglo-Irish Treaty fought each other in a sad example of internecine conflict. Michael Collins gave up his chairmanship of the provisional government to take on command of the Free State Army, which he whipped into a disciplined and effective military force. Under his brilliant leadership and innovative tactics, the anti-treaty forces were on the back foot within months, but the civil war would linger on for another year.

In August 1922, Michael Collins was on a military tour of Cork near his birthplace, when he was ambushed and killed by anti-treaty soldiers. He was only thirty-one years of age. In an incredible display of respect, many soldiers from opposite sides of the civil war attended his funeral in Dublin, as well as soldiers from the British Army and an estimated crowd of nearly 300,000 citizens.

The fate of the newly-independent Ireland hovered close to complete collapse and for several days the British government wondered if it should return in force to take back the country. Thankfully, the pro-treaty forces were quickly able to restore leadership and resume the war that had already been largely won under the brilliance of Collins. Within months both sides decided to end the conflict.

Michael Collins was not a romantic, nor even an idealist. He had a pragmatic notion of what Ireland could realistically achieve in negotiations with the British. It was Collins who believed that a limited form of independence for Ireland was preferable than no independence at all. He was a Catholic, but not devout like so many of the leaders who followed him.

After Collins came a succession of leaders who took Ireland down a conservative, religious, introspective and economically-backward path for decades. It seems that this direction would have been something foreign to Collins. As a man of action, the premature death of Michael Collins was a significant loss to the newly-independent Ireland. What might have been Ireland's future as a country if Michael Collins had lived beyond his thirty-one years?

MONSIGNOR HUGH O'FLAHERTY
(1898–1963)

ROMAN CATHOLIC PRIEST
AND VATICAN OFFICIAL

Hugh O'Flaherty was born in Kiskeam, Co. Cork, the eldest of four children of James O'Flaherty, a sergeant in the Royal Irish Constabulary, and his wife Margaret (née Murphy). As was the custom at the time, Hugh came into the world via his mother's family home, but shortly after the birth, mother and son returned to Killarney in Co. Kerry, where his father was posted, and this is where Hugh was raised.

Ireland was in great political turmoil during Hugh's youth. Home Rule for Ireland had been stalled in the British parliament and there was much agitation among the Irish population against continuing British rule. Hugh's father was a native Irishman who loved Ireland as much as anyone at the time. He became so conflicted between loving Ireland yet working for the British authorities that he resigned from the police force in 1909 to take up a position as steward of the Old Killarney Golf Club. The young

Hugh O'Flaherty was only eleven at the time and his father's sacrifice of a well-paid and comfortable lifestyle on moral principles affected Hugh greatly.

From an early age, Hugh felt a calling to the priesthood. He was educated at a monastery school in Killarney and then at a Jesuit seminary in Limerick. But he was better at sport – particularly golf – than academic matters, and struggled to pass his theological studies. In 1920, while at the Jesuit seminary, four of his friends were shot and killed in separate episodes involving the dreaded 'Black and Tans'.

The 'Black and Tans' were volunteers from Britain, brought to Ireland to suppress Irish nationalism. At best they were an unregulated and ill-disciplined mob of ex-soldiers and ruffians. Assaults, beatings, arson, robbery and the occasional killing became the calling card of these people. O'Flaherty became increasingly appalled at the excessive brutality and barbarity of these men and vowed that in the future he could not idly stand by and watch such excessive behaviour again.

In 1922, Hugh was sent to the Vatican in Rome to complete his theological studies and surprised everyone by excelling academically. Hugh was ordained into the Catholic priesthood in 1925 and spent another two years earning three doctorates in Divinity, Philosophy and Canon Law. He had rapidly become one of the most educated priests to come out of Ireland in a long time.

For the next several years, Hugh worked for the Vatican, handling controversies and writing responses to official requests. He developed an aptitude for diplomacy which was recognised by being awarded the honorific title of Monsignor and being sent on diplomatic missions to Egypt, Czechoslovakia, Haiti, and San Domingo, where he organised famine relief. Whenever he returned to Rome, O'Flaherty played golf regularly with the son of Mussolini (Italy's prime minister) and also with the ex-king of Spain.

Even though the Vatican had a tiny footprint of less than fifty hectares and was completely surrounded by the city of Rome, it had the legal status of a separate country. The Vatican had its own laws, its own military (the famous Swiss Guard), its own money and courts. There were also a small number of countries that had established their diplomatic missions within the Vatican, including Switzerland, Ireland and Great Britain. When O'Flaherty was not dealing with administrative matters in the Vatican or playing golf, he was attending a number of diplomatic events in both the Vatican as well as in the capital of Italy itself. O'Flaherty socialised with the elite of Italy and Rome and these contacts would prove invaluable in the years that lay ahead.

In 1939, Nazi Germany went to war with the rest of Europe, but Italy, which was an ally of Germany, remained neutral until June 1940 when Mussolini (mis)judged that Germany would win the war under Hitler. The Vatican remained neutral throughout WWII, which effectively meant that it was isolated and vulnerable inside a Fascist Italy.

Within a year, O'Flaherty was travelling the countryside touring prisoner-of-war camps helping the Allied prisoners get messages to loved ones back in the UK, Australia and New Zealand. As the winter of 1941 approached, O'Flaherty organised the distribution of thousands of blankets to the prisoners.

In 1942, the Italians and Germans began to crack down on prominent Jews, anti-Fascists and Italian aristocrats who opposed Mussolini. Many of these people had personally known O'Flaherty for years and now they asked him for help. One of the first people he assisted was Princess Nini Pallavicini, who had been found in possession of an illegal radio. She had narrowly avoided arrest by jumping out of a window and had come straight to the Vatican seeking O'Flaherty's help. He found her accommodation in one of the Vatican's nunneries, where she remained safe for the duration of the war.

Soon, others – including escapee prisoners of war – began making their way to the Vatican, looking for his assistance. O'Flaherty made it a habit of standing on the porch of St Peter's basilica every evening, where he could be easily approached. The Catholic Monsignor began hiding people in monasteries across Italy and arranging for others to flee the country under false passports. It was the beginning of an organised smuggling operation that breached the Vatican's neutrality, but was nonetheless condoned by the church hierarchy, including Pope Pius XII. Within months, hundreds of people wanted by the Italian Fascists and German Nazis had been hidden or smuggled out of Italy. Such was O'Flaherty's success that by late 1942 he came to the attention of Hitler's Gestapo chief in Rome, Colonel Herman Kappler.

Kappler began setting traps for O'Flaherty to dare him to venture outside the comparative safety of the Vatican. On one occasion, Kappler even had O'Flaherty surrounded in a Roman *palazzo*, but the Monsignor managed to effect his escape through a coal chute in the building's basement. At another time, Kappler sent two well-built thugs onto the grounds of the Vatican to abduct O'Flaherty, but thanks to a tip-off, the abduction attempt was foiled by the Swiss Guards, who sent the disguised SS officers packing after a very brutal beating.

One of the most daring exploits was when a British serviceman on the run needed an urgent operation to remove a burst appendix. O'Flaherty drove the unconscious soldier, who was dressed as a civilian, to the nearest hospital in Rome, which had only just been commandeered by the Germans for their exclusive use. Somehow, he managed to get the escaped prisoner into an operating theatre, where German surgeons expertly performed an appendectomy. A few hours later the soldier woke up from the anaesthetic surrounded by German soldiers. Before he could react, O'Flaherty calmly wheeled him back to the waiting car and sped off to the safety of the Vatican.

In July 1943, the Americans invaded Sicily and the Italian Fascist administration crumbled. Mussolini was arrested and the Italians agreed to surrender. Within weeks, the Germans occupied Northern Italy and Kappler effectively became the sole ruler of Rome. His first action was to free Mussolini, held by partisans in the Apennine Mountains of Italy, which was brilliantly achieved in no time. Next, he deported over a thousand of Rome's Jews to Auschwitz in October 1943, where only sixteen would survive the war.

Up to this point in his life, Monsignor O'Flaherty had harboured a deep-seated enmity of the British based on his experiences as a young man in Ireland, but when the Nazis herded so many Jews onto railway cattle-cars to their certain deaths, he realised that there were people prepared to commit crimes on a scale that he had never previously imagined.

There were still approximately another 8,000 Jews living in Rome and O'Flaherty redoubled his efforts to protect as many as he could. However, the size of this undertaking made it necessary for the resourceful priest to seek more support than he could possibly organise himself. It arrived immediately and from a most unlikely source. The British had been impressed and grateful for all the help O'Flaherty had already given in organising the escape of mainly

British prisoners of war. When Churchill's government heard about the plight of the remaining Jews in Rome, it immediately authorised the transfer of large sums of money and put at O'Flaherty's disposal men skilled in the art of espionage, forgery and people-smuggling.

Thanks to the combined efforts of the British government working alongside Monsignor O'Flaherty an estimated 5,000 Jews were saved from the gas chambers. Of that number 3,000 alone were hidden in the Pope's official residence, Castel Gandolfo, until Rome's liberation.

In March 1944, the Italian resistance killed thirty-three German soldiers in a bomb attack in Rome. Colonel Kappler responded ruthlessly by machine-gunning 335 Italians in caves outside Rome – people who had been picked at random. Just for good measure he ordered the entrance of the cave dynamited to seal in the dead as well as any citizens left alive.

In June 1944, the Allies broke through the German lines and liberated Rome. Amid the triumphal celebrations, Monsignor Hugh O'Flaherty visited the British Envoy to the Vatican, Sir D'Arcy Osborne, and warmly shook his hand. It was a rapprochement that acknowledged what had been a considerable shift in O'Flaherty's attitude towards the British.

It is estimated that the escape organisation built by O'Flaherty and the British saved the lives of almost 4,000 prisoners of war who were mainly from the British Empire, but also included servicemen from America, Russia and Greece. Some sources also add another 2,000 Italian civilians to that list. Then we must include the estimated 5,000 Jews who were rescued. In total, O'Flaherty was directly involved in saving up to 11,000 people from falling into the hands of enemy soldiers.

For this staggering effort, Monsignor Hugh O'Flaherty was

awarded the US Medal of Freedom and made a Commander of the British Empire. He was offered a lifelong pension from a grateful Italian government, but the humble man declined it.

After the war, Colonel Kappler was tried for war crimes and sentenced to life imprisonment. The only visitor Kappler had was Monsignor O'Flaherty, who came to see him in gaol every month. These visits continued for a number of years, until Kappler asked O'Flaherty for forgiveness and was subsequently baptised into the Roman Catholic faith. Italy's most notorious Nazi had been converted by the very man who he had tried to kill.

O'Flaherty suffered a number of strokes in 1960 and retired to his sister's residence in Cahirciveen, Co. Kerry, where he died in 1963, at sixty-five years of age. In 1983 a TV movie was produced of his life, called *The Scarlet and the Black*, featuring Gregory Peck.

Monsignor Hugh O'Flaherty was a humble man, who was driven to action in wartime by a sense of injustice that had its origins in his youth. His sense of outrage at what Fascists and the Nazis were doing to their fellow human beings would not allow him to stand idly by and watch as thousands were condemned to death. He saved the lives of so many and did so at great personal risk. In the end O'Flaherty's love of God transcended national, religious and ethnic boundaries.

DAME NINETTE DE VALOIS
(1898–2001)

BALLET DANCER AND FOUNDER
OF THE ROYAL BALLET

B orn Edris Stannus on Baltiboys estate, Blessington, Co. Wicklow, Ninette would use her stage name exclusively for most of her long and successful life. She was the second daughter to Thomas Stannus, a major in the British Army and his wife Elizabeth (née Graydon-Smith). The family was of Protestant, Anglo-Irish heritage who had settled in Ireland in the seventeenth century and had prospered.

When Ninette was young, two formative events were to have a lasting effect on her life. She wrote about them in her autobiographical memoir, *Come Dance with Me*. One was a pantomime of *Sleeping Beauty* that her mother took her to see in Dublin. The other was an authentic Irish jig taught to her by a domestic servant on the Baltiboys estate where she lived, which Ninette performed to the accompaniment of a piano in front of a room full of guests on the estate. Normally a shy, diminutive girl, Ninette remembered that from the instant the guests applauded, she knew what she wanted to do for the rest of her life.

The Irish estate was sold in 1905 and the family moved to Kent, England, where, from the age of eight, Ninette was given weekly classical dancing lessons. She showed enough talent for her mother to take her to London and obtain the services of a recently retired ballerina to commence formal training four days a week. There were times when practising was difficult, even painful, but it was put down to the normal price one had to pay for an apprenticeship in this gruelling form of performing art.

While a teenager, she saw many world-class dancers perform at Covent Garden and other theatres in London. On one occasion she witnessed the great Russian ballerina, Anna Pavlova, then at the height of her career, dance the dying swan (*Le cygne*) from *Le Carnaval des Animaux* by Saint-Saëns and knew that this was the person she would imitate (and hopefully surpass) in her own career.

Ninette went on tour in 1913, when she was fifteen, with a company of young people billed as 'The Wonder Children'. The tour was only moderately successful, but it prepared Ninette for life as a ballet dancer. The following year, she successfully auditioned for the lead in an annual performance of ballet at the Lyceum Theatre, London. She would go on to give two performances a day for ten weeks every year for the next five years and earn the not inconsiderable sum of £5 per week while doing so.

It was at this point in her life that, at the urging of her mother, she adopted Ninette de Valois as her stage name, on the basis of some tenuous connection the family might have had with minor French royalty.

In 1917, she received the tragic news that her father, now Lieutenant-Colonel Stannus, had died of wounds commanding the 7th Battalion of the Leinster Regiment in the battle at Messines Ridge, east of Ypres in Belgium. The news devastated Ninette, but after a respectful period of mourning, she was back dancing and training once again. During 1917 and again in 1918, Ninette appeared in the *corps de ballet* during the opera seasons at London's Covent Garden. By 1919, she had become the principal dancer.

Under the Czars, several Russian ballet companies had been liberally sponsored and as a result had become world famous. But with the changes after the Russian Revolution and the execution of the Czar together with his entire family, the ballet companies found themselves without patrons and were forced to look for work outside Russia. One of the best companies – the Ballets Russes dance company, founded by Sergei Diaghilev – moved to Paris, looking for young dancers to bolster its depleted ranks.

Ninette auditioned in 1923 and spent two wonderful years in France honing her skills from some of the 'masters' of classical ballet at the time. When she returned to London, she was at the peak of her career and acknowledged by all who saw her as one of the best ballet dancers to have ever graced the stage. People wrote that she might have even surpassed the great Anna Pavlova herself!

But during this time, the incessant hours of practice and the constant need to leap higher and dance longer on the toes of her feet, kept her in constant pain. She decided to find out why and the result shocked her into doing something she had not thought of doing, at least not at that time. At the age of twenty-eight, she quit performing full time after learning that she was suffering from an undiagnosed case of childhood polio. The disease was beginning to adversely affect her otherwise peerless performances and she did not want the world to remember her in decline. She would continue to dance occasionally, until she finally hung up her dancing shoes for good in her mid-thirties, but increasingly she saw that her direction now lay in producing and directing ballet for others to dance.

Ninette had accumulated enough money to start her own dance school in London in 1926, which became highly successful and was named the Academy of Choregraphic [sic] Art. It was a good start.

Between 1929 and 1931, Ninette commenced a collaborative partnership with the great Irish poet and playwright William B. Yeats in Dublin, who had established Ireland's first centre of performing arts, called Abbey Theatre (*see* p. 170). Yeats wanted to include dance and movement to a number of his plays and it was Ninette to whom he turned to choreograph and occasionally dance in them. This suited Ninette, for she wanted to encourage the development of dance in Ireland. The Abbey Theatre School of Ballet, which she established, would be the forerunner of other dance schools throughout Ireland. She directed this Irish school of dance until work commitments in London prevented her from devoting more time to its needs.

Yeats insisted that the dancing should have an Irish element, so Ninette drew upon the Irish jigs of her childhood to create something unique and different. During this time, she was also being asked to choreograph pieces elsewhere that had ancient Greek, Shakespearean and experimental dance influences. Ninette would never forget the influence of the Russian method of ballet either, where grace was merged with verve. Gradually, Ninette was fusing these different styles into what would become the modern, dynamic and exciting dance idiom of British Ballet, though at the time many people would have thought the idea of a home-grown ballet company ludicrous. There was no tradition of ballet in Britain and virtually all performances there were staged by touring companies from Europe.

When Ninette finally left Ireland and the Abbey Theatre in 1931, to take up the challenge of founding director of the Sadler-Wells Ballet Company in London, Richard Cave wrote in his book *Collaborations*, that Yeats regarded her departure, 'as an irreparable loss to him, and to Ireland'.

De Valois set about trying to change the face of ballet in Britain. Over the next twenty years she staged several exciting ballets that came from overseas, including *Giselle*, *Coppélia*, *Swan Lake*, *The Nutcracker* and *Sleeping Beauty*. She also created new ballets that are still enjoyed today, such as *Job* (1931), *Rake's Progress* (1935) and *Checkmate* (1937). It was during the 1930s and 1940s that de Valois was credited with discovering such names as Robert Helpmann, Margot Fonteyn, Moira Shearer, Beryl Grey, Rudolph Nureyev, Michael Somes and Frederick Ashton.

Many of her ballets were imaginative and exciting, and along with film, literature, plays and music, British culture went through a renaissance in the pre and post WWII period. Sadler-Wells Ballet Company prospered under Ninette de Valois and played to packed houses every season. Ninette was created a Dame of the British Empire in 1951 for services to ballet. Subsequently many other awards and honours were bestowed upon her by other countries and universities. In 1956, Queen Elizabeth II recognised the excellent work that Dame de Valois had achieved in just one generation, by granting the Sadler-Wells ballet a charter, thereby creating the Royal Ballet Company, the first of its kind in British history.

In 1963, Dame Ninette retired as Director of the Royal Ballet, although she remained head of the school until 1972. One day when she was in her eighties, she was invited to return to the ballet school and check on a rehearsal in progress. The young students were terrified at the presence of this living legend as she beat out the steps on the wooden floor with her now ever-present walking stick. Dame Ninette knew the ballet that they were rehearsing intimately – *Rakes Progress* – because she had choreographed it forty years earlier. One of the lead dancers missed her timing and she turned on the dancer immediately, pointing out exactly where she had gone wrong and then, to everyone's amazement, Dame Ninette got to her feet and even performed the move flawlessly for the class. With that masterful display of memory, de Valois exited the room leaving a classroom of students in awe of her.

Ballet companies in Canada, New Zealand, Australia and South Africa were all encouraged in their development and growth by Dame Ninette. She also travelled to Turkey in the late 1940s, at the invitation of its government, to establish the Turkish School of Ballet and the Turkish State Ballet in the capital city of Ankara. For much of the remaining years of her life, she wrote poetry, lectured and of course visited the ballet – especially the Royal Ballet in London which she, more than anyone else, helped to create.

In an interview for the *Los Angeles Times* when she was in her nineties, she jokingly said, 'I'd rather have been a writer than a dancer. And I get more fun out of my poetry than I did out of my choreography.'

De Valois married Arthur Connell, a physician, in 1935. He died in 1986. They had no children. She died at her home in London at the truly remarkable age of one-hundred-and-two. She was featured on an Irish stamp in the year of her death in 2001.

Dame Ninette de Valois left an indelible mark on British dance with her contributions as a dancer, choreographer, teacher and director. Her tireless work led to the founding of one of the world's greatest ballet companies: The Royal Ballet. She was one of the most influential figures in the world of performing arts during the twentieth century.

ERNEST WALTON
(1903–95)

PHYSICIST AND NOBEL LAUREATE

Ernest Walton was born in Epworth Cottage, a thatched dwelling, in South Dungarvan, Co. Waterford, the eldest of two children to the Reverend John Walton and his wife Anna (née Sinton). Anna Walton died in 1906, a year after daughter Dorothy was born and when Ernest was only three years of age. Reverend Walton married again, to Mary Kirkwood in 1909 and had one son in 1919.

As was the custom at the time, Methodist ministers moved to a new congregation every three years or so. This meant that the young Walton children grew up in a number of locations, including Rathkeele, Co. Limerick, Banbridge, Co. Down and Cookstown in Co. Tyrone. Even though the family was Protestant in a mainly Catholic country, young Ernest grew up with a strong sense of national pride in being Irish.

Ernest attended several day schools during this time until he became a boarder at the Methodist College, Belfast in 1915, where he excelled in science and mathematics. In 1922, Walton won a scholarship to attend Trinity College, Dublin where he studied science. He was awarded a Bachelor's degree in Mathematics and Physics, with First-class honours in 1926 and subsequently passed his Master's degree in Science the following year. Along the way he picked up many prizes and awards for academic excellence (seven in all!), which prompted the university to award him a prestigious Research Fellowship to continue his postgraduate studies in physics at Cambridge University, England.

In the late 1920s and early 1930s, the Physics Department of Cambridge University was a leading centre of scientific research in the world. It was led by a brilliant New Zealander, Professor Ernest Rutherford, who had already won a Nobel Prize for pioneering work in nuclear physics. But he was not on his own, there were another three Nobel laureates teaching in the same department at Cambridge. Under Rutherford's leadership the department focussed on unravelling many of the unsolved problems of nuclear physics, which at that time was still essentially a theoretical science.

Initially, Walton worked alone, concentrating on aspects of accelerating sub-atomic particles. The project suggested great promise, but was too much for one person to achieve alone. What Walton needed was a collaborator. At Rutherford's instigation, Walton was paired with John Cockcroft, another dazzling post-graduate student and from 1929 the two men began making immediate progress.

Mankind was still theorising about what lay at the heart of an atom's nucleus. It was thought that if this infinitesimally small object could be bombarded by other equally minute particles then the nucleus might separate into pieces, allowing Walton and

Cockcroft to discover its composition. Walton wrote a full thesis to support this idea, which so impressed his supervisors that he was awarded his PhD in 1931.

To properly succeed, Walton and Cockcroft had to turn theory into practical reality and demonstrate the correctness of their ideas. But to do so, they had to build a device that did not exist at the time – a particle beam accelerator. Cambridge physics laboratory in the 1930s was not well endowed with the necessary equipment to construct an entirely new apparatus, so the two scientists had to make do with what they could beg, borrow or scrounge from other laboratories at Cambridge University. When finished, the grandly named 'particle beam accelerator', was an invention built from bicycle crossbars, plasticine, biscuit tins and sugar crates as well as more recognisable scientific apparatus, such as capacitors, diodes, transformers and vacuum tubes.

On 14 April 1932 the two young scientists switched on the machine for the first time to see what would happen. The device started to hum, belts turned and electricity was generated. When the machine was at full capacity over 700,000 volts of electricity was being created – as much energy as a lightning bolt. Then Walton threw a switch and all that energy bombarded a lithium nucleus that was waiting at the bottom of a vacuum tube.

The nucleus instantly disintegrated, releasing highly energetic particles. Walton would later describe the experiment as 'a wonderful sight, lots of scintillation, looking just like stars' (quote from Waterford County Council Library Service). What the two scientists had witnessed from the safety of a lead-lined observation box was the energy released from an atom as it split apart. This was the first time that man had artificially split the atom and even though the two scientists did not realise it at the time, they had just ushered in a new scientific era – the nuclear age. The primitive machine is today on view at the London Science Museum in South Kensington, London.

The results of their research and experiments were announced to the Royal Society and subsequently published in a number of scientific journals, but the implications remained dormant for several years. In fact, Walton and Cockcroft were initially satisfied that they had validated scientific theory, but slowly the scientific community came to understand the enormity of their achievement.

Over the next couple of years, the two researchers experimented with other elements, such as beryllium, boron, carbon, fluorine and aluminium, which they subjected to bombardment and observed the results. They also obtained a small sample of deuterium: a heavy isotope of hydrogen that had only been discovered in 1931, and used this new substance to bombard others. This created very different reactions and significantly advanced the scientific community's understanding of nuclear physics.

There was one extremely important finding that the two repeatedly observed, that would go on to change the face of the world. Each time an atom was split an enormous amount of energy was produced. When measured, it confirmed precisely Einstein's theory of relativity in that energy and mass are interchangeable. Up to this point Einstein's formula of $E=mc^2$ had only been hypothetical, whereas now Walton and Cockcroft proved that it was a reality. In the process the two researchers had demonstrated that a stupendous new energy source had been discovered, so powerful that theoretically a thimbleful of material could light up a city for a hundred years.

In 1934, Ernest Walton returned to Trinity College, Dublin, where he was appointed Professor and Head of Physics, a position he held until he stepped down from full-time employment forty years later. In the same year that he returned to Ireland, he married his childhood sweetheart Freda Wilson, who was the daughter of an Irish Methodist minister. Ernest and Freda were both thirty-one years of age. The couple had five children, four of whom lived to adulthood. Two of the children would continue their father's passion for science by becoming noted academics in physics in their own right.

The next two decades proved extremely frustrating for Walton as he rejected several offers to continue his nuclear research outside Ireland, wishing instead to build his own department's reputation for excellence. It was also a time of severe funding shortages in Ireland's universities. At one stage during the 1940s, Professor Walton had only three teachers in his department, yet was still expected to perform research experiments, set exams, conduct lectures, publish papers and give public speeches.

Ernest Walton was shocked when he was informed that the United States had dropped two atomic bombs on Japan in 1945 with the stated purpose of ending WWII. He had previously rejected an approach by the Americans to join the 'Manhattan Project' on the basis that he was a pacifist and his beloved physics department simply could not sustain the loss of any more teachers.

For his entire working life in Ireland, Professor Walton would struggle against inadequate funding. He was constantly informed by government officials that public investment in science and technology was not needed beyond the barest minimum. Walton knew that other countries had invested heavily in science and received rich returns through the rise of new industries, but Ireland took no heed.

In 1951, Walton and Cockcroft finally received the recognition that many believed was long overdue. They were jointly awarded a Nobel Prize in Physics for their pioneering work in atomic research. Following the glittering ceremony, a letter of congratulations was sent from the President of Ireland, which Walton used to request that more money be spent on science in the Republic of Ireland. This request, like so many before and after, fell on deaf ears.

Upon his retirement from full-time teaching in 1974, Walton continued to stay in Dublin for many years and was occasionally seen around the university. That is, until the death of his wife in 1983. He then moved to Belfast to live with a daughter and enjoyed a further period of quiet interest in science. He died of old age in 1995, in his ninety-second year.

Walton was much admired and respected, and was a quiet, unassuming man who was at the forefront of nuclear physics. He also tried in vain to convince the Irish authorities that science and technology should be a high priority for government expenditure. In the first area he was recognised with many awards and honours including the Nobel Prize. In the second, he was ignored.

SEÁN MACBRIDE (1904–88)

LAWYER, STATESMAN AND NOBEL PEACE LAUREATE

MacBride was born in Paris and was the only child of Major John MacBride and Maud Gonne. John MacBride was a leading Irish nationalist who had fought alongside the Boers against the British in the South African Boer War (1899–1902) as part of the 'Irish Brigade'. Since then, he had been living in self-exile in Paris. Maude Gonne was at one time a lover of William Butler Yeats (*see* p. 168) and was also an Irish nationalist.

The marriage between MacBride and Gonne was short-lived and tempestuous, with the pair separating in 1905, leaving the infant Seán to be raised by his mother in Paris. John MacBride returned to Ireland where in 1916, he was executed for his part in the Easter Rising of 1916.

Seán received the best education possible in Paris until 1918, when he was fourteen and his mother decided to return to live in Dublin, Ireland, where Seán was enrolled in an Irish boarding school in Co. Wexford. For the rest of his life, Seán would speak English with a pronounced French accent. The young MacBride grew up in a household that lived and breathed the nationalist cause for an independent Ireland and it was not surprising that Seán became a supporter of nationalism too, especially after his father was executed in 1916.

While still a schoolboy, Seán joined the Irish Republican Army (IRA) and was handpicked by Michael Collins (*see* p. 238) to accompany him to Paris during the Anglo-Irish treaty negotiations in late 1920. It helped considerably that he spoke fluent French to facilitate communication with the local French people for everyday necessities.

It would be true to say that at this stage in his life MacBride was a firebrand revolutionary, not interested in any practical or political compromise with the British. So when Collins negotiated a treaty that fell short of MacBride's expectations, he broke ranks with Collins and sided with anti-treaty proponents led by Éamon de Valera (*see* p. 224). He spent time in prison for his beliefs in 1922, escaped and was later rearrested in 1927.

During this period of being in and out of gaol, MacBride started a law degree at University College, Dublin, in 1924, which he completed after many interruptions in 1937. When he qualified as a barrister, this allowed him to represent defendants in court. Also during this period, MacBride married Catalina (Kid) Bulfin in 1925. She was a twenty-five-year old secretary whose parents were Argentinean immigrants. The couple had two children.

Throughout the 1920s and into the 1930s, MacBride continued to rise in the ranks of the IRA to eventually become the organisation's chief of staff in 1936. That same year the IRA resumed a bombing campaign in England, which MacBride opposed as futile. In 1937,

Éamon de Valera, who had been in power since 1932, modified the Irish constitution so as to remove the Crown, through the Governor General, from being the Head of State. This and other changes, effectively made the Irish Free State an independent country. MacBride saw no further justification for the existence of a clandestine guerrilla army and in early 1938 he formally severed ties with the IRA after twenty years of active involvement in the organisation.

MacBride then established an extremely successful practice as a criminal barrister and in a number of spectacularly effective cases caused the de Valera government a great deal of embarrassment over its use of emergency powers during WWII. The more MacBride defended his clients against the actions of de Valera's government, the more that MacBride felt he should enter politics and debate these issues on the floor of the Dáil Éireann (Irish Parliament).

In 1946, MacBride founded a political party called Clann na Poblachta (meaning Clan, or Family of the Republic) in the hope that it would eventually replace Fianna Fáil, which in MacBride's mind had become stale, conservative and economically backward. At the 1948 general elections in Ireland, Clann na Poblachta won enough seats to form a coalition government in the Dáil, thereby replacing the stranglehold that de Valera and his Fianna Fáil party had enjoyed over Irish politics for sixteen years. MacBride was given the post of Minister of External Affairs (Foreign Affairs) at a time when post-war Europe was undergoing massive changes.

Between 1949 and 1950, MacBride chaired a vitally important committee of the newly-formed Council of Europe to draft the European Convention on Human Rights, which was signed by the twelve member states of the Council of Europe in Rome in late 1950. The Convention was a modern version of the Bill of

Rights from England (1689) and the USA (1789), together with a significant contribution from the French Declaration of the Rights of Man (1789).

While impressing commentators of the world stage with his skill and legal expertise, back in Dublin Seán MacBride was instrumental in bringing about a change in Ireland's legal status. In 1949, Ireland declared itself a republic (which for years it had been in all but name only) and left the British Commonwealth. To everyone's surprise, Britain's reaction was quiet acceptance, and even King George VI sent a congratulatory telegram to the President of the new Irish Republic.

MacBride remained in and out of Irish politics for another decade, but his power and influence began to wane. First his Clann na Poblachta party broke up over a spectacular public row between MacBride and its co-leader, Noel Browne, over Browne's proposal to implement a free universal health scheme for all mothers and children under sixteen years of age. The Catholic Church opposed the scheme and MacBride, having a strong Catholic faith, felt he had to support the Catholic Church. The disagreement between co-leaders ended with Browne's forced resignation, a walkout of members of Clann na Poblachta, and the eventual de-registration of the party itself by 1965.

In the 1950s, the IRA resumed its armed insurgency against authorities in Northern Island in what became known as the Border Campaign (1956–62). The campaign involved intimidation, bombing and other acts of violence. The IRA was declared an illegal organisation and many suspects were gaoled indefinitely under emergency provisions. Seán MacBride began appearing for several of the IRA internees and scored a number of notable legal victories against the Irish authorities.

He also began appearing for prisoners internationally. In 1958, MacBride represented Archbishop Makarios, the Greek Cypriot leader, who the British had exiled to the Seychelles. MacBride was successful in getting the order revoked using the European Convention of Human Rights, which he had helped draft years earlier. His growing skill as a human rights lawyer on the global stage convinced MacBride that his future lay in a new direction.

MacBride left Irish politics in 1961 to commence a full-time career in human rights. That year he became a founding member of London-based Amnesty International (AI) and began a long association with that organisation, often representing prisoners of conscience at public trials, which garnered worldwide attention to their plight.

In 1963, MacBride became the secretary-general of the International Commission of Jurists based in Geneva. For the next ten years he became a familiar face on the international scene. In 1973, he was appointed as the United Nations Commissioner for Namibia and assisted that country to transition to independence after almost half a century of South African occupation.

His outstanding work in international affairs, most notably in connection with Namibia, was acknowledged in 1974, when MacBride was awarded the Nobel Peace Prize in Sweden. When his tenure as United Nations Commissioner concluded in 1977, MacBride retired back to Ireland to live out his final days in Dublin.

Seán MacBride died in 1988 after a short illness and was buried in Dublin's Glasnevin cemetery alongside his wife, 'Kid', who had passed away in 1976. MacBride was eighty-three years of age and was survived by a daughter and a son.

Even though Seán MacBride was a political revolutionary, he was also socially conservative. He supported independence for

CHAIM HERZOG (1918–97)

SOLDIER, LAWYER AND PRESIDENT OF ISRAEL

Chaim Herzog was born in Belfast, the only child of Rabbi Yitzhak Herzog and his wife Sara (née Hillman). The parents were Orthodox Jews. When Chaim was born, his father was Rabbi of the small Jewish congregation in Belfast, but the following year Mr Herzog was invited to become Rabbi of the much larger synagogue in Dublin.

Jews had been present in Ireland for hundreds of years, but their numbers were never more than a few hundred in total. However, during the second half of the nineteenth century there was an upsurge in migration of Jews to Ireland, mainly from Eastern Europe, following the Russian pogroms. By the early twentieth century, there were an estimated 5,000 Jews living in Ireland, of which all but a few were concentrated in Dublin (3,000) and Belfast (1,500).

The family settled in Portobello, Dublin, in 1919 where Rabbi

271

Herzog was appointed as the first Chief Rabbi of Ireland, a position he retained until he and his family immigrated to Palestine in 1935. The young Chaim Herzog spent his formative years in Dublin, which was still recovering from the deaths and destruction of the Easter Rising of 1916 and the simmering guerrilla war during the 1920s against British rule in Ireland (see contents for Collins and de Valera pages). Like his father before him, the young Chaim Herzog was a fluent Irish speaker.

Rabbi Herzog earned significant credit for himself and Irish Jewry with his public support of the Irish independence movement during his tenure as Chief Rabbi of Ireland. It would seem that these ideals were absorbed by the young Chaim as he also became a supporter of Irish independence as well as a member of Zionist organisations calling for the establishment of an independent Jewish state in Palestine. Chaim Herzog studied at Wesley College in Dublin and became lifelong friends with many of his fellow students.

When Chaim was seventeen, the Herzog family relocated to Palestine, then a British mandate under the League of Nations. There, Chaim joined the underground paramilitary group called Hagenah (Defence) and fought alongside the British in the 1936–1939 Arab revolt in Palestine. Before the Arab revolt had run its course, Chaim moved to Britain in 1938, where he completed a law degree from University College, London, in 1942 and immediately joined the British Army to fight in WWII.

Herzog initially served as a tank commander in the Armoured Division, but in 1943, he was transferred to the Intelligence Corps. From the time of the D-Day landings in Normandy in 1944, Chaim was engaged on the front line as well as in dealing with interrogations back at Divisional Headquarters in France, Belgium, the Netherlands and Germany as the Allies slowly rolled back the Germans in their push to Berlin. He also participated in the liberation of several Nazi concentration camps, including Bergen-Belsen. One lesser known fact about Major Chaim Herzog is that while interrogating a supposed low-level German prisoner, the perspicacious questioner recognised the man as none other than Heinrich Himmler, a leading member of the Nazi party and the infamous designer of the 'final solution' to eliminate six million Jews from the face of Europe.

Major Herzog witnessed at first hand the untold suffering of Jews at the hands of the Nazis in WWII and returned to Palestine in 1947, fuelled with an overwhelming conviction that Jews should have their own homeland. He re-joined Hagenah, where his experience with the British Army was acknowledged by him being appointed Intelligence Chief for one of its brigades. Also that year, he married Aura Ambache, a fellow member of Hagenah. The couple had four children.

By the time the former British mandate of Palestine was granted statehood by the United Nations in 1948, Herzog had managed to shape the Intelligence section he was responsible for into an effective organisation. This was just as well, because within weeks, a coalition of Arab countries launched an all-out offensive to push Israel 'back into the sea'. The young state of Israel won that battle and as a reward for his good work, Herzog was promoted to the rank of major-general and placed in charge of all military intelligence for the embryonic state of Israel (1950–5).

Herzog went on to serve a tour as military attaché in the United States in the mid-1950s and then was one of three operational heads of the Israeli Defence Force (IDF). When he retired from the IDF in 1962 at forty-four years of age, Herzog moved into the world of publicity as a commentator. During the Six-Day

War in 1967, Herzog became the voice of calm and reason on Israeli radio, giving accurate and insightful commentary on the progress of the war. After the conflict, Herzog was appointed as the first military commander of the newly captured West Bank territory, which included the vitally strategic urban area of east Jerusalem.

In 1972, Herzog founded one of Israel's largest law firms: Herzog, Fox and Ne'eman, but his career away from the public was short-lived. In 1975, he was appointed by the Israeli Prime Minister, Yitzhak Rabin, to serve as Israel's ambassador to the United Nations. During Herzog's tenure, the Arab, Muslim and Communist nations joined together to put forward a resolution condemning Zionism (and indirectly Israel) as a form of racism. Herzog drew international attention for his passionate advocacy against the proposition. He stepped up to the podium and addressed the general assembly of the United Nations by defiantly tearing the resolution into pieces, declaring that 'Hitler would have felt at home on a number of occasions during the past year, listening to the proceedings in this forum.' (Druckman, *The Herzogs*, p. 4 – see references at the end.) Ultimately the resolution was passed 72 votes to 35, with 32 abstentions. It was not one of the most honourable moments in the history of the United Nations.

Following his service in the United Nations, Herzog returned to Israel. He was sixty-three years of age and most people in his position would have considered permanent retirement after such a long and distinguished career. But Chaim Herzog decided to enter politics instead and in 1981, he was elected as a Labor politician to the Israeli Knesset (parliament). The Labor party was in opposition and not considered a threat to the ruling Likud party's dominance. Yet in 1983, when a new President of Israel needed to be elected by the Knesset, it was Herzog who unexpectedly won the ballot over the Likud party's nominee.

Herzog was a well-respected and popular choice. He travelled abroad visiting over thirty countries and improved the profile and image of Israel internationally. He was the first Israeli president to visit a number of countries including the United States, China, Germany and Ireland. He made a historic trip of reconciliation to Spain, marking 500 years since the Jews were expelled from that country. He met with kings and queens, presidents and prime ministers. In Ireland, Herzog inaugurated the Irish-Jewish Museum in Dublin and in Co. Kerry dedicated a statue to his childhood friend, Cearbhall Ó Dálaigh, the fifth President of Ireland who was also a fellow lawyer. Herzog was re-elected unopposed for a second five-year term as president, making him the longest serving Israeli president to date.

In 1993, Herzog bowed out of official life and retired to live out his last years with his wife and to write his memoir, *Living History: A Memoir* (first published in 1996 and re-issued by Plunkett Lake Press in 2015). He died after a long illness in 1997 and was buried in Mount Herzl cemetery in Jerusalem. He was survived by his wife, Aura, who was active in public affairs in her own right. Of their four children, two are active in politics, of whom Isaac Herzog at the time of writing is currently the Leader of the Opposition in the Israeli Knesset.

Chaim was a passionate believer in statehood for emerging countries, whether it be Ireland or Israel or indeed the twelve other countries the United Nations recognised as gaining their independence between the years 1975–8. Even though he was prepared to defend his country and his beliefs with force, he was often described as a warrior who loved peace. Herzog mentioned many times that it was his upbringing in Ireland that taught him about fairness, equality and social justice. He wanted nothing more than tolerance and understanding towards all, especially minorities. Although he knew that in a post-WWII world, which was in such turmoil, that ideal was often difficult to achieve.

JOHN HUME (1937–)

POLITICIAN AND
NOBEL PEACE LAUREATE

Hume was born in Derry, Northern Ireland, the first child of seven born to Sam Hume, an ex-soldier and shipyard riveter, and Annie (née Doherty). Two generations earlier, John Hume's grandfather, a stonemason, had emigrated from Scotland. The grandfather was Protestant, but married a local Catholic girl and all their descendants were raised as Catholics.

John Hume was educated at St Columb's College in Belfast and in 1955 he enrolled at St Patrick's College, Maynooth, Ireland's leading Catholic seminary near Dublin in the Republic of Ireland. Hume initially wanted to become a priest, but after three years of university study, changed his mind when he met and fell in love with a local Belfast woman. In 1960, Hume married Patricia Hone, the daughter of a handyman, and graduated with a Bachelor's degree in French and History.

Hume had become a Francophile at college and the young

married couple spent the next several summers in France, learning to speak the language fluently and absorbing the cornerstone French ideals of *liberté, égalité et fraternité* (liberty, equality and fraternity). John and Patricia returned to Ireland in 1963 and John received a Master's degree from St Patrick's College the following year. His subject was the social and economic history of Derry in the early-to-mid 1800s.

When Hume returned to his native Derry in 1965, he taught in local schools and began looking for other ways to relieve distress in his community. The area of Hume's upbringing and where he returned to live and work was, and still is, known as Bogside, because this once referred to its boggy location outside the city walls of Derry. But even after the area was filled in and populated (by mainly Catholics), the name became synonymous for entrenched discrimination in British-ruled Northern Ireland. There was crushing poverty, simmering tension, the occasional outburst of communal violence and an ever-present sense of hopelessness.

While working as a teacher, Hume became actively involved in the Credit Union movement in his city as a practical way to lift people out of poverty. With a few of his friends, Hume founded the Derry Credit Union, the first credit union in Northern Ireland. This whetted his appetite for more community involvement.

With a backdrop of rising sectarian strife and civil unrest across Northern Ireland during the 1960s (known as the 'The Troubles'), Hume became active in the Derry Citizens' Action Committee and also in the Northern Ireland Civil Rights Association. It was his belief that violence would not solve anything and he drew inspiration from the American Civil Rights movement, led by Martin Luther King.

In 1969, Hume was elected to the Parliament of Northern Ireland as an independent for the seat of Foyle, but his tenure was short-lived, as civil unrest worsened to the point that Britain suspended parliamentary democracy in favour of direct rule in 1972. In 1970, Hume and a few others formed a new party in Northern Ireland: the Social Democratic and Labour Party (SDLP), which believed in achieving Irish unification through constitutional and non-violent means. Britain tried to restore democracy again in 1973 by replacing the old Parliament of Northern Ireland with an Assembly that was based on a more equitable representation of the Catholic minority of Northern Ireland. The SDLP gained a number of seats and became the second most popular party in the Assembly. John Hume was given the Finance Ministry in what quickly turned out to be an unworkable coalition.

The Assembly collapsed due to sustained opposition from the Northern Ireland unionist (pro-union with Britain) parties and authority over Northern Ireland returned to being exercised directly from Britain.

It would be another twenty-five years before parliamentary democracy was handed back to Northern Ireland. Meanwhile John Hume, now leader of the SDLP, was elected to the European Parliament (1979–2004) as well as being the member for Foyle in the British Parliament in Westminster (1983–2005).

Hume continued to advocate for a peaceful solution to Northern Ireland, both inside and outside his country. For example his membership of the European Parliament in Brussels and the British Parliament in London allowed him to constantly place Northern Ireland's 'Troubles' onto the world stage. His main aim was to persuade militant republicans that there was no future in their armed struggle.

These approaches were the first faltering steps taken by Hume to create a new Northern Ireland Parliament that led eventually to an Anglo-Irish Agreement in 1985. Unfortunately, the vast majority of Northern Ireland Unionists rejected the agreement and demonstrated their objections in mass rallies across Belfast. But Hume did not give up and in a perverse way his task was made easier by the worsening bombing campaign of the Irish Republican Army (IRA) that was so extreme it lost backing even among its Catholic supporters.

Hume seized the moment in the late 1980s to commence secret negotiations with Gerry Adams, the Sinn Féin leader in Northern Ireland, and these would subsequently expand to also include representatives from the British and Irish governments. At times US President Bill Clinton played a significant role as a facilitator during the peace process. The negotiations were delicate and lasted almost five years. They were also personally risky for John Hume. Graffiti was scrawled across the front of his home calling him a 'Traitor'. At one point his house and car were firebombed.

Eventually a joint Declaration of Peace was announced in 1993, followed by a most significant announcement in 1994, that the IRA would unilaterally enforce a ceasefire. The ceasefire was broken a few times over the next several years, but compared to the intensity of the violence in earlier times, most impartial observers were satisfied that the IRA had made a genuine effort to end their armed campaign. This easing of civil unrest allowed the political discussions to continue and it is now widely acknowledged that John Hume was the person mainly responsible for bringing about the subsequent treaty known as the 'Good Friday Agreement' in 1998.

The Agreement was a landmark treaty that was signed by most political parties in Northern Ireland and agreed to by the British and Irish governments. It called for a decommissioning of all armed paramilitary groups, and created a new Government of Northern Ireland with Britain devolving many of its powers to it. The main point within the Agreement was the acceptance that Northern Ireland remained part of the United Kingdom, while acknowledging that the minority of Northern Ireland and the majority of the people of the 'island of Ireland' wished to bring about a united Ireland. The Agreement made provision for Northern Ireland to determine by referendum whether it would stay in the UK or join Ireland at some future date.

With the signing of the Good Friday Agreement, 'The Troubles' in Northern Ireland formally came to an end after claiming the lives of over 3,600 people on both sides of a conflict that had lasted thirty years (1968–1998).

At subsequent elections John Hume was elected as the member for Foyle and his party, the SDLP, gained the highest popular vote in Northern Ireland. It was a high point in John Hume's life, which was made even more remarkable later that year when he and John Trimble (the then leader of the Ulster Unionist Party) jointly won the Nobel Peace Prize. Although Hume and Trimble shared the world's most prestigious peace prize, the two were never close. One of the only times the two were pictured together in public was when they attended a concert in Belfast by Irish band U2 in the lead-up to a referendum in support of the Good Friday Agreement. On the stage of the Waterfront Theatre before thousands of adoring fans, John Hume and lead singer Bono raised both their arms like prize-fighters (*see* Bono, p. 308).

Hume retired from the Northern Ireland Assembly in 2001, although he retained his membership of both the UK House of Commons and the European Parliament until 2004. For the next decade he spoke at a declining number of events throughout

Ireland and Europe. In 2014, Hume was visited by ex-President Bill Clinton, who was so instrumental at bringing about the original peace accord in 1994. In a symbolic gesture, the two walked across Derry's new Peace Bridge over the river Foyle, after which Clinton urged the assembled crowd to 'finish the process of peace in Northern Ireland'.

At the time of writing, Hume, now in the autumn of his life, is increasingly suffering from loss of memory. He leads a quiet life in Derry surrounded by his wife Patricia, five adult children (all of whom graduated from university) and friends. He loves walking, speaking French whenever he can and discussing politics, even if he can no longer remember everything about the remarkable contribution he made to it.

John Hume not only brought peace to Northern Ireland, he fundamentally changed attitudes of bitterness and division that had festered for hundreds of years. The change is still fragile, but John Hume has already shown that harmony, a shared vision and a willingness to work together is eminently more preferable to an endless cycle of violence, partition and hatred.

MARY ROBINSON (1944–)

HUMAN RIGHTS LAWYER AND FIRST FEMALE PRESIDENT OF IRELAND

Ms Robinson was born Mary Bourke in Ballina, Co. Mayo, the only daughter of five children to Aubrey Bourke and his wife Tessa (née O'Donnell), who were both medical practitioners. The Bourkes were a well-regarded family with a long and illustrious history stretching back to the arrival of the Normans in the twelfth century. Branches of the Bourke family were both Catholic as well as Protestant (Church of Ireland). Even more confusing, over the centuries various Bourke family members had either fought against British dominion over Ireland, or had staunchly supported it.

Mary grew up in one of the poorest counties in the Republic of Ireland. She witnessed first-hand through her parent's medical practice what the depths of poverty could do to the health of the people living around her. Mary also spent time with her grandfather, Henry Bourke, who had a thriving law practice in Ballina, and the many tales he told of his cases in court infused

Mary with a strong interest in the law and how it could be used to correct injustice.

The young Mary attended a local private school in Ballina and then a Catholic boarding school for girls in Dublin. At one stage, Mary was so impressed by the dedication of the Sacred Heart Sisters at Mount Anville School that she thought of becoming a nun, but her mother prevailed on Mary to get a university education first. She sugar-coated her suggestion by offering the seventeen-year-old Mary a year's final tuition at a French finishing school.

In 1961, Mary spent a very significant year at Mademoiselle Anita Pojninska's finishing school in the heart of Paris. It was liberating, intellectually stimulating and taught her to question many of the beliefs she had accepted as normal back in Ireland. For instance, Mary began to query the role of the Catholic Church in Irish society, especially its attitudes towards women.

When Mary returned to Ireland, she enrolled in Trinity College, Dublin and decided to study law. It was the early 1960s and Irish society, indeed world society, was undergoing fundamental changes. Miss Bourke applied herself diligently to her studies, won a prestigious scholarship and graduated with first degree honours in 1967. She then won a further scholarship to attend Harvard Law School in the United States. Mary Bourke arrived at Harvard to undergo her Master's degree in the middle of nationwide demonstrations against the Vietnam War and about civil rights. The stimulating classroom debates she participated in completed the journey of change she had begun years earlier at the Parisian finishing school.

Mary returned to Ireland in 1969 a political liberal, and secured a part-time position as a tutor in Law at Trinity College, Dublin. Shortly after, she was awarded a professorship and won a seat in the

Republic of Ireland's senate (upper house), which had three seats in its sixty-seat chamber reserved for graduates from Trinity College. To cap off a remarkable few years, Mary Bourke married Nicholas Robinson in 1970. Her new husband was a fellow graduate in law from Trinity College and also was a keen supporter of women's rights. She adopted his surname.

Mrs Robinson used her position as Senator to effect changes to the Irish legislation. In 1971, she tried unsuccessfully to remove the prohibition on the use of contraceptives in Ireland. This created a storm of controversy in which Robinson was heavily criticised by her political opponents as well as by the Roman Catholic Church. The bill was initially defeated, but when she reintroduced it in 1973, Irish attitudes on this matter had significantly altered. In the end legislation was not needed, because the Irish Supreme Court intervened and overturned the thirty-six-year ban on contraceptives as an unlawful violation of marital privacy.

In 1973, Ireland joined the European Community (now, European Union), which opened up the possibly to Robinson of using the European Court of Justice and the European Court of Human Rights to modernise and reform the Republic of Ireland's outdated laws. Over the next seventeen years, Mary Robinson acted in a series of landmark cases, such as the abolition of all-male juries (1976), introducing free legal aid in civil cases (1979), taxation equalisation for married couples (1980) and equal pay for equal work (also 1980).

In 1976, she joined the Labour Party, but since it was mainly trade union-based and overwhelmingly male, a female academic was not made to feel welcome. Nevertheless, Mrs Robinson represented the Labour Party in two unsuccessful attempts at securing a seat in Ireland's lower house, the Dáil Éireann (1977 and 1981). However, Robinson continued to be re-elected to the Irish senate, where, in 1984, she hoped to be promoted to Attorney General in a new coalition government in which Labour was a partner. Her aspiration was cut short when the position of Attorney General went to another person. Further disappointments followed and, disillusioned by her ten-year involvement with Labour, Mary Robinson resigned her party membership in 1985.

During the 1980s, Robinson continued to campaign for women's rights and strongly supported the 'Yes' vote on two unsuccessful referenda on abortion and divorce that convulsed the country between 1983 and 1986. Ireland might have been undergoing great social change, but the established hierarchy of the Roman Catholic Church and middle-aged males were not giving up without a fight. It would not be until 1995 that divorce was permitted, but abortion still remains illegal.

In 1989, Robinson decided not to seek re-election to the Irish senate to concentrate on her academic career at Trinity College, Dublin. But within months of walking away from twenty years of politics, she was approached by the Labour party to consider standing as their candidate in the forthcoming Irish presidential election. Mary Robinson was surprised. Such an invitation was a very great honour and if she was successful the presidency, which was mainly a ceremonial position, would propel her to the very pinnacle of the Irish state for the elected term of seven years. At the urging of her husband, she decided to accept the proposal on one condition: that even though she was nominated by the Labour party, Robinson would still run as an independent candidate.

Mary Robinson was the first woman to run for the Irish presidency and many people gave her little chance of success. But after a brilliantly run campaign she comfortably won the 1990 election by capturing almost 52 per cent of the popular vote. Robinson brought a new quality to the Irish presidency, which had previously been the preserve of retired male politicians.

Mrs Robinson's style was more inclusive than that of any previous president and she invited groups of people from all walks of life to the official residence of the president in Dublin. Community groups, gay and lesbian organisations, the unemployed and the handicapped joined health workers, educators, soldiers and police offices at the regular functions held at the president's residence.

To show people that there was nothing to fear from the Republic of Ireland, Robinson also reached out to politicians in Northern Ireland, as well as to the royal family in England. Her moves of reconciliation and inclusiveness coincided with delicate efforts for a lasting peace to 'The Troubles' in Northern Ireland (*see* Hume, p. 277). When Robinson decided to visit West Belfast in 1993, she unleashed a storm of protest. The area of Belfast was well-known for its support of the outlawed Irish Republican Army and Robinson's visit was seen by some as explicit endorsement of the IRA's bombing and murder campaign. However, Robinson regarded her trip as a necessary part of the much-needed healing process towards a lasting peace.

Robinson travelled widely and specifically targeted the descendants of Irish immigrants in places like Britain, America, Canada, South America, Australia and New Zealand. She was quick to point out that the Irish diaspora was one of the largest movement of people in the history of the world, and that more people of Irish ancestry lived outside their country of origin than currently lived in the Republic of Ireland. In her inauguration address, Mary Robinson said, 'There are 70 million people living on this globe who claim Irish descent. I will be proud to represent them all.'

The more that Robinson travelled, the more she observed human rights abuses that were occurring worldwide. In 1992, she visited Somalia to see for herself what could be done in a country devastated by civil war, drought and famine. In 1994, Robinson became the first head of state to journey to Rwanda after the horrendous ethnic genocide of the Tutsi people there. These trips made this far-sighted president realise that international responses to these crises should be co-ordinated through the United Nations, yet the UN was woefully under-resourced to adequately manage the situation.

As Robinson's seven-year term of office came close to finishing, she faced a choice: to seek a second term in office or else to move on to another challenge, this time possibly with the United Nations. Even though she was immensely popular with the Irish people, with an approval rating reaching an unprecedented 93 per cent, Robinson made up her mind to apply for the UN post of High Commissioner for Human Rights in 1997. With the support of a grateful Irish government, Mary Robinson secured the position and she flew out to the Headquarters of the Human Rights Commission in Geneva on the same day that she completed her last official engagement as President of Ireland.

What greeted the new High Commissioner on her arrival in 1997 was an organisation that had been overwhelmed by the magnitude of the disasters it was trying to manage. There were too few people dealing with too many crises in almost every continent on the globe. Staff morale was at a very low ebb and financial resources were completely exhausted. Robinson quickly obtained pledges of money from donor countries and reinvigorated the staff with a strong sense of purpose and direction. In a short time, this inspiring woman became renowned as a fearlessly outspoken critic of human rights abuses around the world.

MARY ROBINSON (1944–)

Since leaving the position of UN High Commissioner for Human Rights in 2002, Mary Robinson still travels the globe giving speeches and talking to world leaders about women's rights, as well as promoting democracy, the abolishment of child marriage and the promotion of gender equality. She is currently the UN Special Envoy for Climate Change.

In her life she has received numerous awards and honours from universities, societies and governments around the world, including the Presidential Medal of Freedom from President Obama, but throughout all her travels and accolades her heart has always remained in Ireland. She resides there today with her husband and three adult children. Mary Robinson is currently the chancellor of her beloved Trinity College, Dublin, a university she has been associated with for over fifty years as a student, lecturer, professor and finally, Head of the governing body.

Her compassion and leadership has helped Ireland move from being a patriarchal society dominated and, in some cases, held back by, conservative attitudes, to being a more open, inclusive and progressive country.

GEORGE BEST
(1946–2005)

FOOTBALL LEGEND

B est was born the first of six children to Richard ('Dickie') Best, a shipyard worker and his wife Anne (née Withers) in East Belfast, Northern Ireland. The family were proudly Protestant (belonging to the Free Presbyterian Church). Dickie was a member of the Orange Order, a fraternal society established to maintain Protestant dominance in Northern Ireland and named after the Dutch-born Protestant king, William of Orange, who defeated the Catholics in Ireland at the Battle of the Boyne in 1690.

The East Belfast area at the time of George Best's birth was overwhelmingly working-class, Protestant and poor. In the Northern Ireland government elections, the majority of people voted for Unionist parties (political organisations that supported union with the United Kingdom and opposed integration into a united Ireland). The main employers were the heavy industries of shipbuilding, textiles and ropemaking, which had traditionally provided tens of thousands of jobs each year for over a century. However, by the 1950s these industries were in slow decline and people grew more uncertain about their future in the workforce.

Best grew up on the Cregagh estate in East Belfast and played kick-about football (soccer) with his mates in the open fields between the high-rise buildings and terrace houses. In 1957, the academically gifted Best went to Grosvenor High School in Belfast, but being a grammar school it tried to emulate the great grammar schools of England by only offering rugby in winter and cricket in summer. George Best had only known soccer prior to this, and also felt that his slight build was not suited to the more physically combative sport of rugby. He started to truant from Grosvenor High School and after a short time was transferred to a nearby High School, Lisnasharragh Secondary School (now closed), that dealt with 'troubled' or disadvantaged students. Most importantly, the school offered football on its sporting curriculum.

George Best started playing with the school team during the week and then with the local team, Cregagh Boys club, on the weekend. He settled down academically and began showing great promise in the sport he had now come to love. In 1961, when George was still only fifteen years of age, he was spotted by a talent scout from the Manchester United team in England. The scout signed him as a junior for the club and within two years he made his debut with the senior side, scoring his first goal in top-class football in just his second game.

Best's rise as a football professional was phenomenal. After only fifteen appearances for Manchester United, George won his first Northern Ireland 'cap' when he played against Wales in 1964. By way of explanation, the use of 'caps' is a quaint leftover from the English public school system, where the sports of cricket, soccer and rugby all had their beginnings. In the nineteenth century caps were commonly worn in a school to distinguish pupils in different sporting 'houses' (teams). In modern rugby, soccer and cricket, a cap is awarded to a player when he or she first represents a country internationally. Nowadays, a player who has represented their country twenty-five times is said to have earned twenty-five caps, although only one physical cap was awarded at the first appearance.

Best won a Football Association Cup winner's plaque in 1964. Then in 1965, he won a Championship medal for helping Manchester United win the premiership. He did it again in 1967. Best scored two of the winning goals when Manchester United won the much coveted European Champions Cup Final in 1968 (now called the UEFA Champions League Cup Final).

From 1967 to 1971, he scored more goals than any other player in the Manchester United side. In total, Best made 370 appearances for his Manchester United club, scoring 179 goals: on average a superb rate of one goal every two matches! His incredible skill, pace and control bamboozled his opponents and made him Britain's first football superstar. He had become such a huge talent in football that he was voted not only UK Player of the Year for the 1967-8 season, but also European Player of the Year for the same period.

At one time, George Best was receiving up to 1,000 letters per week from fans and had to employ three full-time staff to answer them. But the pressure of superstardom took its toll. Best made ill-judged business investments in nightclubs and fashion shops that lost him a great deal of money. He started missing training sessions, partying to all hours of the night and drinking heavily. It was inevitable that his football career would suffer and after two years of deteriorating performances, Manchester United finally let him go in 1974. Best was only twenty-six years of age.

Over the next ten years, Best journeyed the world playing for many clubs on short-term contracts, but whilever he continued drinking and carousing, he could never recover the miraculous form of his younger days. When Best finally hung up his boots in 1984, he was playing for a lowly ranked team in Northern Ireland.

In his football career, Best played over 700 games for a dozen clubs in Europe, North America, South Africa and Australia, in which he scored over 250 goals. Further, between 1964 and 1978, he represented the national team of Northern Ireland at thirty-seven international games, scoring nine goals.

After retiring from professional football in 1984, Best continued to attract attention for his drinking, gambling and womanising. He spent time in and out of rehabilitation clinics for alcoholism, attended years of meetings with Alcoholics Anonymous, and underwent hypnotherapy and even acupuncture, but after every treatment he would relapse and resume drinking heavily. Later in life he was declared bankrupt and had problems with the Taxation Office over unpaid tax bills.

Years of heavy drinking eventually led to George having chronic liver disease and he had a liver transplant in 2002. Unfortunately, he was not able to overcome his alcohol addiction and, despite everyone's advice and even professional counselling, George resumed drinking. In 2005, he was admitted to hospital with 'flu-like' symptoms, which rapidly deteriorated into organ failure. He died at Cromwell Hospital, London, surrounded by close family and friends. He was only fifty-six years of age.

In keeping with his dying wish, the body of George Best was returned to his beloved Ireland where he was buried alongside his mother in Roselawn cemetery on the outskirts of Belfast. A crowd of over 100,000 people lined the streets as the cortège passed by to pay their respects to this footballing legend. Around the world millions more watched on TV as he was laid to rest.

It is reported that Best's last words to the world were, 'Don't die like me'. To honour his memory and his dying wish, George's married sister Barbara (McNarry) established the George Best Foundation to promote healthier lifestyles and to combat alcoholism. Over the next decade the Foundation gave a total of almost £300,000 in charitable donations, until it was wound up in 2014 because of Barbara's declining health. In 2014, a treasure trove of Best's memorabilia was uncovered in a London bank vault, having being placed there by Best decades earlier. It is hoped these items will become some of the prized exhibits in a planned Ulster Sports Museum.

George Best had two failed marriages and fathered one son, Calum, with his first wife. He was also believed to have an illegitimate daughter in the late 1960s, but her identity has been a very well-kept secret. It is understood that Best never saw his daughter during his lifetime.

To this day George Best is regarded as one of the most prodigiously talented footballers to have ever played professionally in the world. He is consistently ranked as one of the Top 10 players of all time. To sum up the people of Northern Ireland proudly say: 'Maradona good, Pelé better, George Best.'

PIERCE BROSNAN (1953–)

ACTOR AND
SOCIAL ACTIVIST

Brosnan was born in Drogheda, Co. Louth in the Republic of Ireland, the only child to Thomas Brosnan, carpenter and his wife May (née Smith). Brosnan's parents separated when Pierce was an infant and when his mother went to London to find work as a nurse, he was raised by relatives in Navan, Co. Meath. For the next decade, Brosnan's mother constantly sent money home for his upbringing and would return as often as she could to spend her holidays with her son.

When he was eleven, Brosnan left Ireland to be with his mother in the Scottish village of Longniddry, East Lothian, a dormitory suburb outside Edinburgh. Brosnan's mother had recently remarried and his new stepfather took Pierce to see the latest James Bond film, *Goldfinger* in 1964. The film starred Sean Connery and Pierce was impressed by the admiration heaped on a locally-born lad who had reached international stardom. It was at that point that he decided he wanted a career in acting.

Later, after the family moved to London, Brosnan went to a state comprehensive school in Putney in south-west London. He left there at sixteen years of age and set out on his own to be an actor. While busking as a fire-eater, he was hired by a circus agent and after this enrolled as an actor at the Drama Centre, London. He graduated in 1975, aged twenty-two, and worked for the next eight years gaining skills, experience and recognition acting in British films and West End (of London) stage plays.

During this period, Brosnan met Australian actress Cassandra Harris. They married in 1980 and shortly thereafter, she starred as a Bond-girl in *For Your Eyes Only* (1982) which featured Roger Moore as agent 007. During the filming of this Bond movie, Cassandra introduced Brosnan to the film's producer, Albert Broccoli, who would remember Brosnan years later when he was casting for a Bond replacement. In 1982, the Brosnans moved to Southern California in the United States in order for Pierce to further his film career.

The young actor's arrival in Hollywood coincided with NBC Television casting for a debonair conman-turned private investigator, in a forthcoming production called *Remington Steele*. Brosnan fitted the bill perfectly. He went on to play the character Steele opposite Stephanie Zimbalist (daughter of actor Efrem Zimbalist Jnr) in the popular TV series for ninety-four episodes over five seasons. It launched Brosnan's career internationally.

In 1986, Brosnan was chosen by Albert Broccoli to replace the aging Roger Moore as James Bond, Secret Agent 007, but his NBC contract prevented him from accepting, so the studio went ahead and cast Timothy Dalton in the role instead. A year later, in 1987, *Remington Steele* ceased production, but unfortunately this happened too late for Pierce to play James Bond. Brosnan starred in a number of big-budget movies, such as *The Fourth Protocol* (1987), *The Heist* (1989), *The Lawnmower Man* (1992) and *Mrs Doubtfire* (1993). Each film and television appearance (there were several guest spots) enhanced his reputation for playing handsome, cultured and slightly dangerous characters. Fortuitously, this was just what the makers of the Bond 007 series were still looking for in 1994, when Dalton's two Bond films were regarded as relative failures at the box office.

This time, Brosnan was available and signed for a three-film contract with an option for a fourth. His first Bond film, *Goldeneye* (1995) grossed over US$500 million worldwide (adjusted for inflation), reversing a declining trend in gross box-office receipts (adjusted) that had developed under previous Bond actors Roger Moore (1973–1985) and Timothy Dalton (1987–9). The public immediately warmed to Brosnan's interpretation of the 'spy with a licence to kill' in *Goldeneye* and elevated him to the 'best' James Bond character since the legendary, and some say iconic, Sean Connery back in the 1960s and early 70s.

After the success of his first Bond film, Brosnan followed up by starring in *Tomorrow Never Dies* (1997), *The World Is Not Enough* (1999) and *Die Another Day* (2002). Every one of these Bond films grossed over US$400 in the box office (adjusted) and collectively won a number of Golden Globe and BAFTA awards. For the four films in the Bond series featuring Brosnan, he was estimated to have been paid more than US$40 million in total.

While still being contracted to play James Bond, Brosnan was allowed to work on other projects, including one or two he created with his own film production company, 'Irish Dream Time' that Brosnan formed in 1996. *Dante's Peak* (1997), *Grey Owl* (1999) about one of Canada's first environmentalists and *The Tailor of Panama*

(2001), were some of the twelve feature films he either starred in or produced during the period he was filming the Bond series. It showed that Brosnan could not only play a spy, but that he could also perform comedy, action dramas, thrillers, and romance. In *Grey Owl* in particular, he further showed a growing interest and commitment to the environment and conservation of nature.

When Brosnan finished filming *Die Another Day*, he was approaching his fiftieth birthday and was now considered a megastar who could virtually guarantee box-office success with any movie he performed in. Yet the producers of the Bond franchise and even Brosnan himself questioned whether his age might work against him continuing to perform the character of James Bond. After a delay of a few more years, it was accepted by mutual agreement that another, younger, Bond should replace Brosnan. In 2005, that person was Daniel Craig who, as the sixth actor to play James Bond in fifty years, has reinvented and reinvigorated the character yet again.

After leaving the part of Bond, Pierce Brosnan has gone on to make or produce many more movies. At the time of writing, he has seventy-five films to his credit. If anything, the mature, still incredibly handsome actor, appears to have increased his workload in the last decade ... and he has also enhanced his popularity still more. Apart from the James Bond series, Brosnan's later films have attracted much critical acclaim and certainly rank among his most popular. Some examples are *Evelyn* (2002), *Seraphim Falls* (2006), *The Ghost Writer* (2010) and *November Man* (2014).

In 1991, Brosnan's wife Cassandra Harris died in his arms after a four-year battle with ovarian cancer. She was forty-three years of age. It was a devastating loss for Pierce and their three children: Sean, who was born in 1983 and Charlotte and Christopher –

Cassandra's two children from a previous marriage, who Brosnan had adopted as his own in 1986. Three years later in 1994, Brosnan met American journalist Keely Shaye Smith and after a long relationship the couple were married in Ireland in 2001. They have two sons, Dylan, born in 1997 and Paris, born in 2001. In a macabre coincidence, Brosnan's stepdaughter Charlotte from his first marriage, also died of ovarian cancer in 2013, when she was only forty-one years of age.

As Brosnan's wealth and influence grew, so did his commitment to a number of social and environmental causes. In fact, since the mid-1990s, Pierce and Keely had been passionately involved in making this planet a better place. The couple have donated large sums of money to build playgrounds and schools around the world, and to fight environmental cases in court and to actively campaign for same-sex marriage, gay adoption and gun control.

Pierce Brosnan says he has been very lucky in his life. He still loves acting and in his sixties remains at the top of his profession. His lifestyle is extremely comfortable, with a house in Malibu, California and property on the island of Kauai, Hawaii. He takes yearly trips back to Ireland to meet friends, to catch up with his staff in his film production company of 'Irish Dream Time', and to relax by reading, fishing and taking walks along Ireland's spectacular landscapes.

This is a man who is proud to be Irish. He has introduced his Irish heritage, Irish art and culture to all his children. Even though he became an American citizen in 2004, Brosnan never gave up his Irish passport. It holds a special place in his heart.

Yet he is acutely aware of his own physical limitations and mortality. In 1984, he suffered a bout of 'Bell's Palsy' (facial muscle paralysis) from which he made a full recovery. But it is the death of his first wife and daughter from cancer that has made the deepest impact on him personally. When time allows, Brosnan devotes as much time and effort as he can to social and environmental causes. He successfully campaigned against the destruction of marine mammal habitat off the coast of California and Mexico. Brosnan is Chairman for the Entertainment Industry Foundation that annually distributes millions of dollars to women and children in need.

Brosnan returned to his first vocation – drawing and painting – in the late 1980s and now produces a small number of paintings a year. Profits from the sale of his paintings and prints are given to the Brosnan Trust, which supports a number of social and environmental causes. Pierce Brosnan has been an ambassador for UNICEF (United Nations Children's Fund) since 2001 and he personally has contributed to over thirty different charities worldwide. Despite his globetrotting, and the fame and fortune that came from all his movie roles, it has been the personal tragedies that have shaped him into the man that he is today: a hard-working, generous person with a heightened social conscience.

VERONICA GUERIN
(1958–96)

INVESTIGATIVE JOURNALIST

Veronica Guerin was born in the Dublin suburb of Artane, the second youngest in a family of three girls and two boys. Her father, Christopher, had his own accountancy practice and Veronica's mother, Bernadette (née Paris), stayed at home to look after the children. Veronica was educated at the local Catholic school where she excelled in sport, playing both football and basketball for Ireland in her teens. One of her heroes was the Manchester United footballer Eric Cantona. She treasured a photograph taken at Manchester United's home ground of Old Trafford during a visit in 1995, in which she and Cantona were filmed together.

Guerin graduated from Trinity College, Dublin with an accountancy degree in 1980 and worked for three years in her father's practice. Following the latter's death in 1983, Veronica started a public relations company, which she ran successfully for seven years. At this time, she also developed a lifelong fascination with Irish politics and for a while, during the mid-1980s, became the research assistant to Charles Haughey the Taoiseach (Prime Minister) of the Republic of Ireland.

Charles Haughey liked his bright, enthusiastic and capable assistant. Soon the Haughey and Guerin families became close friends. In 1984, Haughey appointed Veronica to the position of secretary of the Fianna Fáil delegation to the New Ireland Forum, a multi-party think tank and discussion group that aimed to find solutions to 'The Troubles' in Northern Ireland. It was an initiative of John Hume (*see* p. 277). This position propelled Guerin, then twenty-six years of age, into the centre of Ireland's politics.

The following year, Veronica married Graham Turley, a construction engineer-turned-builder, whom she had been close to for several years, since they were both in the youth wing of Fianna Fáil. Charles Haughey, along with a number of other prominent Irish politicians attended their wedding as guests. Guerin and Turley had one child, a son, Cathal in 1990. Veronica continued to use the surname 'Guerin' after her marriage because she felt that in her career she had built up a high degree of recognition under her maiden name.

Ireland during the 1980s and 90s was a very different place from the economically struggling and socially conservative country that had existed for the previous half century or more. Starting in the 1980s, economic reforms by way of lower taxes, higher competition and privatisation of government services fundamentally transformed Ireland into an export-oriented, service-based economy. The nation prospered, unemployment fell and individual incomes rose. The Republic of Ireland was even referred to as the Celtic 'tiger' because its remarkable growth rates matched that of the Asian 'tiger' countries.

But along with rising incomes came a whole range of problems Ireland had not faced before, or at least not to the same degree. Entrepreneurs evolved who took advantage of the fast, changing and essentially under-regulated economy to make themselves rich at the expense of others. The areas of major concern were moneylenders and property developers. Even worse were the drug lords, who were poisoning ever-increasing numbers of people with (mainly) heroin.

After Cathal's birth in 1990, Guerin switched careers again, this time becoming a business reporter with the *Sunday Business Post*, a general paper with a strong emphasis on covering financial and political affairs. She quickly built up a network of trusted sources within government and the business community. Her disarming ability to elicit information from people allowed Veronica to file stories that were startling for their accuracy and detail. One of her early reports was an exposé she wrote about Aer Lingus Holidays.

Following her stint with the *Sunday Business Post*, Guerin was engaged by the *Sunday Tribune* as a senior reporter. There, she wrote a series of stunning interviews with Bishop Eamon Casey, who was living in self-imposed exile secretly in Ecuador. When it became public knowledge that Bishop Casey had had a long-term sexual relationship with an American divorcee and had fathered a son with her years earlier, he fled Ireland. Veronica Guerin tracked him down to the South American country, flew there and recorded her meetings with him in a series of exclusive interviews.

In 1994, Guerin transferred to the *Sunday Independent*, one of Ireland's largest selling newspapers, as the news and crime reporter. It was from this point that her 'nose' for a good news story drew her inexorably towards Ireland's dark underbelly. Guerin noted with alarm how illegal drugs had rapidly penetrated Ireland's society to become a major scourge with the urban youth. It seemed that while the police had been preoccupied with the activities of armed militant nationalists, the illicit drug trade had grown virtually unchecked.

The more she shone a light on the dark recesses of the drug trade, the more the drug lords became upset at this upstart interfering with their privacy. But Guerin remained undaunted by the threats to her wellbeing that were either whispered through intermediaries or left as messages on her answering machine. She forged on, exposing more of the drug barons' practices, writing in her paper: 'They are destroying lives and they are practically untouchable' (*The Irish Times*, 29 June 1996).

In October 1994, the threats turned into violent action, when two bullets were fired through a bedroom window of her home in a classic 'drive-by' gangster shooting. No one was injured, but it was the bedroom of four-year-old Cathal and his mother had just walked out of the room after tucking him in bed for the night. The incident left her quite shocked. Still, she refused to be silenced and wrote more damning articles.

Just a few months later in early 1995, Guerin published an article exposing the man suspected of masterminding the largest robbery in Ireland's history. The very next day she opened the door to her home to find a man standing there with a pistol in his hands. Not a word was said between the two, but he raised the gun and pointed it directly at Guerin's head. He then slowly ran the barrel of the pistol down Guerin's body until it pointed at her thigh. He then pulled the trigger. The assailant fled and was never identified. As the ambulances and Gardaí (Irish police force) rushed to her house, Veronica was left beside her front door, bleeding profusely from a serious gunshot wound to the leg.

She recovered and arrangements were put in place to install an expensive surveillance system in her home, as well as to provide her with round-the-clock police protection, but Guerin cancelled the police escort after only a few days, claiming that it hindered her work. She subsequently received the International Press Freedom award from the Committee to Protect Journalists, an organisation based in New York.

Later in 1995, Guerin turned up uninvited to the €5 million house and equestrian centre of John Gilligan near Enfield, Co. Meath. Gilligan allegedly became uncomfortable at questions about the source of his wealth. Guerin alleged that she was assaulted and pressed charges against Gilligan, but the case was still before the court when the next and final incident happened to the courageous journalist.

Veronica Guerin was driving her car on her way back to Dublin from an interview in June 1996, when she stopped at traffic lights. While she was on the phone to a police friend two males on a high-powered motorcycle drove up beside her and the pillion passenger fired five rounds of a handgun into her body at point-blank range. She died instantly. Guerin was thirty-seven years old, and married with a six-year-old son.

The nation was completely traumatised by Guerin's murder – the first time a journalist had been killed in Ireland's history. Thousands of people flocked to her funeral and thousands more placed flowers at the gates of Leinster House, Ireland's House of Parliament, turning the front railings into a floral shrine. The Press and the people demanded that the government do something to rein in organised crime, which the public now rightly recognised was out of control.

Within a week the Irish parliament passed the Proceeds of Crime Act (1996) and the Criminal Assets Bureau Act (1996). For the first time in Ireland's history, these two pieces of legislation gave authorities the legal power and the investigative strength to confiscate any asset purchased with the proceeds of crime.

The Gardaí was also stunned into action and mounted one of the largest investigations ever done by the Irish police force. Over 150 arrests were made for many gang-related activities. The crackdown of organised crime resulted in many criminals leaving Ireland or ceasing their criminal activities for good. The following year it was reported that drug crime in Ireland dropped by a remarkable 15 per cent.

As for Guerin's murder investigation, the police identified four people who were central to her murder, all of whom were part of a drug gang whose members had threatened Guerin in the past. As the police investigation started to close in on these criminals, some fled Ireland. Eventually two suspects would be given life sentences for their part in Guerin's murder. Of the remaining two suspects, one was convicted on different charges after being acquitted of Guerin's murder and the other died in a UK prison in 2009 whilst serving sentences for unrelated crimes.

After her death, one of her brothers, Jimmy, picked up where Veronica left off, becoming the crime reporter for the *Sunday Independent* newspaper in Dublin.

Veronica Guerin came to journalism late in her life, but she not only excelled at it, she loved it. It gave her a great sense of satisfaction knowing that she was exposing drug lords and crime bosses to the general public. 'I am simply doing my job' she once said and it was clear that by doing so she was highlighting the failings of the police and the authorities to combat crime.

Some say she was reckless, while others say that she was brave. Perhaps both of these opinions are correct, but there is one matter of which there can be no doubt: Veronica Guerin paid the ultimate price for her pursuit of the truth.

At her funeral, her son Cathal lovingly placed the framed photograph of Veronica taken at Manchester, standing alongside her football hero Eric Cantona. What else could a six-year-old do to show how much he loved his mother and how much he would miss her?

BONO (PAUL HEWSON)
(1960–)

MUSICIAN AND
SOCIAL ACTIVIST

Hewson was born and raised in Dublin, the second son of Brendan Hewson, postal worker and his wife Iris (née Rankin). Brendan was Catholic and Iris was Protestant (Church of Ireland). It was agreed that the firstborn child would be raised as a Protestant and the second child raised as a Catholic. It did not work out that way. The young Paul was so attached to his mother and brother that he kept on following them to the local Church of Ireland and grew up a Protestant too, although it would be fair to say that for most of his life he has been more spiritual than religious.

The young Hewson grew up on Cedarwood Road, Ballymum, Dublin, along with several other lads who would remain his closest friends and lifelong influences. Growing up in the 1960s and 70s, the boys did not fit the usual description of typical Irish youths. They were eccentric, artistic and rebellious against the stultifyingly repressive society that had dominated Ireland for decades. The boys gave themselves nicknames to emphasise their difference from the rest of the community and Hewson's best friend, Derek Rowan (better known as 'Guggi'), dubbed Hewson 'Bona Vox' after a local store that sold hearing aids. Hewson originally objected to the name until it was pointed out that it meant 'good voice' in Latin. It was indeed an attribute that Hewson possessed and had already demonstrated to his friends over previous years. In no time the nickname was shortened to 'Bono', the designation by which the world came to know him.

In 1974, when Bono was fourteen years old, his mother Iris died suddenly of a brain haemorrhage caused by an aneurism. It devastated the young teenager and several songs he wrote later in life, including 'I will Follow you', 'Mofo' and 'Iris (Hold Me Close), reflect the love and the loss he felt for his mother. Two years later in 1975, Bono responded to an advertisement to form a rock band that had been posted on the bulletin board of his local high school. When he was asked if he played guitar, Bono answered yes. At the time, he could not even strum a chord. Thankfully two of his best friends managed to join the band and at their urging, Bono was accepted too.

The band secured the occasional engagement where they played cover versions of popular 'heavy' rock bands, but their performances were mediocre. Also, the members could not settle on a name for their group. After a year or so, one of the band members left to form his own punk rock band called The Virgin Prunes. This allowed the remaining four members of the ensemble to focus on mainstream rock and write their own material. The first thing the band did was settle on a permanent name and 'U2' was selected, being a reference to the downing of the American U2 spy plane over Soviet territory in 1960. From the start, the band was making a political statement about who they were and what they stood for.

In 1979, U2 released a grouping of three singles which were made as the result of winning a band contest that included an opportunity to record in a professional recording studio. The band followed up this moderate success with more studio releases, albums including *Boy* (1980), *October* (1981) and *War* (1983). Each one was more successful than the previous record and gained the band more fans and a growing national reputation.

In 1982, Bono felt financially secure enough to marry his high-school sweetheart, Alison Stewart. They had four children: two girls, Jordon (1989) and Memphis Eve (1991), and two boys, Elijah (1999) and John Abraham (2001).

More albums were produced during the 1980s, during which Bono grew to become the creative inspiration and driving force of the band, being the lead singer and writing virtually all the lyrics for the songs. U2 participated in the Live Aid concert for Ethiopian famine relief in 1985, organised by Bono's friend Bob Geldof. The band performed live in front of 72,000 fans at Wembley stadium in London and was watched by a global television audience estimated at more than two billion people.

Bono started injecting more of his personality into the band's performances, often getting audience members to come onto the stage and sing or dance with him. It was at this stage that he adopted his most obvious feature of dress: his coloured glasses. Bono once explained this accessory was necessary as glaucoma had left him with eyes that were very sensitive to light, especially that from camera flashes.

The band's life changed irrevocably in 1987 with the release of their next album, *The Joshua Tree*. One track on the album, 'I Still

Haven't Found What I'm Looking For', became an international hit single and propelled U2 onto the world stage, taking the sales of the album with it into the stratosphere. They were now a commercial and critical success and tours followed of North America, Europe and the United Kingdom. People around the world suddenly noticed that Ireland was producing world-class rock music (other bands and individuals such as Clannad, Sinéad O'Connor, The Corrs and The Cranberries reinforced this opinion, producing major international hits of their own).

Having secured huge national and international fame, Bono took the opportunity to make political statements and began campaigning for causes that had always been close to his heart. For example, in 1987 Bono condemned the Provisional Irish Republican Army for the Enniskillen bombing that left eleven innocent people dead and sixty-three injured. In retaliation, the Provisional IRA threatened to kidnap Bono and IRA supporters attacked one of the band's vehicles. But this intimidation only spurred Bono on to make further comments about terrorism and other sensitive subjects.

More hits and more albums followed and over the last three decades of performances, tours and recordings, U2 has become one of rock music's most successful bands, and Bono one of the industry's most influential artists. Bono has had audiences with prime ministers, presidents and popes and is regularly interviewed by international press and media.

At the time of writing, the band has so far released thirteen albums and sold more than 170 million records worldwide, making them one of the most successful rock bands of all time. U2 has won over twenty-two Grammy awards, a Golden Globe award in 2003, and were inducted into the American Rock and Roll Hall of Fame in 2005.

Since 1999, Bono has campaigned to relieve third-world debt and increasing foreign funding with surprising success. In 2002, President George Bush unveiled a US$5 billion increase to America's aid package to Africa that included a significant amount of debt to be forgone. For his efforts in trying to alleviate financial suffering in Africa and other third-world regions, Bono was nominated for the Nobel Peace Prize in 2003.

It is difficult to quantify all the causes and campaigns to which Bono has lent his name and efforts. But in summary, it ranges from financial relief, environmental and conservation improvements, and ending discrimination against ethnic minorities, women and religious groups. Finally, Bono has been at the forefront of a massive international effort to reduce the incidence of AIDS and disease in sub-Saharan Africa. Thanks to his efforts, millions of people in Africa have received retroviral drugs to fight AIDS who would not have got them otherwise, and many more millions have received mosquito nets to prevent them from contracting malaria.

Somehow, amid a blizzard of philanthropic activity over more than twenty years, Bono has managed to produce a continual stream of bestselling records, organised blockbuster world tours and secured astute financial investments that have made him a billionaire in his own right. For all his fame and riches, he is a decent person genuinely devoted to doing all he can to alleviate some of the world's most intractable problems.

One of the latest initiatives Bono had been involved in was the 2015 Global Citizen Festival, in which hundreds of prime ministers, presidents, world leaders and activists met at the United Nations in New York and pledged to end extreme poverty in the world by 2030.

BRIAN O'DRISCOLL
(1979–)

INTERNATIONAL
RUGBY STAR

The Irish still love their national games of curling and Gaelic football, but over the last century, other forms of ball games – particularly soccer and rugby – have also been enthusiastically embraced by the Irish people. Each of these 'foreign' codes have produced their own Irish champions, such as George Best in football (*see* p. 290), but arguably none have excelled or have achieved as much as Brian O'Driscoll has done in the sport of rugby.

Brian Gerald O'Driscoll was born in Clontarf, Dublin to Frank O'Driscoll, a medical practitioner, and his wife Geraldine (née Barrett), also a doctor. The family was thoroughly steeped in the game of rugby at the highest levels. Brian's father and two uncles played tests for Ireland, with one of the uncles being selected to play for the much coveted British and Irish Lions. Yet, for all that pedigree Brian played Gaelic football when he was growing up and did not start playing rugby until he went to the local high school.

Blackrock College had a strong tradition in rugby and Brian's innate understanding of ball games was recognised and nurtured. In his final two years at Blackrock College he captained the senior team and was selected to play for the Irish Schools in 1996. The following year, after leaving high school, he played in the Ireland U-19 (under nineteen) side, which won the Under 19 Rugby World Championship and marked him out as a rising star in the world of rugby.

O'Driscoll then attended University College Dublin, where in between studies in Sports Management he played for the university's top rugby team and continued to be selected for Ireland's U-20 and then U-21 teams. Up to this point in his rugby career, O'Driscoll had played in the fly-half position, but the rugby coach saw more potential in moving Brian out to a centre position in the backs, giving him more room to play his naturally expansive running game. With this simple change, Brian O'Driscoll's already stellar career now became meteoric.

As a balanced centre he had everything – pace, strength and equal ability to dominate in both attack and defence. Over a career spanning almost two decades Brian O'Driscoll made 141 appearances in international rugby, 133 for Ireland and eight for the British and Irish Lions, making him the second most capped player in rugby history (surpassed only by the great Richie McCaw from New Zealand with 147 games, reached during the Rugby World Cup in 2015). O'Driscoll captained Ireland eighty-three times and scored a record number of forty-six tries for his country and another for the British and Irish Lions.

One of his career highlights is the performance he put in against France in 2000 during the 5-Nations Championship. That day in Paris, Brian O'Driscoll could do no wrong, scoring an incredible hat-trick of tries to propel Ireland to a resounding win. His extraordinary feat turned him into a household word in his homeland and considerably raised the profile of rugby in Ireland.

Brian O'Driscoll became so popular that T-shirts were sold in their thousands emblazoned with the words 'In BOD We Trust'. Yet, O'Driscoll never let all the adulation go to his head. He has remained humble and self-deprecating. Perhaps the unexpected suicide of his best friend and one-time roommate, Peter Twomey, in 2008 contributed to O'Driscoll's own sense of mortality and for him to focus on the more meaningful aspects of life, such as family, health and happiness.

Between duties with the Irish national team and the Lions, O'Driscoll played 186 games for his beloved club Leinster, taking them to numerous championship trophies in the Celtic League, Heineken Cup and European Cup Challenge.

In 2014, when Brian O'Driscoll finished his last game of professional rugby he had assembled an impressive record of achievement that some say will not be matched for a very long time – if ever. A few of the many accolades heaped on O'Driscoll include being shortlisted three times for the International Rugby Player of the Year (2001, 2002 and 2009) and being named 'Player of the Decade' in *Rugby World* magazine. Even America's President Barack Obama, not noted for his knowledge of rugby, described O'Driscoll as 'legendary' in his St Patrick's Day address in 2014.

After leaving rugby as a full-time player, Brian joined Irish radio network Newstalk as a commentator and also signed on as an expert analyst for BT Sport. In 2014, he joined the Oversight Board, leading Ireland's bid to host the 2023 Rugby World Cup, which is a joint initiative of The Irish Rugby Football Union, the Irish Government and the Northern Ireland Executive.

Brian O'Driscoll leads a busy life with wife, Irish actress Amy Huberman, two young children and his business interests, but he has always devoted a large portion of his time to helping those less fortunate than himself. His two favourite charities are the Temple Street Children's Hospital in Dublin and the Irish Society for the Prevention of Cruelty to Children (ISPCC). In late 2013, O'Driscoll held a gala benefit night where his efforts raised almost €700,000 to assist the work done by these two organisations.

Recently, he has made a commitment to tackle poverty and social deprivation in the underprivileged areas of Belfast. Linking with local organisations, Brian is meeting and inspiring young people to seek employment and improve their lives. Apart from giving his time, he also contributes financially to the programme. Brian considers that his actions are enriching his own life and feels privileged to be able to give something back to his society.

Since 1879, Irish Rugby has had no restrictions of class, religion or county on selection to the Irish team. In this regard the sport of rugby has shown the rest of Ireland what could be achieved in a land without prejudice or bigotry. O'Driscoll believes in this idea and is a living example of it. His friends are Protestants and Catholic; they come from the Republic of Ireland and from Northern Ireland.

Brian O'Driscoll is a modest and unassuming man who is regarded as one of the greatest rugby players to have ever graced the game. He continues to be actively engaged in promoting the sport of rugby to a domestic audience as well as working with the underprivileged youth of Ireland.

It is appropriate that we finish this book on *50 Great Irish Heroes* with Brian O'Driscoll, because in many ways he represents Ireland's future. Economically, O'Driscoll epitomises how Ireland has over the centuries transitioned from an agrarian economy, through a post-industrial one, to become a service-based marketplace. Professional services, art, tourism, science, entertainment, sport, retail and business now dominate Ireland's jobs. Agriculture, mining and manufacturing are still important, but the combined total of people employed in these industries today are less than 20 per cent of the total workforce.

O'Driscoll also symbolises how Ireland's turbulent and at times violent past has been replaced by compassion, co-operation and a high degree of tolerance for each other's politics, religion and lifestyle. The great unknown in Ireland's future is whether the northern and southern parts of the country will come together to form one united Ireland. It is more likely to happen if both sides reach out in mutual respect and understanding, rather than succumb to the threats of criminals with bombs.

BIBLIOGRAPHY
AND SOURCES

GENERAL REFERENCES

bio.: www.biography.com

Collins English Dictionary (10th ed. 2010)

Commire, A., Klezmer, D. (eds.), *Women in World History: A Biographical Encyclopedia*, Yorkin Publications, Gale Group, USA, 1999

Cronin, M., and O'Callaghan, L. (eds.), *A History of Ireland* (2nd Edition), Palgrave Macmillan UK, 2015

Donelly, J. S., Jr (ed.), *Encyclopedia of Irish History and Culture*, Macmillan Library Reference USA, 2004

Encyclopaedia Britannica (online edition 2015)

Hall, S. (ed.), *Hutchinson Illustrated Encyclopedia of British History*, Routledge, 1999

Macquarie Dictionary, Macmillan Group, 6th edition, online version (published 2013)

McGuire, J., and Quinn, J. (eds.); *Dictionary of Irish Biography* (9 volume set): *From the Earliest Times to the Year 2002*, CUP, 2009

McMahon, S., *Great Irish Heroes*, Mercier Press, Cork, Ireland, 2008

Concise Oxford English Dictionary, OUP 11th ed. 2008

Matthew, H.C.G., and Harrison, B. (eds.) *Oxford Dictionary of National Biography: From the Earliest Times to 2000*, OUP in Association with the British Academy, 2004

Ruckerstein, L., and O'Malley, J.A (eds.), *Everything Irish: The History, Literature, Art, Music, People, and Places of Ireland, from A to Z*, Ballantine Books, 2003

Wikepedia: www.wikipedia.com

SPECIFIC REFERENCES
Saint Columba

Haggerty, B., 'St Columcille of Iona' found at http://www.irishcultureandcustoms.com/ASaints/Columcille.html

Mommsen, T. (ed.), *Prosperi Tironis, Epitoma chronicon* [Chronicles of Prosper of Aquitaine], apvd Weidmannos, Berlin, 1892, found at https://archive.org/details/chronicaminorasa11momm

Tertullian, *Adversus Judaeos* [*An Answer to the Jews*], Chapter VII, translated by Sydney Thelwall, found at http://en.wikisource.org/wiki/Ante-Nicene_Fathers/Volume_III/Apologetic/An_Answer_to_the_Jews/The_Question_Whether_Christ_Be_Come_Taken_Up

Brian Boru

Cavendish, R., 'Brian Boru, High King of Ireland, killed', *History Today*, Vol. 64, 2014, found in http://www.historytoday.com/richard-cavendish/brian-boru-high-king-ireland-killed

Green, M., 'Brian Boru', *The Information about Ireland* Site, 2014

found in http://www.ireland-information.com/articlesbrian
boru.htm

Grace O'Malley

Chambers, A., *Granaile: Grace O'Malley: Grace O'Malley – Ireland's Pirate Queen*, Gill & Macmillan, 2006

'Grainne O'Mailley, The She-Pirate', *Dublin University Magazine*, Vol. 55, 1860, found online at http://search.proquest.com

Hardiman, J. (ed.), 'Irish Minstrelsy', Vol. II, Joseph Robins, London, 1831, found at https://archive.org/details/irishminstrelsy01curr goog

'O'Malley, Grace', *Irish Cultural Society of the Garden City Area*, 1988, found in http://www.irish-society.org/home/hedgemaster archives-2/people/o-malley-grace

Robert Boyle

Davis, E. B., 'Robert Boyle's Religious life, Attitudes and vocations', *Science and Christian Belief*, Vol. 19, No. 2 (pp. 117–38)

MacIntosh, J. J. and Anstey, P., 'Robert Boyle', in Edward N. Zalta (ed.), *The Stanford Encyclopedia of Philosophy*, Fall 2014 Edition, found at http://plato.stanford.edu/entries/boyle/

Maddison, R. E. W., *The Life of the Honourable Robert Boyle*, Taylor & Francis, 1969

Patrick Sarsfield

Birkhead, A., 'Tales of Irish History', Le Roy Phillips, Boston, 1911, Chapter *'Patrick Sarsfield, Defender of Limerick'*, 2015 found in http://www.heritage-history.com/index.php?c=read&author= birkhead&book=irish&story=limerick

'Patrick Sarsfield', *A Compendium of Irish Biography, 1878* found in http://www.libraryireland.com/biography/PatrickSarsfield.php

Wauchope, P., *Patrick Sarsfield and the Williamite War*, Irish Academic Press Ltd, 2009

Kit Cavanagh

Dowie, M. M., 'Women Adventurers', T. F. Unwin, London 1893, electronic version found at *National Library of Australia* in http:/catalogue.nla.gov.au/Record/6501372

Wilson, J., *The British Heroine: or, an Abridgment of the Life and adventures of Mrs. Christian Davies, commonly call'd Mother Ross*, Globe London, 1742, electronic version found at *National Library of Australia* in http://catalogue.nla.gov.au/Record/3176908

Turlough O'Carolan

McCormack, M., 'O'Carolan', Echoes of Irish History, 1990, found at Irish Cultural Society of the Garden City Area in http://www.irish-society.org/home/hedgemaster-archives-2/people/o-carolan

Nelson-Burns, L., 'The Folk Music of England, Scotland, Ireland, Wales and America', site, found at http://www.contemplator.com/carolan/

'Turloch O'Carolan, Irish Harper 1670–1738' found at the *Old Music Project*, 2015 at http://www.oldmusicproject.com/OCC.html

Yeats, G., *The Complete Collection of Carolan's Irish Tunes,* Ossian Publications, Dublin, 1984

Ambrosio O'Higgins

Minster, C., 'Biography of Ambrosio O'Higgins', *Latin American*

History, 2015, found at http://latinamericanhistory.about.com/od/thehistoryofchile/p/10ambroseohiggins.htm

Murray, E., 'O'Higgins, Ambrose [Ambrosio]', *Dictionary of Irish Latin American Biography*, 2007, found at http://www.irlandeses org/dilab_ohigginsa.htm

Wolfe Tone

McCormack, J., 'Tone, Theobald Wolfe', Irish Cultural Society of the Garden City Area, 1998 found at http://www.irish-society. org/home/hedgemaster-archives-2/people/tone-theobald-wolfe

'Theobald Wolfe Tone', quotes found at http://en.wikiquote.org/wiki/Theobald_Wolfe_Tone

Tone, W.T. (ed.), *The Life of Theobald Wolfe Tone* [...etc], Gales & Seaton, Washington, USA, 1826

Tone, W.T. (ed.), 'Narrative of the third and last expedition for the liberation of Ireland and of the capture, trial and death of Theobald Wolfe Tone', found at http://iol.ie/~fagann/1798/tone.htm

Tone, T. W., 'An Address to the PEOPLE OF IRELAND on the present important crisis', found at http://iol.ie/~fagann/1798/tone7.htm

Mary Ann McCracken

'Discovering Women in Irish History', *Women in History,* found at http://womeninhistory.scoilnet.ie/content/unit2/1798.html

O'Neill, M., 'The Life and Times of Mary Ann McCracken', article found at http://iol.ie/~fagann/1798/o_neill.htm

'The Famous Faces of North Belfast', found at North Belfast Partnership in http://www.northbelfastpartnership.com/images/

custom/pageimages/118/3347/The%20Famous%20Faces%20 of%20North%20Belfast.pdf

The Madden Papers, 'United Irishmen, their lives, and times', 2nd Series Vol. II (1843), held in the Public Record Office of Northern Ireland (http://www.proni.gov.uk/)

Sir Francis Beaufort

Ireland, Dr J. De C., 'Francis Beaufort, (Wind Scale)', *National Maritime Museum of Ireland* found at http://www.mariner.ie/ history-3/articles/people/beaufort/

Daniel O'Connell

Birkhead, A., *Tales from Irish History*, Le Roy Phillips, Boston, 1911, chapter 'Daniel O'Connell, Liberator' found at http:/ www.heritage-history.com/index.php?c=read&author=birkhea d&book=irish&story=oconnell

Gladstone, W. E., 'Daniel O'Connell', *The Nineteenth Century*, Vol. 25, January 1889, pp. 149–68, found at http://search.proquest. com/docview/2638415?accountid=13902

Kinealy, C., 'O'Connell and Anti-Slavery', *History Today*, Vol. 57, 2007 found at http://www.historytoday.com/christine-kinealy/ liberator-daniel-o%E2%80%99connell-and-anti-slavery

'O'Connell, Daniel', Irish Cultural Society of the Garden City Area, 1986, found at http://www.irish-society.org/home/hedgemaster-archives-2/people/o-connell-daniel

Charles Bianconi

'Bianconi: Early years in Italy', found in *Ask About Ireland* at http:// www.askaboutireland.ie/reading-room/environment-geography/transport/bianconi/early-years-in-italy/

'Carlo Bianconi – A True Rags To Riches Story From Tipperary', found in *Thurles Information* at http://www.thurles. info/2008/12/31/carlo-bianconi-a-true-rags-to-riches-story-from-tipperary/

Igoe, B., 'Charles Bianconi and The Transport Revolution, 1800–1875' found in *The Irish Story* at http://www.theirishstory. com/2012/12/14/charles-bianconi-and-the-transport-revolution-1800-1875/#h

O'Connell, M. J., *Charles Bianconi: A biography, 1786–1875*, Chapman and Hall, London, 1878, found at http://archive.org/ stream/charlesbianconib00oconiala/charlesbianconib00ocon iala_djvu.txt

Ryan, T., Ryan, M., *Bianconi: a Boy with a Dream: The Pioneer of Irish Transport*, Ryan Publications, 2007

Mary Aikenhead

Atkinson, S.A., *Mary Aikenhead: her life, her work and her friends*, M. H. Gill, Dublin, 1879

Rudge, F.M., 'Mary Aikenhead' in *The Catholic Encyclopedia*, Vol. 1. New York: Robert Appleton Company, 1907, found at http:// www.newadvent.org/cathen/01234a.htm

Twohig, Sr Miriam, 'A Short Synopsis on the Life of Mary Aikenhead', 2013, found at http://www.rsccaritas.ie/mary-aikenhead-her-spirit-and-mission

James Gamble

Gamble, J.N. (speech, 3 May 1890), 'James Gamble's Journey from Ireland to Ivorydale' found in *P&G Heritage* at http://www. pg.com/en_US/company/heritage/featured_stories.shtml

'James Gamble (Industrialist)', found at http://pages.rediff.com/
james-gamble--industrialist-/424950

Procter & Gamble, 'A Company History, 1837–Today', found at
http://www.pg.com/translations/history_pdf/english_history.
pdf

'Procter Meets Gamble', found at P&G Heritage in http://www.
pg.com/en_US/company/heritage/featured_stories.shtml

http://news.pg.com/blog/procter-meets-gamble

George Boole

Harrison, E., 'George Boole – the Lincoln Genius', Lincoln
Cathedral guide, 1993, found at http://www.rogerparsons.info/
george/boole.html

Lerner, K.L., and Lerner, B.W. (eds.), 'George Boole', *Computer
Sciences*, USA, 2013

Machale, D., *George Boole: His life And Work*, Boole Press, 1985

Catherine Hayes

Noy, G., 'The Swan of Erin: The Enduring Legacy of Kate Hayes',
Snowy Range Reflections (Journal of Sierra Nevada History &
Biography), Vol. 1 no. 3, Fall 2008, Sierra College Press found at
http://www.sierracollege.edu/ejournals/jsnhb/v1n3/hayes.html

Shoesmith, D., 'Hayes, Catherine (?–1861)', *Australian Dictionary
of Biography*, Vol. 4, (MUP), 1972, found at http://adb.anu.edu.
au/biography/hayes-catherine-3736

Walsh, B., 'Catherine Hayes, 1818–1861', found at https://basilwalsh.
wordpress.com/tag/opera-in-dublin-in-the-19th-century

Walsh, B., 'The Irish Diva & Giuseppe Verdi', The Friends of
Kensal Green Cemetery, *The Magazine*, Issue 45, Spring 2007

William Thomson

'Sir William Thomson Baron Kelvin of Largs', University of Glasgow, found at http://www.universitystory.gla.ac.uk/biography/ ?id=WH0025&type=P

'Sir William Thomson, Lord Kelvin (1824–1907)', *BBC History*, 2014, found at http://www.bbc.co.uk/history/historic_figures/kelvin_lord.shtml

Thomson, E., 'William Thomson, Lord Kelvin (1824–1907)', *Proceedings of the American Academy of Arts and Sciences*, Vol. 51, No. 14 (Dec. 1916) pp. 896–9, found at http://www.jstor.org/stable/20025642

Thomas D'Arcy McGee

A People's History, 'The Assassination of Thomas D'Arcy McGee', found at *CBC Canada* series at http://www.cbc.ca/history/EPCONTENTSE1EP9CH1PA2LE.html

Burns, R., Block, N., 'Thomas Darcy McGee', *The Canadian Encyclopedia,* 2015 found at http://www.thecanadianencyclopedia.ca/en/article/thomas-darcy-mcgee/

Davis, W.G., 'Thomas D'Arcy McGee: Irish Founder of the Canadian Nation', found at http://gail25.tripod.com/mcgee1.htm

McMurray, Hon. Edward, speaker of Canadian Parliament, 'Thomas D'Arcy McGee' an address to the Empire Club (Toronto) 2 April 1925, found at http://speeches.empireclub.org/62641/data

Eliza Lynch

Carroll, C, "Villain' of Brazil-Paraguay war was misunderstood hero, says new book', *The Guardian*, 2009, found at http://www.theguardian.com/world/2009/nov/08/eliza-lynch-paraguay-brazil

BIBLIOGRAPHY AND SOURCES

Lilis, M., 'The True Origins of Eliza lynch', *The Irish Times*, 2014 found at http://www.irishtimes.com/culture/heritage/the-true-origins-of-eliza-lynch-1.1719349

Murray, E., 'Eliza Lynch (1835-1889): Courtesan and Unofficial First Lady of Paraguay', *Irish Migration Studies in Latin America* (Vol. 4 No. 1, 2006), found at http://www.irishargentine.org/dilab_lynchea.htm

Vila, L., 'Eliza Lynch; Paraguay's Peron', *The Culture Trip*, found in http://theculturetrip.com/south-america/paraguay/articles/elisa-lynch-paraguay-s-peron/

Wilson, J., *The British Heroine: or, An Abridgment of the Life and Adventures of Mrs. Christian Davies, commonly call'd Mother ROSS*, Globe, London, 1742

John Philip Holland

Holland, J.P., 'The Submarine Boat and Its Future'. *The North American Review*, Vol. 171, No. 529 (Dec, 1900) pp. 894–903, found at http://www.jstor.org/stable/25105099

Whitman, E.C., 'John Holland father of the modern Submarine', *Undersea Warfare*, Summer 2003, found at http://www.public navy.mil/subfor/underseawarfaremagazine/Issues/Archives/issue_19/holland.htm

Thomas Barnardo

'Barnardo's Around the World – Our History', *Barnardos.com* site found at http://www.barnardos.com/dotcom_history.htm

James, 'Dr Barnardo: Facts and Information', *Primary Facts*, 2012 found at http://primaryfacts.com/234/dr-barnardo-facts-and-information/

Smith, M.K., 'Thomas John Barnardo ('The Doctor')', the *Encyclopedia of Informal Education,* 2012 found at http://infed.org/mobi/thomas-john-barnardo-the-doctor/

Michael Davitt

Bryan, W.J. (ed.), 'On the Irish Land League by Michael Davitt 1889', *The World's Famous Orations*, Vol. VI, Ireland (1775–1902), 1906, found at http://www.bartleby.com/268/6/22.html

'Michael Davitt and the Land league: An Irish Revolution' found at http://www.lookleftonline.org/2010/11/michael-davitt-and-the-land-league-an-irish-revolution/

'Michael Davitt (1846–1906): An exhibition to honour the centenary of his death' found at http://www.mayolibrary.ie/files/combinedseries.pdf

Moody, T., *Davitt and Irish Revolution, 1846–1882*, OUP, 1982

Charles Parnell

Birkhead, A., Tales from Irish History, Le Roy Phillips, Boston, 1911, Chapter *'Home Rule for Ireland'* found at http://www.heritage-history.com/index.php?c=read&author=birkhead&book=irish&story=rule

'Charles Stewart Parnell', *Clare County Library*, found at http://www.clarelibrary.ie/eolas/coclare/people/parnell.htm

Green, M., 'Charles Stewart Parnell', *Ireland Information* (online), 1998, found at http://www.ireland-information.com/articles/charlesstewartparnell.htm

Pelling, N., *Anglo-Irish Relations, 1798–1922*, Routledge, London, 2002

BIBLIOGRAPHY AND SOURCES

Michael Cusack

Anglim, P., 'Nationalism and the GAA in Limerick between the years 1887–1924', *Limerick GAA History*, 2013, found at http://limerickgaahistory.blogspot.com.au/2013/11/nationalism-and-gaa-in-limerick-between.html

Cusack, M., "A word about Irish Athletics', printed in *United Ireland* newspaper, 18 October 1884.

'Michael Cusack (1847–1906)', *Clare County Library*, found at http://www.clarelibrary.ie/eolas/coclare/people/cusack.htm

Oscar Wilde

'Official Website of Oscar Wilde', *CMG Worldwide* website, 2015 found at http://www.cmgww.com/historic/wilde/bio1.htm

'Oscar Wilde Biography', *Oscar Wilde online* found in http://www.wilde-online.info/oscar-wilde-biography.htm

George Bernard Shaw

Frenz, E.H. (ed.) from *Nobel Lecture, Literature 1901–1967*, 'George Bernard Shaw Biographical', Elsevier Publishing Company, Amsterdam, 1969, found at *Nobelprize.org*, in http://www.nobelprize.org/nobel_prizes/literature/laureates/1925/shaw-bio.html

William B. Yeats

Foster, R. F., *W. B. Yeats: A Life*, Oxford University Press, 2005

Frenz, E. H. (ed.) from *Nobel Lecture, Literature 1901–1967*, 'William Butler Yeats – Biographical', Elsevier Publishing Company, Amsterdam, 1969, found at *Nobelprize.org*, in http://www.nobelprize.org/nobel_prizes/literature/laureates/1923/yeats-bio.html

'W. B. Yeats at Lissadell', The Yeats Gallery Exhibition 2010, found at *lissadell online* in http://lissadellhouse.com/index.php/yeats/william-butler-yeats/

Constance Markievicz

'Constance Markievicz Facts', *Encyclopaedia of World Biography*, The Gale group, Inc., 2010 found in http://biography.yourdictionary.com/constance-markievicz

'Countess Constance Markievicz 1868–1927', found at *BBC History* – '1916 Easter uprising – Profiles' in http://www.bbc.co.uk/history/british/easterrising/profiles/po10.shtml

'Countess Markievicz a brief introduction and the Constance Markievicz Exhibition at Lissadell...2007', found at *lissadell online* in http://lissadellhouse.com/index.php/countess-markievicz/

Walsh, J., 'Countess Constance Markievicz', *Irish Cultural Society of the Garden City Area* found at http://www.irish-society.org/home/hedgemaster-archives-2/people/countess-constance-markievicz

Eva Gore-Booth

'Eva Gore Booth, Poet & Suffragist 1870–1926' found at *lissadell online* in http://lissadellhouse.com/index.php/eva-gore-booth/

Tiernan, S., 'Challenging Presumptions of Heterosexuality: Eva Gore-Booth, A Biographical Case Study', *Historical Reflections*, Vol. 37, Issue 2, Summer 2011

Tiernan, S., *Eva Gore Booth: An Image of Such Politics*, Manchester University Press, 2013

Kathleen Lynn

McCoole, S., 'Seven Women of the labour Movement 1916', found at http://www.labour.ie/download/pdf/seven_women_of_the_ labour_movement1916.pdf

Stokes, T., 'Naming National Children's Hospital', found at *The Irish Republic* article, 2011 in https://theirishrepublic.wordpress. com/tag/madeleine-ffrench-mullen/

'The Secret Diaries of Dr. Kathleen Lynn', found at http://loopline com/htm/23_kathleen_lynn.htm

Ernest Shackleton

Service, R. W., *Spell of the Yukon and other Verses*, Barse & Hopkins, 1907

Shackleton, J. and MacKenna, J., *Shackleton: An Irishman in Antartica*, Lilliput Press, 2012

'Sir Ernest Shackleton – Antarctic Explorer', *Royal Museums Greenwich* website, found at http://www.rmg.co.uk/explore/sea-and-ships/facts/explorers-and-leaders/shackleton

Hanna Sheehy Skeffington

McCoole, S., 'Sheehy Skeffington, Hanna', found online at http://www.hannashouse.ie/index.php?option=com_content &task=view&id=3&Itemid=2

Margaret Cousins

Candy, C., 'Relating Feminisms, Nationalisms and Imperialisms: Ireland, India and Margaret Cousins's Sexual politics', *Women's History Review*, Vol. 3, No. 4, 1994

Cousins, J. H., and Cousins, M. E., *We Two together*, Ganesh, Chennai, 1950

Eichelberger, S., '1878 – Birth of Margaret Cousins', *Halla Mor*, 2013, found at http://www.hallamor.org/1878-birth-of-margaret-cousins/

Patrick Pearse

O'Farrell, M., 'Pearse whistled as he came out of his cell: diary of a 1916 executioner', *The Irish Times* site, 2014 found at http://www.irishtimes.com/culture/heritage/pearse-whistled-as-he-came-out-of-his-cell-diary-of-a-1916-executioner-1.1885073

'Pádraig Pearse (1879–1916)', *Easter 1916.ie* website, found in http://www.easter1916.ie/index.php/people/signatories/p-h-pearse/

'Patrick Pearse 1879–1916', found at *BBC History* – Wars & Conflict, '1916 Easter uprising – Profiles' in http://www.bbc.co.uk/history/british/easterrising/profiles/po11.shtml

Pearse, P., *Three Lectures on Gaelic topics*, M. H. Gill & Son, Dublin, 1898, found at https://archive.org/details/threelecturesong00pearuoft

Éamon de Valera

'Éamon de Valera 1882–1975', found at BBC History – Wars & Conflict, '1916 Easter uprising – Profiles' in http://www.bbc.co.uk/history/british/easterrising/profiles/po06.shtml

Longford, F. P. (Earl of Longford), O'Neill, T.P., *Éamon de Valera*, Hutchinson, 1970 (online edition 2006)

Sweeney, M. D., Excerpt from 'Irish Neutrality in World War II: Éamon de Valera's Struggle to Protect Eire' An Independent Study, 2009 found at http://history.hanover.edu/hhr/09/irishneutrality.pdf

Harry Ferguson

Gibson, H., 'Harry Ferguson, Inventor and Pioneer', *Dromore District Local Historical Group Journal*, found at http://lisburn.com/books/dromore-historical/Journal-2/journal-2-3.html

'Harry Ferguson', *Grace's Guide* website, 2015, found at http:/
www.gracesguide.co.uk/Harry_Ferguson

'Story of Harry Ferguson', *Harry Ferguson Legacy* website, found at
http://www.harryfergusonlegacy.com/

Michael Collins

Conroy, J., 'Collins, Michael: The Big Fellow', Irish Cultural
Society of the Garden City Area, 1996 found at http://www.
irish-society.org/home/hedgemaster-archives-2/people/collins-
michael-the-big-fellow

McDowell, M., 'Michael Collins Biography', *RTE ONE Ireland's
Greatest* website, 2015 found at http://www.rte.ie/tv/irelands
greatest/michaelcollins.html

'Michael Collins 1890–1922', found at BBC History – Wars &
Conflict, '1916 Easter uprising – Profiles' in http://www.bbc.
co.uk/history/british/easterrising/profiles/po03.shtml

'The Anglo-Irish War', found at BBC History – Wars & Conflict,
'1916 Easter uprising – Profiles' in http://www.bbc.co.uk/history/
british/easterrising/aftermath/af04.shtml

Hugh O'Flaherty

Fleming, B., *The Vatican Pimpernel: The Wartime Exploits of
Monsignor Hugh O'Flaherty*, Collins, 2014

'Hugh O'Flaherty', *County Kerry* website, found at http://www
rootsweb.ancestry.com/~irlker/scarlet.html

Hugh O'Flaherty Memorial Society, found at http://www
hughoflaherty.com/index.cfm/page/biography

Vandessel, J., 'Monsignor Hugh O'Flaherty', 2010, found at http:/
msgrhughoflaherty.50webs.com/index.html

Walker, S., 'The Priest who converted his enemy', *Catholic*

Herald, 2011, found at http://www.catholicherald.co.uk/features/2011/04/13/the-priest-who-converted-his-enemy/

Ninette De Valois

Cave, R. A., *Collaborations: Ninette de Valois and William Butler Yeats*, Dance Books 2011

'Dame Ninette de Valois', *The Oxford Dictionary of Dance,* found at http://www.oxfordreference.com/view/10.1093/oi/authority.20110803115118562

Daunt, J., 'Ninette de Valois: The Irish Mother of Modern British Ballet', found at *The Culture Trip*, in
http://theculturetrip.com/europe/ireland/articles/ninette-de-valois-the-irish-mother-of-modern-british-ballet/

De Valois, N., *Come dance with me: a memoir, 1898–1956*, (paperback version), Lilliput Press, London, 1992 (reprinted 2015)

Walsh, J., 'Interview: Dame Ninette de Valois: Doyenne of dance', *The Independent,* 1998 found at http://www.independent.co.uk/life-style/interview-dame-ninette-de-valois-doyenne-of-the-dance-1163145.html

Ernest Walton

Dicke, W., 'Ernest T. S. Walton, 91, Irish Physicist, Dies', *The New York Times – Obituaries*, 1995, found at http://www.nytimes.com/1995/06/28/obituaries/ernest-t-s-walton-91-irish-physicist-dies.html

Duke, S., 'The Atom Splitter: Ernest Walton', *Careers, Ireland's greatest Physics, Science Spinning*, 2011 found at http://seanduke.com/2011/05/04/the-atom-splitter-ernest-walton/

Duke, S., 'How Irish Scientists Changed the World', Londubh Books, 2013

'Ernest T. S. Walton – Biographical', *Nobelprize.org*, Nobel Media AB 2014, Web 2 June 2015, found at http://www.nobelprize.org/nobel_prizes/physics/laureates/1951/walton-bio.html

Waterford County Council Library Service, 'Ernest Walton (1903–1995)', found at http://www.inarchive.com/page/2012-01-18/http://www.waterfordcountylibrary.ie/en/localstudies/waterfordscientists/ernestwalton1903-1995/

Seán MacBride

Byrne, J., 'The Extraordinary Life and Times of Seán MacBride: Part 1', December 1982, found at *politico.ie* website, from http://politico.ie/archive/extraordinary-life-and-times-sean-mcbride-part-1

Pilger, J., (interview), 'The Outsiders – Seam MacBride [1983]', *YouTube,* 2013 from www.youtube.com/watch?v=3NqTn6S0pe8

Chaim Herzog

'Chaim Herzog 1918–1997', The Famous Faces of North Belfast, page 57, *North Belfast Partnership* from http://www.northbelfastpartnership.com/images/custom/pageimages/118/3347/The%20Famous%20Faces%20of%20North%20Belfast.pdf

Druckman, Y., 'The Herzogs: Three generations of Israeli leadership', *YNetnews.com* website, 2015, found at http://www.ynetnews.com/articles/0,7340,L-4637599,00.html

Herzog, C., *Living History: A Memoir*, Plunkett Lake Press, New York, 2015

Isseroff, A., 'Biography of Chaim Herzog', *Zionism and Israel – Biographies* website, found at http://www.zionism-israel.com/bio/Chaim_Herzog_biography.htm

John Hume

O'Callaghan, M., 'John Hume: Politician and Co-recipient of the 1998 Nobel Peace Prize', *RTÉ ONE Ireland's Greatest* website, 2015, found at http://www.rte.ie/tv/irelandsgreatest/johnhume.html

'The Nobel Peace Prize 1998', *Nobelprize.org* website, found at http://www.nobelprize.org/nobel_prizes/peace/laureates/1998/hume-facts.html

'Who is John Hume?', *Your Dictionary* website, 2015, found at http://biography.yourdictionary.com/articles/who-is-john-hume.html

Mary Robinson

'Mary Robinson', *The Elders* website, 2015, from http://theelders org/mary-robinson

Mary Robinson Foundation Climate Justice website, 2015, found at http://www.mrfcj.org/

McWilliams, D., 'Mary Robinson: Former Irish President and United Nations High Commissioner for Human Rights', *RTÉ ONE Ireland's Greatest* website, found at http://www.rte.ie/tv/irelandsgreatest/maryrobinson.html

Robinson, M., *Everybody Matters: A Memoir*, Hodder & Staughton, 2012

George Best

De Menezes, J., 'George Best wasn't called George, according to his birth certificate', from *The Independent*, at http://www.independent.co.uk/sport/football/news-and-comment/george-best-wasnt-called-george-according-to-his-birth-certificate-10236583.html

'George Best', *IMDb Biography*, found at http://www.imdb.com name/nm0078928/bio

Pierce Brosnan

Pierce Brosnan Official Website, found at http://www.piercebrosnan com

'Pierce Brosnan', *IMDb Biography* website, found at http://www imdb.com/name/nm0000112/bio?ref_=nm_ov_bio_sm

Veronica Guerin

O'Reilly, E., *Veronica Guerin: The Life and Death of a Crime Reporter*, Random House UK, 1998

'Tireless Fighter Whose Good Luck Finally Ran Out', *Irish Times*, 29 June 1996

'Veronica Guerin', *Encyclopedia of World Biography*, The Gale Group, Inc., 2010, found at http://biography.yourdictionary.com/ veronica-guerin

'Veronica Guerin', *Telegraph Media Group Limited*, 2015, found at http://www.telegraph.co.uk/news/obituaries/7733654/Veronica-Guerin.html

'Veronica Guerin, Ireland: World Press Freedom Hero (Honoured in 2000)', *International Press Institute*, found in http://www.free media.at/awards/press-freedom-heroes/veronica-guerin.html

Bono (Paul David Hewson)

Eagleton, T., 'The Frontman: Bono (In The Name of Power) by Harry Browne – review', The *Guardian* online, 2013, found at http://www.theguardian.com/books/2013/jun/26/frontman-bono-harry-browne-review

Fanning, D., 'Bono: Musician and human Rights Campaigner',

RTE ONE Ireland's Greatest website, 2015, from http://www.rte.ie/tv/irelandsgreatest/bono.html

Fry, M., 'Bono Biography', *@U2* website, found at http://www.atu2 com/band/bono/

Brian O'Driscoll

Bray, A., 'Charities delighted as BOD's night raises €670k', *Independent Ireland*, 2013, found in http://www.independent.ie/woman/celeb-news/charities-delighted-as-bods-night-raises-670k-29724061.html

Flannagan, M., 'Farewell to Irish Legend Brian O'Driscoll', found at *Sydney Morning Herald*, (Australia) 2014 found in http://www.smh.com.au/rugby-union/union-news/farewell-to-irish-legend-brian-odriscoll-20140313-hvic8.html

O'Driscoll, B., *The Test: My Autobiography*, Penguin, 2014.

Stead, M., *Legend – The Biography of Brian O'Driscoll*, John Blake, 2013